Values-Centered Entrepreneurs and Their Companies

A new brand of entrepreneurs has arrived on the business scene. These entrepreneurs carry with them a whole new set of values. Their mission is to be socially responsible, protect the planet, and do the right thing for all of their stakeholders. They aim to achieve a balance between profits and one or more causes of their choosing, and view for-profit entrepreneurship as a vehicle for social change. Their approach to management questions our basic assumptions about how businesses should be run and what their role should be in society. The authors call these pioneers "values-centered" entrepreneurs.

This book explores how these highly unorthodox leaders have built their profitable and socially responsible business enterprises. The authors examine a group of over 40 entrepreneurial companies and how each balanced the profit objective with social responsibility in key aspects of their business operation—from their initial company formation, through growth, to exit—to build successful triple bottom-line companies. The book presents ten of the most dominant and interesting commonalities with a focus on those policies and decisions that departed from conventional business practice.

David Y. Choi, Ph.D., is Associate Professor of Management and Entrepreneurship and an Associate Director of the Fred Kiesner Center for Entrepreneurship at Loyola Marymount University.

Edmund R. Gray, Ph.D., is Professor of Management at Loyola Marymount University.

Values-Centered Entrepreneurs and Their Companies

David Y. Choi and Edmund R. Gray

Routledge
Taylor & Francis Group

NEW YORK AND LONDON

First published 2011
by Routledge
270 Madison Avenue, New York, NY 10016

Simultaneously published in the UK
by Routledge
2 Park Square, Milton Park, Abingdon, Oxon OX14 4RN

Routledge is an imprint of the Taylor & Francis Group, an informa business

Typeset in Minion by RefineCatch Limited, Bungay, Suffolk
Printed and bound by TJ International Ltd, Padstow, Cornwall

Library of Congress Cataloging-in-Publication Data
Choi, David Y.
  Values-centered entrepreneurs and their companies / David Y. Choi, Edmund R. Gray.
    p. cm.
  Includes bibliographical references and index.
  1. Social responsibility of business. 2. Social entrepreneurship. 3. Entrepreneurship—
  Moral and ethical aspects. I. Gray, Edmund R. II. Title.
  HD60.C48 2010
  658.4′08—dc22   2010000654

ISBN13: 978–0–415–99760–7 (hbk)
ISBN13: 978–0–415–99761–4 (pbk)
ISBN13: 978–0–203–88350–1 (ebk)

(DYC) To my parents

and

(ERG) To my grandson, Alexander

Contents

Figures and Tables

Figures

Tables

Preface and Acknowledgements

"Greed ... is good," Michael Douglas's character, Gordon Gekko, famously proclaimed in the 1987 movie, *Wall Street*. Certainly, profit is a critical element in our free enterprise system but the most prominent business headlines of the new millennium suggest that unbounded greed has become the paramount motivator in business (Karl Marx must be wryly smiling from his grave). Of course, business has never been perceived as the most idealistic of professions but its public image, we would venture to say, has shrunk to a new all-time low.

And, no wonder business has such a poor image. We have seen bankers willing to put the entire financial system at risk to maximize their bonuses, observed pharmaceutical companies making drugs unaffordable to millions of people, and learned about oil companies paying lobbyists to create artificial doubts about solid science, just to name a few reasons for business's poor standing. And these actions are deemed justified and understandable in the name of capitalism! (It is equally amazing to see nice, honest people going to work every morning at these corporations.) But besides the problem of public image, the prevailing self-serving view of business does not really serve anyone, not people, planet or even business itself, at least not in the long term.

As teachers as well as practitioners, we have a rather different view of business's potential; one that involves individuals starting companies to pursue their dreams for a better world, not just for themselves and their families but also for their customers, partners, and communities. One that employs and empowers people and treats them with dignity. One that shares good fortune with the less fortunate and endeavors to leave behind a better world for the next generation.

Too idealistic? Too impractical? We don't think so! As we dug into our research, we found more and more entrepreneurial companies whose philosophy and admirable business policies fit our view of business and in many cases exceeded our expectations. Their leaders refused to blindly follow the conventional role of business in society and operated their companies according to an alternative set of values. Their cause-orientation combined with entrepreneurial passion inspired innovative and often unorthodox management practices worthy of public attention. Our article, "Socially Responsible Entrepreneurs: What Do They Do (To Create and Build Their Companies)?" published in 2008 in *Business Horizons* focused on these practices and became a springboard to this book.

Our "values-centered" entrepreneurs (as we came to call them) clearly demonstrate that businesses can be an integral part of society, not just as employers and revenue generators (certainly very important functions), but through the use of a wide range of interesting business strategies and management practices. These include offering more sustainable products, building a totally different supply chain, inventing a new brand of promotional strategy, and fostering an extraordinary relationship with employees. This book brings to light the major commonalities as well as best-in-class practices—thereby providing some insight into how these entrepreneurs juggle their multi-faceted objectives successfully. Our hope is that these findings will serve as a framework that a new generation of entrepreneurs can build upon.

The book starts with a brief discussion of our research objectives and methodology—and then presents an overview of the theoretical underpinning of the study. The central core of the book is a comprehensive discussion of ten commonalities in management practice that we distilled from our research. We devote a chapter to each commonality. The book concludes with in-depth case studies of four companies, highlighting their unique business philosophies, policies and practices.

Many people have contributed to this book. John M.T. Balmer, of Brunel University, was an early collaborator. He worked with one of the authors in developing pragmatic lessons from a study of four "sustainable" entrepreneurial companies. Several of our students including Nancy Marcello, Mathew Carroll, Jonathan Mentzer, Mauricio Rivera, and Jose Limon helped with company research and proofreading. Further, we particularly want to acknowledge Catherine M. Dalton of Indiana University, editor of *Business Horizons*, who helped us frame the study and provided valuable suggestions in developing the aforementioned article. Other academics including Jeff Robinson of Rutgers University and Fred Kiesner of Loyola Marymount University have supported our project and offered suggestions. We should also note that our current Dean, Dennis Draper and our former Dean, John Wholihan provided us with the supportive academic environment needed for completing the research and writing the book.

Over the years, the following work-study students helped type our evolving manuscript: Hugo Lopez, Jessica Lopez, Ankita Patel, Aimee Afad, Stephen Ma, and Carolina Sanchez. We thank them for their efforts. We specially want to single out Cissy Easter who oversaw the typing of multiple drafts of the manuscript and managed much of the administrative work necessary for putting the book together.

We are grateful to all of our values-centered entrepreneurs who have provided the inspiration for this book. Many of them have offered their time and wisdom. A special thank you goes out to, among others, Gary Erickson (Clif Bar), Timothy Haahs (Tim Haahs & Associates), Eric Henry (T.S. Designs), Chris King (King Cycle Group), Robert Milk (Novica), Laura Scher (Working Assets), Kristin Groos Richmond and Kirsten Saenz Tobey (Revolution Foods), Sarah Endline (Sweet Riot), and Jeff Pink (EV Rental) who have helped with key insights that we have incorporated in our book. We especially appreciate Seth Goldman (Honest Tea) and Marc Benioff (Salesforce.com) for their strong endorsement of our book. Executives in many of the other companies, such as AgraQuest, King Cycle Group, Novica, Pacific Community Ventures, Rhythm & Hues, and Tom's Shoes, have also provided valuable information.

Finally, we are privileged to have worked with a great team at Taylor and Francis. The team includes John Szilagyi, Nancy Hale, and Sara Werden. A special thanks goes to our copy-editor Jane Olorenshaw whose superb work exceeded our expectations. The team has helped make our book better.

Part 1
Toward a New Breed of Entrepreneurs

1

Introduction

The reasonable man adapts himself to the world. The unreasonable one persists in trying to adapt the world to himself. Therefore all progress depends on the unreasonable man.
—Playwright and essayist George Bernard Shaw[1]

A New Brand of Entrepreneurs

In the Southern California beach community of Hermosa Beach, two young women, Gina Williamson and Melissa Scheurermann, have created a unique product and started a new business—making and selling biodegradable wax for surfboards. Their compelling purpose was to provide an environmentally safe alternative to traditional surfboard waxes which contain a variety of harmful chemicals. They hope this venture will contribute to keeping their beloved South Bay clean and, in the process, they wouldn't mind making a few dollars.

Gina and Melissa are entrepreneurs by almost any credible definition of the word. They have identified a potential opportunity in the marketplace and set up a business to exploit it. They have committed resources to this end. Although they didn't quit their day jobs, they did spend approximately two months of their free time developing the product, BT Wax. They also invested their own money in supplies of beeswax and other ingredients. They manufactured their merchandise in Gina's kitchen and delivered it personally to a handful of local surfboard stores. Before that, they had to convince the shop proprietors to give their products shelf space. And, of course, they hope to grow their business and eventually run it on a full-time basis.[2]

In most respects these young women are no different from the millions of others who have embarked on entrepreneurial ventures through the years. They are unusual in one way, however; their principal motivation in starting the business was to protect the environment. It's not that they don't like money. But they believe that they can protect the environment and make money at the same time. The vast majority of entrepreneurs go into business for more selfish (albeit socially well accepted and perfectly respectable) reasons, such as increasing their income and escaping the drudgery or oppression of working for someone else. But these conventional reasons are just part of the motivation for people like Gina and Melissa. We may call them idealistic, selfless, or unreasonable. They think they can make money and improve society at the same time. In fact, they believe that the two goals will feed off each other.

Our research over the last five years has uncovered a statistically small but still surprisingly sizable and fast-growing group of entrepreneurs whose motives and business philosophy are similar to those of Gina and Melissa. These so-called social, socially responsible, ethical, sustainable, or "values-centered" entrepreneurs endeavor to "do good" and concomitantly "do well." They have built profitable companies that significantly contribute to the greater good of society—an outcome which many of them believe traditional capitalism has been ineffective in producing. In this book we aim to examine the motivations, philosophies, and business policies and practices of these "values-centered entrepreneurs" (as we will refer to them from here on out) to learn what commonalities exist amongst them and what lessons ("best practices") can be learned from them. We hope that our findings will offer helpful guidelines for those (whether they may be students, corporate employees, or entrepreneurs) who aspire to follow in their footsteps.

A Growing Movement

The concept of social or responsible entrepreneurship is not completely new. It has been around several decades. Some of the more well-known firms in this category are The Body Shop, Ben & Jerry's, Stonyfield Farm, Patagonia, and Newman's Own. Other widely recognized successful responsible ventures (no longer "ventures" per se) include large U.S. public companies run by their founders, such as Interface Carpets, Starbucks, and Whole Foods. In recent years, however, the pace of development of values-centered ventures has increased. While difficult to quantify (there is no registry for them), increasing numbers of socially responsible firms are being established. Even some of today's hottest technology companies such as Google and Salesforce-.com exhibit a heavy values-centered or social bent. For example, Salesforce.com founder, Marc Benioff, has written two books, *Compassionate Capitalism* and *The Business of Changing the World*, and set up the Salesforce.com Foundation to pro-actively give to causes. Following in Salesforce.com's footsteps, Google set up a foundation early on and has invested in wind energy and other environmental/social projects. Moreover, an increasing number of venture capital and lending institutions, including Pacific Community Ventures, RSF Social Finance, Gray Matters Capital Foundation, and Shorebank (originally Shoreline Bank), have been established to finance social ventures. Even Kleiner Perkins Caulfield & Byers, the legendary venture capital firm that financed internet pioneers like Netscape, Amazon, and Google, has increased its focus on alternative-energy projects.[3]

The passion toward responsible entrepreneurship is growing, particularly among young adults. Universities and MBA programs nationwide, in particular, are finding a strong interest among students for courses in social entrepreneurship. In response to this trend, Brock et al. (2008) report, there are more than "250 professors . . . actively teaching or researching in social entrepreneurship from more than 35 countries, with 29 different competitions, with over 800 different articles and 200 cases used in social entrepreneurship courses."[4] The recent Global Social Venture Competition, a business plan competition among MBA students held in April 2009 at the Haas School of Business at UC Berkeley, received more than 200 entries (compared to the usual 20–50 entries in most competitions).

A New Sense of Urgency and the Role of Entrepreneurship

In recent years, especially with the advent of the new century, the idea of "sustainable development" has come to the forefront of societal issues. Sustainable development was initially defined as "development that meets the needs of the present without compromising the ability of the future generation to meet their needs."[5] Over time, sustainability, as it is frequently called, has become a multidimensional concept that extends beyond environmental protection to encompass economic development and social equity, domestically and abroad.[6]

Today, there is mounting scientific evidence that the quality of human life is at risk due to global environmental deterioration, dramatic economic inequality, and the immense scale of Third World poverty. At a pragmatic level, it means that we must arrest the acceleration of global warming, reverse the deterioration of our life-sustaining ecosystems, and raise standards of living in the Third World (not just because of our moral responsibility but also because ecosystem deterioration and social/political stability are implicitly tied to it).

Based on our observation, there seems to be an overall trend in the developed and even developing economies toward increased consciousness about the natural environment, human health, the treatment of people, and economic inequities around the world. More than ever, people seem concerned about corporate responsibility and transparency. They are asking concrete questions about the manufacturing practices of clothing and shoe companies, fair-trade purchasing practices of coffee chains, and environmental practices of the extractive industries, among others. Consumers seem more receptive than ever to sustainable seafood, organic farming, natural foods, and homoeopathic remedies—all closely tied to the health of the environment. In response, even a large industrial conglomerate like General Electric has said that it "wants to instill values in everything the company does—without compromising the profit principle."[7]

The sense of urgency for action, by consumers and the public at large, is compounded by the fact that, while the concern for sustainability and responsible business practice has risen in recent years, the expectation that governments or multinational corporations will sufficiently address these issues has diminished. Although many large companies have started or expanded their corporate social responsibility (CSR) programs, most people also recognize that these won't be nearly enough to have much impact given the magnitude of today's problems. Indeed, today's mounting societal and environmental problems seem to require a vastly different approach to business. As eBay co-founder and billionaire Pierre Omidyar put it, "I have learnt that if you want to have a global impact you can't ignore business. I don't mean corporate responsibility programs, but business models that provoke social change."[8] Considering the impact that business has on people and the environment, it is apparent that anything like global sustainability will be impossible without the engagement of industries and markets. The question however is: Who will show leadership in bringing about critical changes in business practice? Perhaps our entrepreneurs!

Our values-centered entrepreneurs are individuals who have felt compelled to take action. They make it their business to address the world's social and environmental problems. They are idealists who understand and exploit the power of the capitalistic market system. Or, perhaps, they should be considered first and foremost social activists who instead of carrying picket signs make their statement through responsible business practices. As Gunter Pauli, President of Ecover, a Belgium-based maker of ecological cleaning products, plainly states, "We don't lead boycotts. We don't run Greenpeace campaigns. We are not in business to attack Proctor & Gamble. We are not in the world to punch Unilever in the nose. We want to be positive. We offer solutions."[9]

Our values-centered entrepreneurs also challenge a fundamental notion about business and social values. They do not accept the widely held belief that there need be a dichotomy between how one conducts business and how one improves society. They demonstrate that it is possible, and in some cases more profitable, to build businesses and exercise their social values concurrently. To our delight, we have learned that they are also eager to share their stories—their dreams, challenges, and successes. They all seem to share our belief that, to address the magnitude of today's problems, all businesses, small and large, need to be environmentally and socially aware and responsive. But they also fully understand that they must be profitable if they are going to be able to stay around and do good works.

The Pursuit of Values-Centered Entrepreneurship

In spite of the urgency of today's challenges and the rapidly growing social venture movement, to most people in the business community, values-centered entrepreneurship remains a mystery. Common questions include: Is it *really* possible for a company to be good and do well? What are the real motivations and objectives of these entrepreneurs? Do they want to make money or serve a mission? Do they want to beat competition and grow or do they feel guilty about it? Where on earth do they obtain the needed financing? How do they balance making profits versus serving their cause? How do they treat their employees, the environment, and their communities? How do they build responsible companies in face of today's fierce competition? Do they sell their companies for profit? Do they give much to charities?

While stories and anecdotes have been written about values-centered entrepreneurs, e.g., through autobiographies by the founders of some of the values-centered companies, few, if any, books or research projects have systematically examined the answers to the above questions. To our knowledge, ours is the first study to methodically examine the business strategies and practices of a relatively large and diverse sample of values-centered companies—46—throughout the key stages of their development and growth. We analyze their financial and non-financial objectives, financing methods, hiring practices, organizational design, marketing strategies, growth and exit patterns, and giving programs. We focus in on the policies and practices that have worked for our sample companies, particularly those that departed from conventional methods, and summarize these empirically derived commonalities in the form of ten specific lessons/guidelines. Although the book is grounded on years of academic research, it is mostly composed of inspiring examples and practical guidelines for aspiring entrepreneurs and managers to follow as they build their values-centered ventures.

The key principles or lessons/guidelines that we obtained from our research, which also provide the fundamental framework of the book, are summarized below. Each of these principles is discussed in detail in Chapters 3 through 11. Chapter 2 sets the theoretical framework for our study.

1. **Commit to a (Meaningful) Purpose**. View the business enterprise as a vehicle for not only achieving personal financial goals but also for pursuing social/environmental missions. (Chapter 3)
2. **Raise Capital with Mission in Mind**. Find and work with the right kind of investors who share similar views to build authentic, purpose-oriented, financially successful companies. (Chapter 4)
3. **Hire Talented Employees with Shared Values**. Place heavy importance on job candidates' personal values, in addition to their professional competencies. This will help build a principled and coherent organizational culture —which, in return, will play a significant role in marketplace success. (Chapter 5)
4. **Promote Your Company's Values**. Publicize your values and sustainable business practices as an integral component of your marketplace differentiation. Promote your brand's soul! (Chapter 6)
5. **Build a Cohesive, Dedicated Team**. In addition to hiring staff with personal values similar to yours, utilize creative or even highly unconventional methods to earn employee loyalty and strengthen commitment to the company and its mission. (Chapter 7)
6. **Make Money, but Also Make Exceptions**. Don't hesitate to increase profits by raising prices, cutting costs and pursuing growth, but also be open to making certain calculated exceptions to exercise your values, and accomplish your non-financial goals. (Chapter 8)
7. **Minimize Your Environmental and Social Footprints**. Take proactive— when financially feasible, extraordinary—steps to reduce your firm's negative impact on the environment and society. (Chapter 9)
8. **Stay With It for the Long Haul**. Be willing to stick around and accomplish what you set out to do. Don't be seduced into flipping the business for short-term profit. When it comes to selling, find the right buyer to maintain dedication toward your mission. (Chapter 10)
9. **Make Giving a Priority**. Make donating company profits and time not an afterthought but a principal reason for being and an important function of the business. (Chapter 11)

10. **Be a Role Model for Others.** Willingly share your business philosophy, principles, and experiences with other aspiring entrepreneurs. Make being a role model a priority and an important measure of success. (Chapter 12)

We hope that the readers, whether they may be students in college, employees of corporations, or entrepreneurs, will find the lessons and their protagonists as interesting and inspiring as we did.

2

The Values-Centered Entrepreneur

In contrast to [Milton] Friedman, I do not believe maximizing profits for the investors is the only acceptable justification for all corporate actions. The investors are not the only people who matter. Corporations can exist for purposes other than simply maximizing profits.
—John Mackey, founder and president of Whole Foods[1]

Manhood is taking care of your family and being able to bless other people. Not yourself—but whether you can bless other people. That's what we've been able to do at my company.
—Magic Johnson[2]

The Conventional Approach to Business

Milton Friedman arguably was the most famous and most influential economist of the second half of the twentieth century. In 1970, he wrote a much-celebrated article for the *New York Times Magazine*, the title of which succinctly summed up his message, "The Social Responsibility of Business is to Increase Profits."[3] He was responding to what most classically trained economists saw as a growing alien threat—the concept of Corporate Social Responsibility (CSR, for short). Friedman argued that since corporate managers legally are agents of the owners (shareholders), to do anything other than try to maximize their financial gain would, in essence, be stealing from them. On a more theoretical plane, many other classically trained economists going back to Adam Smith, the father of capitalism, have asserted that if funds are spent on projects not intended to maximize profits, the efficiency of the market mechanism, or what Smith called "the invisible hand," would be compromised and resources misallocated within the economy. The result would be that less wealth is created within the overall economy.

The reasoning of these economists is well accepted today in the business community. Their theories are taught in basic economics courses in colleges and even high schools around the world: The objective of a business is to maximize profits. Efficiency and profits are the most important measures of success. Concerns for the welfare of employees, the environment, or local communities are "externalities" of secondary importance that the magic of the capitalistic market will eventually take care of on its own. The pursuit of gain for one's self-interest benefits all in society.

Well, the purpose of our book is not to fuel another debate on profit maximization versus corporate social responsibility. Numerous other books and articles have discussed this issue at length. Nonetheless, before moving on, we should mention that most observers today, economists included, acknowledge that the capitalistic market does not work as perfectly as Adam Smith imagined. As champions of capitalism, Friedman and Smith had very optimistic views of the world and believed that efficient markets would create wealth that would work its way through the system and eventually solve the great social problems of the time. Today, it is more obvious that their generalizations about the efficient markets do not apply in all circumstances. As Muhammad Yunus, a trained economist, founder of Grameen Bank and Nobel Laureate, has observed, "The conventional thinking that capitalism breeds wealth creators and competitors who spread that wealth by creating jobs and opportunities for the good of societies has not worked out very well for the majority of the world."[4] Bill Gates, founder of Microsoft, concurs, saying that although capitalization has benefited the lives of billions, "it has left out billions more."[5] Additionally, it appears that corporations are unable to deal with some of the issues that affect their very existence, such as global warming and ecosystem decline.

The Values-Centered Approach

Although classical economics is the theoretical underpinning of our economy and considered gospel by many people in today's business world, a surprisingly large number of intriguing, though not widely studied, entrepreneurs have adopted a modified business philosophy. The entrepreneurs whom we have termed "values-centered entrepreneurs" endeavor to "be good as well as do well" by simultaneously achieving economic (profit), environmental, and social goals—the so-called triple bottom-line.[6] They build profitable companies while also contributing to the greater good of society—an outcome which, they believe, traditional capitalism has been ineffective in producing.

We should mention at this point that we had no intention of introducing a new business phrase ("values-centered entrepreneurs"). Heaven knows the world does not need more business jargon. As explained below, however, we identified such clear differences in the perspective and action among our group of entrepreneurs that we felt they deserved an appropriate classification.

Values-centered entrepreneurs exercise quintessential entrepreneurship: They are eager to challenge and defy convention. They want to change the world. Consequently, they have been called naïve, idealistic, or unreasonable in pursuit of their goals. Many are also willing to adopt unconventional criteria of success that encompass objectives beyond the financial. As John Williams of Frog's Leap, a sustainable Napa Valley winery, remarks on his company website,

> We will succeed as a business, measuring our success with unique criteria. We will both respect and challenge conventional wisdom, growing our company the way we grow our

vines. We will enhance the quality of our lives and the lives of those who work with us, never forsaking our belief that wine is a wonderful part of life, not life itself.

Values-centered entrepreneurs operate with a fundamentally different view of the role of business. They believe that business is deeply rooted in society and has multi-dimensional responsibility to it. They believe in self-interest but also understand that business must be part of the solution to society's ills. Unlike many economists and business people, they believe that business values are and should be integrated with personal values. In their mind, business is not just an entity for maximizing one's financial objective but also a vehicle for pursuing matters of conscience. See Table 2.1 for the contrast between the conventional and values-centered views.

Values-centered entrepreneurs have, in effect, adopted for themselves a higher standard of ethics and conduct. Whereas Adam Smith held that, "Every man, as long as he does not violate the laws of justice, is left perfectly free to pursue his own interest his own way . . .," our values-centered entrepreneurs want to do more than stay within the boundary of the law.[7] The values-centered entrepreneurs believe in self-interest but also trust in the basic goodness of human beings. They assume that a business can be both profitable and benevolent. They want to build for-profit companies that are not just for profit. They believe that consumers prefer buying products from companies with a higher standard of ethics and social performance and that employees will be more motivated to work for a cause than a paycheck or a promotion. They practice ethical, open, values-centered management, not because someone demands it of them or because it is easy (it is usually more difficult) but because they have set for themselves a different and higher measure of success.

As mentioned earlier, our values-centered entrepreneurs challenge the fundamental

Table 2.1 The Role of Business

Conventional View	Values-Centered View
Social responsibility of business is to increase its profits.	Business is deeply rooted in society and has multi-dimensional responsibility to it.
The capitalistic market will take care of the welfare of employees, their communities, and the natural environment.	"The conventional thinking that capitalism breeds wealth and creates jobs and opportunities for the good of societies has not worked out very well for the majority of the world." (Muhammad Yunus).
The pursuit of gain for one's self-interest will benefit all in society.	The pursuit of gain for one's self-interest without the consideration of others can damage society and the environment.
Business is business.	Business is integrated with personal values.
Business and one's moral beliefs do not mix. If you believe in a cause, join a nonprofit on the weekends.	Business is a place one can exercise his/her beliefs and matters of the heart.
Entrepreneurship is a traditional vehicle for technological and business innovation.	Entrepreneurship can also be an agent of social and environmental change.

assumption that work and personal values do not mix (i.e., "business is business"). Conventional business people tend to dichotomize where and how they make their money versus where and how they help society. Some even see making money as a sin and "giving back" as the penance. Our entrepreneurs see nothing wrong with making money, unless it hurts people and the surroundings. They happen to see giving back as the greater good.

In this book, we examine the business practices of values-centered entrepreneurs by investigating the key non-conventional policies and decisions they have employed in building successful triple bottom-line companies. We believe that the findings will offer helpful guidance for those who aspire to follow in their footsteps.

For clarification, we should mention that our values-centered entrepreneurs are similar to "social entrepreneurs," who have received a great deal of recognition in recent years. Social entrepreneurs are commonly defined as a broad category of entrepreneurs who found and manage non-profit or for-profit organizations to serve specific social purposes or causes. Our values-centered entrepreneurs, on the other hand, conceive and run profit-making companies with an added social/environmental mission; but, they are first and foremost subject to market discipline. Certainly, there are ventures that fall into both categories. To illustrate, Nobel Peace Prize recipient Muhammad Yunus is typically described as a social entrepreneur but we view him also as a values-centered businessman. His Grameen Bank and other "social" enterprises follow a for-profit business model. They are subject to the discipline of the market and must, over the long haul, be profitable. Thus, values-centered entrepreneurs would constitute a subset of the social entrepreneurs.

The Relationship to Corporate Social Responsibility (CSR)

CSR, values-centered entrepreneurship's theoretical underpinning, is not a new concept, nor was it in 1970 when Friedman took dead aim at it. Generally, it is believed that Howard Bowman enunciated the first definition of CSR back in 1953 as "the obligation of businessmen to pursue those policies, to make those decisions, or to follow those lines of action which are desirable in terms of the objectives of our society."[8] Joseph McGuire, a decade later, added that "the idea of social responsibilities supposes that the corporation has not only economical and legal obligations but also certain responsibilities that extend beyond these."[9] Archie Carroll, building on McGuire, delineated four distinct categories of business responsibilities: economic, legal, ethical, and discretionary or philanthropic.[10]

We rather like the historical evolution of the notion proffered by Hay and Gray (one of your authors) who saw CSR thinking progressing through three distinct but overlapping phrases (see Figure 2.1).[11] Phase I was the Smith/Friedman perspective of profit maximization. This notion of business responsibilities was prevalent in the United States of the nineteenth and early twentieth centuries. During this period, the nation was poor and implicitly the paramount national priority was economic development. Capitalism was seen as the path to wealth creation. Profit maximization as an essential component in the theory of capitalism was embraced by business and at least tolerated by the majority of the population. The prevalent feeling was that the system created jobs and improved the lifestyle of the average person even though the lion's share of the largess went to the greedy businessmen of the day.

Phase II, trusteeship management, emerged in the 1930s. The stock market crash of 1929 and the "great depression" that followed shook the public's faith in the capitalist system. Some observers began to question whether the owner's self-interest should be the sole objective of business; after all, there are other parties who also have significant stakes in the business. These include customers, workers, suppliers, communities, and government. Furthermore, several of them were growing in power to rival business, especially workers through the trade union movement and the (U.S.) government with the advent of the "New Deal." Sociologists call this phenomenon "pluralism," i.e., multiple centers of power in society.

Structural changes in the economy also stimulated the emerging trusteeship view. The business scene by the 1920s was dominated by giant corporations with highly diffused stock ownership. To illustrate, it was found that the largest shareholders in corporations such as AT&T, U.S. Steel, and Pennsylvania Railroad each owned less than 1 percent of the total shares outstanding in those companies. Similar dispersion of stock ownership was prevalent in many other large corporations. Given these circumstances, it was senior management not the owners (shareholders) who were in control of these corporations. The average shareholder had no say in the direction of the firm. If the shareholder was dissatisfied with management's performance there was little effective recourse other than selling the stock. Hence, a logical question was, "To whom is corporate management responsible?" The trusteeship concept provided a ready answer. The corporation should be managed in a balanced fashion taking into

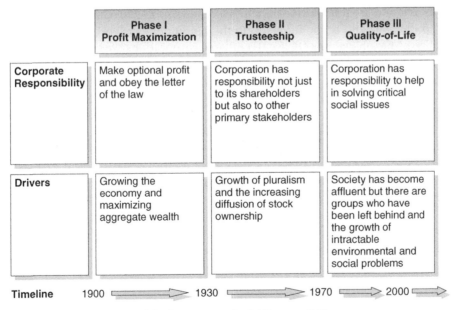

Figure 2.1 Three-Phase Model of Corporate Social Responsibility

Source: Derived from Hay & Gray (1974).

account the interest of all principal resource contributors—shareholders, customers, employees, creditors, suppliers, and plant communities. This philosophy would later be expanded to include all groups with a stake in the company and called "Stakeholder Management."

The third phase, quality-of-life, emerged in the 1960s as the national priorities in the U.S. came into question. America had become what John Galbraith called in his best-selling book, *The Affluent Society*.[12] The vast majority of people were middle class, and aggregate scarcity of goods and services was no longer the dominant problem. But there were vexing social issues that were forging major societal divides. Some of these issues were directly influenced by business, and others only indirectly, but it was becoming increasingly evident that business was operating in an expanded orb of societal expectations. In the 1970s, the big problems included environmental pollution, deteriorating inner cities, minority employment, product safety, worker health and safety, and truth in advertising. New laws and regulations addressing these issues were put in place that required compliance from corporations. But beyond this, there were growing expectations that businesses expand what Carroll called their range of discretionary responsibilities. The composition of quality-of-life issues grew and changed over time. By the 1990s, the range of issues embodied corporate governance, general business ethics, global climate change, ecosystem decline, and Third World poverty. More recently, the bulk of these issues have come to be subsumed under the broad concept of "sustainability."

Returning to the CSR versus profit maximization controversy, as the model on the evolution of CSR clarifies, the Smith/Friedman perspective of Phase I may be an outdated notion in today's world (so yesterday!). Although some people, both economists and practitioners, may be stuck in the 1970s (Phase II), others, like a generous handful of multinationals and our values-centered entrepreneurs, have moved to Phase III and beyond. Thanks to the rise in public expectations, the evolving quality-of-life obligations (Phase III) of large corporations are generally accepted or at least given lip service by their senior executives. But entrepreneurs and small business owners, typically, are not held to the same standard as large corporations because of their firms' modest resources and perceived limited potential for social/ environmental impact. However, in sharp contrast to the prototypical entrepreneur, the values-centered leaders of our firms have put environmental and social performance front and center in their mission to deliver triple (or at least dual) bottom-line performance. We regard these values-centered entrepreneurs not as rarities or odd-balls, as some might, but rather, as frontrunners in the evolution of corporate responsibility.

Toward a New Model of the Business Enterprise

The notion of values-centered entrepreneurship has also caused us to rethink the generally accepted typology of ventures or enterprises. Traditional business enterprises, i.e., corporations, are designed to maximize profits. Non-profit organizations serve causes and make no attempt to generate measurable revenues from the sale of products or services. Thus, it used to be easy to distinguish between businesses and non-profit organizations. Everyone clearly recognized, for instance, that IBM was a business corporation and the March of Dimes was a charity. With the new breed of values-centered entrepreneurs and the increasing interest of nonprofits in finding new sources of revenue, the line between businesses and nonprofits is generally blurring.

For example, Newman's Own is a venture operating at the intersection of two categories. It is legally a non-profit organization but it vies in a competitive industry and operates like a business corporation. Its profits are donated to a multitude of worthy causes because this is what the late Paul Newman[13] and his partner, A.E. "Hotch" Hotchner, wanted. Companies such as Patagonia, Tom's of Maine, or Timothy Haahs & Associates, on the other hand, are legally for-profit enterprises that make rigid commitments to give a substantial fraction of their incomes to charities and causes.

Our values-centered entrepreneurs have built enterprises that are also in between the traditional corporations and traditional charities, as shown in Figure 2.2. Non-profits that act like businesses such as Newman's Own or Goodwill Stores may be categorized as Business Model Charities. Other values-centered ventures, including Ben & Jerry's, Whole Foods, and Clif Bar can be viewed as triple bottom-line companies, or as one of our entrepreneurs preferred, not-just-for-profit companies.

But even this typology leaves out some organizations that lie in between the categories. Consider the example of Homeboy Industries founded by Father Greg Boyle, a Jesuit priest, with the mission "to assist at-risk and former gang-involved youth to become contributing members of our community."[14] Fr. Boyle's organization has two distinct parts: One in a nonprofit job referral and counseling center for former gang members in East Los Angeles. The newer segment is a collection of business ventures

	Traditional Charities	Business Model Charities	Triple Bottom-Line Firms	Traditional Corporations
Source of Income	Donation, grants, sale of products	Sale of products & services	Sale of products & services	Sale of products & services
Use of Income	Expenditures for social purposes	Operating expenses, investment, social purpose expenditures	Expenses, investment, social purpose expenditures, return to owners	Expense, investment, return to owners
Examples	United Way Red Cross	Newman's Own Edun Apparel	Patagonia Tom's of Maine	Microsoft Toyota Exxon

Figure 2.2 Continuum of Enterprise Models

that hire the most at-risk individuals to equip them with the work habits and skills needed to find gainful employment. As of 2008, Homeboy's enterprises included a bakery, a silkscreen operation, a diner, and a small merchandise business. It is doubtful that these popular services or any of Homeboy's other businesses ever turned a profit; after all, their principal purpose was to assist transitioning gang members into civil society. In 2003, less than 20 percent of Homeboy's total revenue was derived from its business ventures; the remainder came from contributions, grants, and government contracts. In a similar vein, also consider Help the World See (HTWS),[15] a social entrepreneurship organization created to furnish eyeglasses and eye care for needy people in Third World countries. After several years of struggling and experimenting, the organization settled on the business model of establishing self-sustaining eye clinics that charged below-market fees that were sufficient, once breakeven volume was exceeded, to create a small profit which would be used to further subsidize people unable to afford even the reduced fees. To support its growth and overheads, HTWS continued, however, to solicit outside contributions. These two organizations seem to lie somewhere in between the Traditional Charities and Business Model Charities. Further, major corporations with more than token social responsibility activities might be thought of as residing somewhere betwixt the triple bottom-line and the traditional corporation categories.

The point here is that there are different types of organizations out there, even if our current legal system does not distinguish amongst them. We should not be stuck in our thinking with just the two legal models, for-profit and non-profit. There is room for everyone with different ideas and motivations to build organizations to make an impact. The legal definitions must not stifle our imagination or be a hindrance to the type of organizations that are created to meet the needs of people.

The Study

In choosing the companies for our study, we used what is often called a judgment sample. We looked for firms that met three specific criteria. The first criterion was that the candidate firm must have a strong social/environmental focus. If a company did not meet this standard, we simply moved on. The second criterion was that the company had to be profitable or at least been profitable for some years.[16] This was important to us because we wanted to distill lessons from financially successful organizations. The third criterion was that the firm had to have been founded by an entrepreneur or entrepreneurs (rather than be a fully-owned spin off from a large corporation) and run by him or her through, at least, its principal growth stages. We applied this test because we wanted to study the thinking of the entrepreneur as much as we did the policies and practices of the firm. In fact, as it turned out, in most cases they were highly intertwined.

Our search process was hardly scientific but we did cast a broad net. We dug into academic case studies, books, and journal articles. We regularly perused business magazines and the business section of a variety of daily newspapers. We watched television news with an eye toward potential leads. We queried our colleagues and gave our students assignments to identify and analyze appropriate companies. We were not particularly systematic in our search but we were persistent. In the end, we found close to 100 firms that seemed to meet our criteria. We then narrowed our own list down to 46 entrepreneurial organizations (see Tables 2.2 to 2.4) that we believed were especially interesting or exemplary. We also tried to have as representative a sample as possible; consequently, we sought, to the extent possible, to balance our sample in terms of size, stage of development, and nature of the business.

Our sample, as mentioned, includes several corporate brands that almost everyone will recognize, such as Ben & Jerry's, The Body Shop, and Starbucks. We purposely included these companies because they are considered leaders in socially responsible business practice. We have called these "Pioneers," because they have pioneered responsible management practices when very few others dared to do so. Other leaders, like Clif Bar and Salesforce.com, with shorter histories, have been categorized as "New Role Models." Additionally, we have identified a group of small ventures such as Dancing Deer Baking and Iggy's Bread of the World that are practically unknown outside of their particular industries and locales but are exemplary in their responsible management practice. We have named them the "Up & Comers." Our companies ranged widely in size, from revenue of under $2 million to over several billion. The sample intentionally embraced firms in various stages of the development cycle. Furthermore, albeit the vast majority of the companies come from the United States, we did examine several overseas firms, including the large Swiss supermarket chain, Migros, the up-and-coming British beverage firm, Innocent Drinks, and Bangladesh-headquartered, Grameen Bank, among others. Also, we noted that for over half of our firms, the environment was a principal cause, reflecting the current gravity of this issue.

We believe that all of the companies in our sample have made noteworthy efforts to do social good and are useful examples for others to heed. But we also realize that some of our choices may be controversial. Take The Body Shop, for example. Although the company has promoted itself as a paradigm of socially responsible capitalism, its critics, and it has had many over the years, have charged that the company has not lived up to its lofty claims. For instance, they have contended that its products were not "all natural" and at some point had been tested on animals (both violate the principles stated in the company's publicity). Critics have also asserted that its claims of helping poor, indigenous communities around the world were highly exaggerated. Underlying the various specific criticisms was the theme that The Body Shop founder, the late Anita Roddick,[17] was insincere and shamelessly promoted the company's social/environmental image to sell products and make money. Because of the criticisms, the company's Board of Directors, in 1995, commissioned an independent audit of its social performance. The consultant, former Stanford University professor Kirk Hanson, concluded that the company's intentions were essentially "pure." But, he also found that its management was overstretched, resulting in inattention to day-to-day operation and ineffective communication with stockholders.[18]

It goes without saying that neither The Body Shop nor any of the other companies in our sample, or any of their founders, are perfect. But all of them have made strong, and, we believe, sincere commitments to making a genuine contribution to society and have made significant progress in implementing their visions. For these reasons, they are included in our study.

To gather and organize the necessary information, we developed (in some cases lengthy) case studies for each of our 46 entrepreneurs and their companies. Information came from both direct interviews with the founders and secondary sources such as books and newspaper articles. With the use of these case studies, we examined how the companies balanced profit objective with mission in key business functions throughout their development cycle—from initial company formation, through growth, to exit—to build and maintain successful triple bottom-line companies. In particular, we analyzed how their commitment to quality-of-life issues affected their company mission, hiring and human resource policies, marketing strategies, financial practices, exit choices, and giving programs—and vice versa. We also took note of all their innovative and unconventional approaches that appeared to be fruitful in their endeavors. After reviewing all available information and learning how each of our 46 companies dealt with the above key decision areas, we were able to distill a set of commonalities. The remainder of the book presents and discusses the ten most

Table 2.2 The Pioneers

	Company	Main Business Area	Main Cause	Headquarters
1	Ben & Jerry's	Ice Cream	Environment, Peace, Community	Vermont
2	The Body Shop	Personal Care	Environment & Human Rights	United Kingdom
3	Calvert Group of Mutual Funds	Asset Management	Community, Employees, Environment	Maryland
4	Grameen Bank	Microloans	Poverty	Bangladesh
5	Interface Carpets	Floor Covering	Environment	Georgia
6	Migros	Food Retail	Social Equity and Community	Switzerland
7	Newman's Own	Salad Dressing & Sauces	Social Equity	Connecticut
8	Patagonia	Outdoor Clothing	Environment	California
9	Starbucks	Coffee Retail	Worker Rights	Washington
10	Stonyfield Farm	Organic Yogurt	Environment, Community	New Hampshire
11	Tom's of Maine	Personal Care	Environment, Community, Employees	Maine
12	Whole Foods	Food Retail	Environment, Community, Employees	Texas

Table 2.3 New Role Models

	Company	Main Business Area	Main Cause	Location
13	Broad Air Conditioning	Appliance	Environment	China
14	King Cycle Group	Bicycle Components	Environment	Oregon
15	Clif Bar	Energy Bars	Environment, Health	California
16	Craigslist	Classified	Community, Nonprofit Organizations	California
17	Ecover	Cleaning Products	Environment	Belgium
18	Eileen Fisher Clothing	Apparel	Women's & Human Rights	New York
19	Explore Inc.	After-School Programs	Education	Maryland
20	Green Mountain Energy	Energy	Environment	Vermont
21	Innocent Drinks	Juice Drinks	Environment, Health	U.K.
22	Magic Johnson Enterprises	Real Estate	Inner City Development	California
23	New Belgium Brewery	Beer	Environment	Colorado
24	Novica	Home Decor	Poverty, Culture Preservation	California
25	Rhythm & Hues	Entertainment	Work Environment	California
26	Salesforce.com	Software	Various	California
27	Seventh Generation	Household Products	Environment	Vermont
28	Sterling Planet	Energy	Clean Energy	Georgia
29	Timothy Haahs & Associates	Architecture	Community	Pennsylvania
30	White Dog Cafe	Restaurant	Community, Environment	Pennsylvania
31	Working Assets	Telecom & Financial	Peace, Equality	Georgia

Table 2.4 The Up & Comers

	Company	Main Business Area	Main Cause	Location
32	AgraQuest	Pest Management	Environment	California
33	Berkeley Mills	Furniture	Environment	California
34	Dancing Deer Baking	Baked Goods	Homeless (housing & jobs)	Massachusetts
35	EV Rental	Car Rental	Environment	California
36	Frog's Leap	Winery	Environment	California
37	Gaia Napa Valley Hotel	Hotel	Environment	California
38	Honest Tea	Beverage	Social Equity	Maryland
39	Iggy's Bread of the World	Bakery	Environment, Worker Rights	Massachusetts
40	Pacific Community Ventures	Private Equity Investment	Worker Compensation	California
41	Revolution Foods	Healthy Meals for Schools	Health	California
42	Shorebank Pacific	Bank	Environment	Oregon
43	Small Dog Electronics	Computer Sales & Service	Various	Vermont
44	Sweet Riot	Chocolate	Environment	New York
45	Tom's Shoes	Shoes	Poverty	California
46	T.S. Designs	Screen-printing	Environment	North Carolina

significant and interesting commonalities found. They clarify how values-centered entrepreneurs and their companies depart from conventional business practice, as well as providing insight into how they make money while achieving their social mission. We have structured the ten commonalities as guidelines/lessons in hopes that, in this form, they will be more instructive and helpful to those who hope to follow in their footsteps.

Part 2
The Lessons/Guidelines

3

Commit to a (Meaningful) Purpose

We started this business for conventional reasons, to make money for investors with a product that doesn't compromise on quality, and for unconventional ones, to be a force for social change.

—Gary Hirshberg, co-founder, Stonyfield Farm[1]

The core of entrepreneurship is about making meaning. If you make meaning, you will probably make money. But if you set out to make money, you will probably not make meaning, and you won't make money.

—Guy Kawasaki, founder and managing director of Garage Technology Ventures[2]

Committed to a Cause

Most entrepreneurs, values-centered or otherwise, start businesses for honorable reasons. Many have great visions of the future. Others want to be their own boss and be financially rewarded for their achievements. They are passionate about their ideas and work tirelessly to achieve their goals. Most of them take tremendous personal risks. Some even succeed in improving people's lives through their innovative new products and services. We applaud all of them for their courage to pursue their dreams. For many years, our school, Loyola Marymount University, like many other universities, has been giving awards to successful entrepreneurs so that they would share their stories with our students. We want more of our students to become entrepreneurs because we believe almost all successful entrepreneurs make a positive contribution to the economy and society.

But our values-centered entrepreneurs are a very special breed. They don't want economic and social contribution to society to be a by-product of their businesses' success, but rather, a significant and direct objective. Yes, they do want to make money and do want to be their own boss. But they also envision a better society—with fulfilled employees, happier communities, and a cleaner environment, among other achievements. These are not afterthoughts but critical components of their entrepreneurial ambition. They don't want to be their own boss for the sake of control, but because they want the freedom to exercise their beliefs. To many of our values-centered entrepreneurs, entrepreneurship does not mean just starting a business, it also represents an opportunity for self-expression and ultimately social change.

The values-centered entrepreneurs we examined have been and are deeply committed to one or more meaningful, non-commercial causes. Their causes include, among others, protecting the environment, reducing Third World poverty, empowering workers, and developing inner cities. For example, Yvon Chouinard of Patagonia, an outdoor apparel and equipment company, was highly concerned about the deteriorating state of the natural environment and wanted his business to become a role model for how business can be responsible. Ben & Jerry's, legendary ice-cream chain named after the founders, has actively protested against a wide range of issues including the Cold War, nuclear energy, and guns. Magic Johnson of Magic Johnson Enterprises and the founders of Shorebank Corporation have been determined to develop the inner cities to improve the lives of those who live there.

Pretenders not welcome
Critical Question for the Aspiring Entrepreneur:

Are there social or environmental issues that you are
<u>really</u> passionate about?

More than Great Products

The values-centered entrepreneurs are in no way less concerned about the quality of their products than other entrepreneurs. In fact, one of the key commonalities among the companies in our sample is the high quality of products they make and their high-end positioning in the marketplace. Consider for example, Chris King Precision Equipment, a quality leader in the cycling equipment industry; Stonyfield Farm, a high-end, natural yogurt producer; or even Starbucks, known for charging $4–5 for a great cup of coffee.

But our values-centered entrepreneurs endeavor to do more than just offer the best products and services. They want to effect change too. They want their business to have meaningful impact on the world—through their products, processes, policies, people, and management practices.

Our mission-oriented entrepreneurs seem to operate with a different view of success. To illustrate, Marc Benioff, founder of Salesforce.com, a technology company with $7 billion in market valuation, is quoted as saying that his key philosophy is that "to recognize success, it needs to be shared . . . [and] the key to being successful in business is giving back."[3] This philosophy is integrated into every facet of Benioff's strategic vision for Salesforce.com and was the primary motivation for establishing the Salesforce.com Foundation one year after the company was founded.

Albeit creating great products and running a business are extremely challenging tasks, our values-centered entrepreneurs want to do even more. Timothy Haahs, founder of Timothy Haahs & Associates, Inc., an architectural firm specializing in the design of mixed-use buildings containing parking structures, speaks incessantly about giving back but seldom mentions offering high-quality products or service. "Those things are given," explained the Philadelphia Ernst & Young Entrepreneur of the Year in an interview, "but we want to do more."[4] The values-centered entrepreneurs seem to exhibit even more ambition and drive than most entrepreneurs—a genre already renowned for these attributes.

Business as a Solution

Our values-centered entrepreneurs are driven by concerns about social and environmental problems, many of which have been caused or exacerbated by corporations. Yet, unlike typical activists or protestors, they utilize the business enterprise as the vehicle of choice to pursue their goals. It is interesting that, in contrast to the negative press about the detrimental impact of business on the environment and its lack of social conscience, our entrepreneurs have an immensely positive view of what business can accomplish.

Consider Magic Johnson, the former superstar professional basketball player and now a real estate mogul, who wanted to develop the inner cities—that were being neglected by the mainstream businesses—in part to offer its residents the kinds of retail and entertainment services he felt they deserved. He also believed that the job opportunities his businesses would bring to the inner cities would be more effective in helping disadvantaged youth than any social program. But perhaps most importantly, he wanted to prove that there was money to be made in the inner city, and encourage other businesses to follow his example, creating still more jobs and more development.

Yvon Chouinard of Patagonia was determined to use his business to inspire and implement solutions to the environmental crisis. While building a recognized brand over the course of well over 20 years (with approximately $240 million in revenue and 1,200 employees), he pioneered many environmentally innovative business practices and served as a role model for many other environmentally concerned entrepreneurs. Chouinard pioneered, among others, the use of organic cotton, green office buildings, and corporate day-care centers. He institutionalized his values by imposing on his company an "Earth Tax" that committed one percent of the company's revenue or 10 percent of profits yearly for needy "green" causes. In 1999 Chouinard was recognized as a "Hero for the Planet" by *Time* magazine because of his leadership in environmental work and his efforts to effect social change.[5]

Muhammad Yunus, the winner of the 2006 Nobel Peace Prize, came to believe that business would be the most effective vehicle to fight poverty. Transforming himself from an academic to an entrepreneur, he has built a financial institution that lends money to the poor, believing in and relying on the innate entrepreneurial capacity of individuals. Yunus notes, "At Grameen Bank, credit is a cost effective weapon to fight poverty and it serves as a catalyst in the overall development of socio-economic conditions of the poor who have been kept outside the banking orbit on the ground that they are poor and hence not bankable." As of 2007, Grameen reported that it had made loans to 7.39 million borrowers, and that more than half had escaped poverty.[6]

Another remarkable story is Stonyfield Farm, a leading yogurt maker, with revenues of about $250 million in 2006. Samuel Kaymen founded Stonyfield Farm in Wilton, New Hampshire, in 1983 as a vehicle to help fund Kaymen's Rural Education Center and to provide support for small family dairy farmers in New England. Kaymen, an early advocate of organic farming, had established the Rural Education Center to educate farmers, as well as the general public, on the merits and techniques of organic farming. Kaymen wanted a marketable product to raise funds for the Center and settled on adapting his grandmother's Ukrainian yogurt recipe.

Perhaps Ray Anderson, founder and Chairman of Interface Carpets (a $1 billion floor covering company) best articulated the rationale for companies adopting social or environmental causes:

> While business is part of the problem, it can also be a part of the solution. Business is the largest, wealthiest, most pervasive institution on Earth, and responsible for most of the damage. It must take the lead in directing the Earth away from collapse, and toward sustainability and restoration.[7]

Deep Personal Convictions

For our values-centered entrepreneurs, it was their personal convictions that caused them to start their companies or implement leading-edge management practices. Consider again the case of Timothy Haahs, who founded his Philadelphia-based architectural firm to "serve others." His sense of service may have had deep roots: Haahs spent the first 12 years of his life in South Korea living in a leper colony where his father served as a Christian missionary. But during his early adult years, Haahs was focused on having a traditional career and living the American dream. After earning his engineering degree from the University of Pennsylvania, and then working for a company that designed nuclear power plants, he climbed the corporate ladder for 10 years, advancing to Principal with Philadelphia-based Walker Parking Consultants.

Haahs' life changed in 1992 when a previously undiagnosed heart defect caused him to lose consciousness while driving on the New Jersey Turnpike. In January 1993, after waiting in the hospital for six months, he received a new heart. The surgery and hospitalization caused him to exceed his lifetime insurance maximum. It also led him to adopt a new perspective on life. "What came upon me," he says, "is that life is really about helping other people, and I wanted to do something with that. To have that kind of impact, I decided to build my own company, and make its purpose to serve others."[8]

Thus, Haahs established Timothy Haahs & Associates, Inc. with a mission statement beginning with the words, "We exist to help those in need." Today, Haahs and his 48 employees translate this mission into donating at least 20 percent of profits, both directly, and through the Timothy Haahs Foundation, to charities and churches serving the needy in the Philadelphia area. Principals and employees of the firm are encouraged to participate in philanthropic activities ranging from food drives and charity walks, to serving on boards of non-profit organizations. In 2002, Haahs moved his office into a building he designed to include a 12,000 square-foot community center with an auditorium and meeting space, which he makes available to non-profit agencies free of charge.

Personal values were pivotal in starting the business for the founders of Novica, a profitable web-based business that features the products created by master artisans in developing countries. Co-founder Armenia Nercessian de Oliveira, a former United Nations officer, spent decades resolving conflicts and defending human rights in war-torn countries around the world. She was formerly stationed with the U.N. High Commissioner for Refugees team that won the 1981 Nobel Peace Prize for its work. Co-founders Robert Milk (Armenia's son-in-law) and Andy Milk are sons of a Peace Corps officer and have had a lifelong interest in artisans in developing countries. Even with such a rich tradition of public service in the family, co-founder and CEO Robert Milk, a member of an investment firm at the time, asked himself many "Why" questions, before diving into this entrepreneurial venture. Today, Milk believes that it makes sense for all aspiring values-centered entrepreneurs to ask similar questions (see Table 3.1) before committing to a new venture.

What made his decision more difficult was, as Robert Milk recalls, that:

> Everyone said it couldn't be done: simultaneously establish offices in countries all over the world, pay artisans more than they have ever made before, ship purchases directly to customers worldwide—from countries all over the world, with no U.S. warehousing, and design a patent-pending back-end system to handle all the complex logistics, international tracking, and tariffs and customs coding so customers could enjoy seamless, low cost, fast, and efficient shipping.

What gave Milk courage to commit to the new venture was a thirst to create something new and contribute to the world, which were core values that had been developed through his background and life experiences. He explains:

> Had it not been for these core values, I may not have been interested in starting Novica. The company had such a far-reaching mission and elaborate infrastructure that would literally require working around the clock for years, and require an incredible sacrifice of time and stamina, that had it not been for mission/values, we would not have wanted to take the plunge. For this reason, I definitely consider myself a social entrepreneur, applying business rules to social issues. Novica is at its very essence a social company, delivering value to artisans and customers worldwide, as well as to shareholders.[9]

Others in our sample followed their personal convictions in a similar fashion, starting their enterprises with a notion of a social good to which they could contribute.

Table 3.1 Robert Milk's "Questions to Ask Yourself before Jumping In"

- Why should I spend the next decade of my life doing this?
- Why would I leave a lucrative corporate job to do this?
- Why does this need to exist?
- Why me? What does my particular background/skill set have to offer in this sector?

The idea for Berkeley Mills, a small California furniture manufacturer, for example, emanated from an idealistic desire to forge a realistic harmony between a wood-worker's livelihood and forest preservation. Therrell Murphy of Sterling Planet who called himself a "practical idealist" had the vision of "leading the migration to sustainable energy that was good for the environment, the economy, and all current and future generations,"[10] and John Hughes founded Rhythm & Hues with the vision of a stable and friendly work environment for artistic talents in the notoriously harsh entertainment industry. Milton Davis, James Fletcher, Ronald Grzywinski and Mary Houghton, the founders of Shorebank Corporation, America's first community bank, believed that a bank could effectively revive underserved neighborhoods.

Before moving on we should note that as it has become "hip" in recent years for companies to claim to be socially responsible; it has also become more difficult to differentiate the truly values-centered firms from what might be called "pretenders" or "opportunists." It takes a little more time to make sure that a company is indeed committed to the cause(s) it claims to be serious about. One aspect of the method-ology that we follow is to assess the founders' level of personal conviction and under-stand where that conviction comes from. Of course, we also look at their actions, not just words, and the extent to which they go out of their way to pursue their missions.

Unconventional Backgrounds

Not surprisingly, many of the entrepreneurs' value systems were shaped as a result of experiences they had prior to starting their companies. Gary Erickson, founder of Clif Bar, was a free spirit who enjoyed outdoor adventures and had a true appreciation for wilderness. He formed the philosophy that would guide his future company after a life-altering experience in Nepal. While trekking, Erickson was troubled by the amount of resources and energy that climbing expeditions consumed for the perhaps egotistical purpose of reaching the summits of the world's highest peaks. Moreover, he was appalled by the tons of waste left behind by the climbers at the base of the mountains. It seemed almost hypocritical that these climbers who claimed to have a love of the mountains would have such a disregard for preserving their quality. He came to the epiphany, "If getting to the top or making the bottom-line means you can't do it without polluting the earth, then don't climb that mountain. Climb another mountain, or climb a different way."[11] So, Erickson decided early on that he wouldn't pollute the earth in developing a successful business. He would find another way!

As one might expect, many of our entrepreneurs exhibited a strong sense of social or environmental consciousness before starting their business careers. Douglas Hyde, founder of Green Mountain Energy, was an attorney for the poor. Tom Chappell of Tom's of Maine was a devout Episcopalian with life-long personal beliefs in the worth of people and nature. Paul Newman was a self-proclaimed environmentalist. Anita Roddick, of The Body Shop, was a librarian and a United Nations worker.

Interestingly, most of our entrepreneurs in our sample did not have extensive business experience before they started their companies. Only five of our 46 sample company founders had business degrees and only a handful had related management experience before starting their successful ventures. For example, Paul Newman, whose company, Newman's Own, has annual revenues over $100 million, was a famous actor and a race-car driver, but had no experience in business. Gary Hirshberg of Stonyfield Farm with over $250 million annual revenue was an educator and environmental activist. Magic Johnson, who now owns a real estate empire estimated to be worth over $500 million, was a professional basketball player. Anita Roddick had zero business or cosmetics experience before founding The Body Shop.[12] Actually, very few in our sample even envisioned themselves as "entrepreneurs" or "business people" before they started their businesses. In fact, Patagonia's Yvon Chouinard, with all his commercial success, still does not see himself as a businessman. Similarly, Ben Cohen and Jerry Greenfield of Ben & Jerry's have often talked about how they had no intention of going into "business." They both claim that it did not come easily to admit to being a businessman.[13] In fact, the founders recall:

> When we first started Ben & Jerry's, we had no intention of going into "business"—we saw it as pretty much a lark . . . When we were introduced to people and they asked, "What do you do?" there came a point when the answer was not "I'm a homemade ice-cream shop owner" but "I'm a businessman." And I had a hard time mouthing those words.[14]

Table 3.2 lists a few of the most successful values-centered entrepreneurs and their unconventional backgrounds.

Another interesting example is John Mackey, the founder of Whole Foods Market, with 270 locations and more than 54,000 employees. His uniform is a short-sleeved shirt, shorts, Teva sandals, and a ruddy tan acquired while roaming the 720-acre ranch outside Austin that he shares with his wife, not the suit and tie one would expect of the traditional CEO.[15] He does not have a diploma from a prestigious Ivy League college or hold an MBA. Rather, he is a dropout from two different Texas universities and never took a business class. He identifies himself as a vegan, ex-hippie who has

Table 3.2 Unconventional Backgrounds

Entrepreneur	Company	Noteworthy Background	Extensive Business Experience
Anita Roddick	The Body Shop	Librarian, UN Worker	No
Ben Cohen & Jerry Greenfield	Ben & Jerry's	Potter, Medical Student	No
Douglas Hyde	Green Mountain Energy	Attorney for the Poor	Yes
Gary Erickson	Clif Bar	Outdoor Adventurer	No
Gary Hirshberg	Stonyfield Farm	Educator, Environmental Activist	No
John Mackey	Whole Foods	College Dropout	No
Magic Johnson	Magic Johnson Enterprises	Basketball Player	No
Paul Newman	Newman's Own	Actor, Race Car Driver	No
Yvon Chouinard	Patagonia	Blacksmith	No

forged his own philosophy for being successful in business. That philosophy advocates making customer and employee needs the highest corporate priority and placing stockholder interests in the backseat.

It is very probable that most of our entrepreneurs would never have started their values-centered companies had they had a more traditional business background. Certainly all MBAs and most business graduates "understand" that mixing profits with social mission is "bad" business. Without any conventional business background, our values-centered entrepreneurs didn't seem to know how unusual their goals and methods were.

Growing Convictions over Time

While our entrepreneurs' value systems were formed in their earlier years, many have become more committed to their cause(s) over time as their businesses stabilized. In 1981, Calvert Wayne, co-founder of Calvert Funds—a pioneer and recognized leader in the socially responsible investing movement—was looking to somehow integrate the values of the Baby Boom generation (which were the product of the civil rights, environmental, and anti-war movements of the late sixties and early seventies) into a financial product. The company was becoming larger, and it had money and resources which Wayne very much wanted to deploy in keeping with his social values. But to make this happen, he first had to overcome internal skepticism and outright opposition.

> My partners told me in no uncertain terms that they thought I was on drugs. But I felt that this was really something I wanted to do, and I told my partners that I would throw a real tantrum if they tried to stop me. This was basically a chairman's pet project, because even though the vote at the meeting was five against one, as chairman I got five votes, so I won.[16]

Fortunately for Wayne and his investors, and for the future of socially responsible investing, the renamed Calvert Social Investment Fund, prospered.

Ray Anderson, founder of Interface Carpets, one of the largest flooring (carpet manufacturing) firms in the United States with more than $1 billion in revenue, was an exception to our general observation: Unlike most of our entrepreneurs, Ray Anderson had founded his company without any particular concern for or commitment to the environment. But Anderson made a dramatic turn as he became more aware of the environmental damage his firm was imparting. He decided not just to reduce his firm's pollution but to become an outspoken champion for sustainability in his industry. Anderson's commitment to reducing environmental burden is expressed in the company's vision statement which reads as follows:

> To be the first company that, by its deeds, shows the entire industrial world what sustainability is in all its dimensions: People, process, product, place and profits—by 2020—and in doing so we will become restorative through the power of influence.[17]

Anderson, a late-bloomer in environmental awareness, has continued to make his operations more sustainable or, in his words, "restorative." Today, Anderson is recognized as one of the world's most environmentally progressive leaders in the business community. He has served as co-chairman of the President's Council on Sustainable Development during the Clinton administration, been recognized by Mikhail Gorbachev with a Millennium Award from Global Green, and received the prestigious George and Cynthia Mitchell International Prize for Sustainable Development.

Writing the Mission Statement

A key commonality we observed among the values-centered companies is that they have written inspiring mission statements that clearly articulate their aspirations and commitments. The mission statements vary in content, length, and style. Ben & Jerry's is one of the shortest and perhaps the most general—and perhaps most applicable to many companies. It is a broad three-pronged declaration emphasizing product, social, and economic missions (environment is included in the social mission) as seen in Table 3.3 below.

The Product Mission and Economic Mission sound pretty much like parts of mission statements of conventional companies with the obvious exception that the company's business (ice cream) is never mentioned. The social mission, by far the longest of the three, receives the most emphasis. It expresses the company founders' view that business plays a "central role" in society and that it can improve "quality of life of people everywhere."

Ecover, a growth-oriented washing and cleaning products company, has similar content but is more inclusive in its mission statement. The company's goals are expressed through a combination Mission/Vision/Values/Strategy Statement as shown in Table 3.4.[18]

Other mission statements get fairly specific in enunciating the particular beliefs of their founders. The Body Shop's mission statement (Table 3.5), for instance, commits the firm to operating in an ecologically sustainable manner and asserts that it is opposed to animal testing in the cosmetics and toiletries industries. Interestingly, this is the only reference to the company's business focus (cosmetics and toiletries) in the entire document.

Table 3.3 Ben & Jerry's Mission Statement[19]

Product Mission
To make, distribute, and sell the finest quality product.

Social Mission
To operate the company in a way that actively recognizes the central role that business plays in society, by initiating innovative ways to improve the quality of life of the local, national, and international communities.

Economic Mission
To operate the company on a sound fiscal basis of profitable growth.

Table 3.4 Ecover's Mission/Vision/Values/Strategy Statement

Mission
Ecover strives to provide effective, sustainable solutions for the hygienic needs of people.

Vision
Ecover is a company that desires to optimize **economic value**. We regard the **environment** as an inseparable part of the economy. Negative impacts on the environment are reduced by means such as stimulating and conducting research on new technologies and raw materials. In the **social** area, Ecover regards job performance as a means to foster the social well-being and personal development of its direct and indirect employees.

Values
Integrity, Respect, Commitment

Strategy
We give substance to our mission statement by developing strong brands in the following specific areas: Detergents and cleansing agents; Personal care products; and Accessories for healthy houses and ecological quality of life. We provide solutions for both domestic and professional use.

Akin to the others, Timothy Haahs & Associates' social mission to "help those in need" clearly overshadows its business mission.[20] Specifically, the Haahs mission statement (as shown in Table 3.6) makes it clear to employees and outsiders that the purpose of the company is to serve those in need and that its professional skills are tools to achieve this end. The company's Core Value Statement ends with, "We will never forget our primary reason for being by continuing to support a variety of charitable causes."

Writing a passionate mission statement obviously does not necessarily lead to business success. But it is an excellent exercise for focusing one's thoughts and setting ambitious triple bottom-line goals. A good mission statement can also inspire employees and other stakeholders, as well as explain the company's *raison d'être* to the outside world.

Table 3.5 The Body Shop International's Mission Statement

To dedicate our business to the pursuit of social and environmental change.

To creatively balance the financial and human needs of our stakeholders, employees, customers, franchisees, suppliers, and shareholders.

To courageously ensure that our business is ecologically sustainable: meeting the needs of the present without compromising the future.

To meaningfully contribute to local, national and international communities in which we trade, by adopting a code of conduct, which ensures care, honesty, fairness and respect.

To passionately campaign for the protection of the environment, human and civil rights, and against animal testing within the cosmetics and toiletries industry.

To tirelessly work to narrow the gap between principle and practice, whilst making fun, passion and care part of our daily lives.

Table 3.6 Timothy Haahs & Associates' Mission Statement

We exist to help those in need.

We emphasize assisting those medical, religious, and charitable organizations (as well as individuals) directly involved with helping those who are in need.

We believe that the best way to accomplish this mission is to become a recognized leader in our chosen field and profession, and to provide engineering and architectural services that are not merely adequate, but distinguished.

We will use to the best of our abilities our God-given talents in Architectural Design, Structural Engineering, Parking Consultation, and Project Management.

Commitment, Determination, and Success

When viewing these mission statements, we are reminded of a study on longevity undertaken by the long-established Royal Dutch Shell Company many years ago.[21] The company wanted to find out why some firms endured for centuries, especially those whose principal business focus had changed drastically or been yanked from under them by external events. A key conclusion was that these companies survived the upheavals of the marketplace and the world at large because they had "being" goals rather than "doing" goals. These businesses were centered on a way of interacting with the world, not on providing specific products or services.

As evident in mission statements, our values-centered entrepreneurs also are more focused on how they interact with their milieu than on providing specific products or services (some of the statements barely mention them). They appear to be more concerned about what they want to be than what products they want to make and sell. Tom and Kate Chappell, for instance, founded Tom's of Maine in 1970 based on the underlying philosophy of having an ethical company with natural products but without a clear idea about how to make them. Their firm's original product was a non-phosphate laundry detergent which was later abandoned. Natural toothpaste, Tom's principal product line today, was not introduced until 1975.

Although being committed to non-financial objectives can seem naïve or even risky, our values-centered entrepreneurs' passion and commitment to their mission, i.e., their desire for being a force for change, may well be a determining factor in long-run viability of their companies. Many of them persevered through periods of slow growth and financial difficulty in part because of their unrelenting determination to make a difference. Starbucks's Howard Schultz, for example, was not discouraged from building the type of company his father would have been proud to work for, even after being turned down by more than 200 investors.[22] Others in our sample exhibited similar determination. Thus, it is entirely possible that being values-centered actually improved their chances for financial success—at least in a number of instances we observed. Later chapters of this book will present more examples of many entrepreneurs who have benefited financially by exercising their values. (Particularly see Chapters 6 and 8, Promote Your Company's Values and Maximize Profits . . . With Some Exceptions.)

Chapter Takeaways

- Make sure that you are really committed to a cause. Ask yourself tough questions, e.g., can I really commit to doing this for an extended period of time?
- Understand that business can really be a solution to many of the world's problems.
- Write an inspiring mission statement for yourself and all others who will work with you.
- Don't worry about not having all the necessary background but be determined to learn and to persevere through some very difficult times.

4

Raise Capital with Mission in Mind
Be Strategic, Resilient, and Cautious

Money won't create success, the freedom to make it will.

—Nelson Mandela[1]

We didn't know beans about beans at the beginning, but we had $40,000 and a challenge that we thought would be fun.

—Paul Newman[2]

Special Challenges for Values-Centered Entrepreneurs

Capital is a critical resource for all entrepreneurial companies. Study after study has identified insufficient capital as a primary cause for venture failure.[3] Raising sufficient capital to start or grow a company, however, can be a daunting task. Most entrepreneurs severely underestimate the time and effort it takes to obtain the necessary financing.

Our research reveals that raising capital for socially conscious entrepreneurs can be even more challenging for several reasons. First, it is difficult for them to be taken seriously by the investment community because most professional venture capitalists and even "angel" investors perceive them as idealistic and naïve, lacking the pragmatic, real-world business sense to run a company effectively. Second, investors, even if they believe the entrepreneur has the requisite ability, fear that he/she will be more interested in the social mission and spend less time on running the business. These widely held preconceptions make it difficult for values-centered entrepreneurs to get investors' attention, much less their financial support.

Complicating the matter further, many values-centered entrepreneurs tend to be selective about the source of financing, i.e., which investors they want to work with. They suspect, often correctly, that professional investors with traditional business views would impede their ability to pursue their non-financial objectives. Several of the entrepreneurs in our sample explicitly stated that they were reluctant to receive financing from institutional investors, because institutional participation could adversely affect the entrepreneurs' management style, level of freedom, and exit decision. Some feared that involving venture capitalists would, down the road, compel them to either sell their companies or pursue an IPO (Initial Public Offering) prematurely—and thereby negatively affect the companies' missions.

Our research illustrates that our sample of values-centered entrepreneurs employed a broad range of strategies to raise capital—as any group of entrepreneurs might. As a group, they exploited most of the conventional types and sources of financing listed in Table 4.1. However, they also utilized approaches that were quite innovative and different from those of conventional entrepreneurs. In this chapter, we highlight some of the most fruitful approaches and strategies utilized by our sample companies. We also summarize the key lessons learned from their experiences.

Start Small and Bootstrap

The majority of our values-centered entrepreneurs did not start out raising a large amount of capital. Like many conventional entrepreneurs, most of our entrepreneurs did not mind starting small. They bootstrapped, i.e., started with very little seed financing, exercised tight cost control, and managed growth through the cash flows generated. For instance, Tom's of Maine started with a loan of only $5,000. Anita Roddick of The Body Shop borrowed £4,000 from a bank to inaugurate her product line. Innocent Drinks, another U.K.-based company, with a current 70 percent market share in smoothies, began modestly with £500 in fruit for its first stall at a music festival in London. Judy Wicks of the famous White Dog Cafe in Philadelphia launched her restaurant out of the kitchen in her apartment. Tim Haahs of Timothy Haahs & Associates began his flourishing architectural office with no money and one computer—that was bought by his brother. Haahs recalls:

> When I was first talking about starting my own business I had no money [just having been released from hospital after two heart transplants]. I was having a conversation with my younger brother one day and I was telling him about how I hoped to start a firm that existed for a more important purpose than simply earning money. We talked about how in order to start this firm I really didn't need any capital, but all I would really need is a computer. The next week I came home to find a box sitting at my front door. Inside was a brand new computer which my brother had ordered and sent to me. That is how the firm was started.[4]

Many of our values-centered entrepreneurs were very patient and accepting of hardships and a slower pace of growth in the initial years. Some might call them "old

Table 4.1 Common Types and Sources of Financing for Entrepreneurial Firms

Types of Financing	*Sources of Financing*
Loan: Money paid back with interest	Bootstrap & business earnings
Micro-loan: Small loans given to entrepreneurs, often in developing countries	Personal savings & credit
	Banks
Equity: Investment that acquires ownership interest in the company	Friends & Family
	Angel investors
	Venture capital firms

school." For example, Chris King operated his bicycle components business as a side venture for 14 years until it was sizable enough for him to make the jump into running the company as a full-time occupation.

Given limited resources, most of our entrepreneurs had no choice but to immerse themselves in every aspect of their operation and build the business with "sweat equity." For instance, the two founders of Stonyfield Farm, Samuel Kaymen and Gary Hirshberg, handled all facets of the business including milking cows, delivering yogurt, stocking shelves, repairing equipment, and developing new products. After the first year, as the on-site milking operation was consuming too much of their time, the partners decided to sell their cows back to local farmers and focus on the company's core yogurt operation. Although sales in the first year were only $90,000, Kaymen and Hirshberg remained totally committed and optimistic.[5] Even when Kaymen fell sick and was briefly hospitalized, he continued to work from his hospital bed.

The founders of Innocent Drinks went through a similar experience. In the early days, they could not afford to hire external agencies to design and develop the company's look and feel, although this task was very important for a consumer products company like Innocent Drinks. The company bootstrapped a solution to the problem by employing at below market wage a close friend with artistic talent, who helped them with logo and packing design. The founders had no choice but to be hands-on in their design process and actually do some of their design work themselves. Additionally, other friends and acquaintances served as the company's focus group to test the efficacy of the designs.[6]

Bootstrapping has an additional benefit: It tends to build an efficient operation. Michael Lutz, former CEO of Gammalink in a *Harvard Business Review* article recommended that entrepreneurs bootstrap at first to build an efficient operation before seeking capital.[7] His article makes the point that "bootstrapping can often be highly beneficial by revealing early on the strengths and weakness in one's business." Lutz continues,

> [Bootstrapping] reveals what may otherwise be hidden problems and forces the company to solve them. Rather than throw money at a problem, the company has no choice but to fix them and thereby strengthen its processes. With low overhead, frugal means, and fragile budgets, entrepreneurial businesses can't buy their way out of problems. They have to learn their way out.[8]

Without an ample amount of capital in their checking accounts, the majority of our sample companies had to focus on keeping their "heads above water." They started small and had to keep growth to a rate they could financially support. They were forced, essentially, to make smart choices in terms of market entry and customer acquisition. They couldn't, for instance, take on marginal customers just to grow. They were forced to minimize inventory. They couldn't hire employees with top credentials, but found "diamonds in the rough" overlooked by other companies. They worked to obtain favorable terms from their suppliers and timely payment from customers. In other words, the companies developed sound business habits as a result of early financial hardship that helped sustain them throughout their life cycles.

Put Your Own Skin in the Game

Most of our values-centered entrepreneurs, like many other entrepreneurs, demonstrated their commitment to their businesses by putting their personal finances on the line. For example, the founders of Ben & Jerry's, Clif Bar, and Sweet Riot labored for months (if not years) without adequate income to build their successful businesses. Others took lower salaries after quitting corporate jobs to start their ventures. These included the founders of Salesforce.com (Marc Benioff was a top salesperson at Oracle) and Honest Tea (Seth Goldman was a marketing executive at Calvert Group). Assuming significant personal risk, Muhammad Yunus of Grameen Bank co-signed the micro-loans that the local bank made to indigent women entrepreneurs in Bangladesh. Such personal sacrifice on the part of entrepreneurs tends to comfort angel investors and venture capitalists because it communicates seriousness and commitment. Demonstrating such commitment is usually considered an integral part of a good financing strategy as it bespeaks a deeply vested interest in the success of the operation to institutional investors.

Magic Johnson, the former NBA star, was frustrated when a string of potential business partners turned down his overtures to redevelop Los Angeles' inner city. "A lot of them wanted my autograph and a picture with me," Johnson said. "But they didn't want to invest with me."[9] Some investors asked Johnson, "If you believe in urban American so much, why don't you invest your own money and prove it?"[10] So, Johnson did just that in 1995, taking an equity stake along with what was then the Lowes chain in a 12-screen movie theater in Baldwin Hills. To the surprise of many, the first of what later became a chain of Magic Johnson Theaters was a big success. Soon, CalPERS (California Public Employees' Retirement System), California's largest asset management company, stepped in, after it had turned Johnson down at first. Other investors followed suit.[11]

Interestingly, Johnson put "his skin in the game" not just by investing his own money in the venture but by getting his hands dirty in protecting his investment. He took part in an unusual meeting with South-Central LA gang leaders from the Bloods and the Crips. Would gang members, he asked, be kind enough not to shoot up his movie theater? "I just laid it out to them that I am building this theater for the community," he recalled. "You can't have anything happen at this theater because we're going to hire your cousins, your mothers, your sons, and daughters. You come here and shoot up the place; it might be your own relatives inside."[12] The theater stands peacefully to this day, largely untouched by violence.

Start with Family and Friends

Family and friends serve as the primary source of early stage financing for the majority of entrepreneurs in most parts of the world. Over the years, we have heard some of our students say "I don't want to do business with friends and family." Our response: "Who else would you want to do business with—your enemies?"

When it came to raising capital, the lion's share of our values-centered entre-preneurs, like conventional entrepreneurs, obtained financial assistance from family and friends. Judy Wicks, of the famous White Dog Cafe in Philadelphia, got a $75,000 loan from a friend to build a small kitchen with a grill. Igor and Ludmilla of Iggy's borrowed money from family and friends to open their first bakery, Pain d'Avignon. Ben and Jerry put in $8,000 of their own money along with $4,000 in the form of a loan from their parents to start their ice-cream empire. Much of the $500,000 seed money for AgraQuest, the natural pest management company, came from the founder's family members, friends, and acquaintances from the local area.

Family and friends' investments are usually relatively small and typically used in the initial stages of company development. Many of our entrepreneurs had to find innovative ways to stretch the limited money they raised to get their business started. Eileen Fisher is an example. In 1984, with $350 in the bank, Fisher showed four of her clothing designs at a show in New York, and received $3,000 in orders. But no bank would lend her the working capital she needed. So, she made a deal with her friends, borrowing money from them to buy fabric and deliver on the order. When she received payment for delivery, she paid them back with interest of 2 percent a month. Three months later, Fisher received $40,000 more in orders. Again, she went to her friends for short-term capital. She continued this process until her business eventually outgrew her friends' resources.

Find the Right Angels

Several of our values-centered entrepreneurs have successfully obtained financial assistance from angel investors (usually wealthy individuals) for the needed seed or growth capital. In most cases, financing occurred when there was a meeting of the minds—in terms of shared similar values and/or objectives.

Innocent Drinks' three founders got a lucky break when they were introduced by friends to a wealthy American businessman, who liked their concept and subsequently provided the venture with a £250,000 loan. Explore Inc., the high-quality after-school program that successfully raised $5 million in equity financing, did so from private investors who shared the founder's views about education.

When Working Assets sought capital for its credit card business in 1985, there were no formal organizations of angel investors focused on socially responsible investing as there are today. The company's credit card division, whose business concept at the time was to give 5 to 10 cents to charity for each credit card transaction, was successful in obtaining an angel investment from a family foundation that in return received preferred stock in the company. The family foundation provided the financing because it believed in Working Assets' mission, even though it was unsure of the feasibility as a business concept. A few years later, Working Assets was able to buy out the investor and have shares returned to the company. Later in 1991, when Working Assets developed its phone services business unit, it raised another round of financing, this time mostly in the form of debt, from investors who again believed in the organization's mission. Because these investors prized its mission, the company's management was never asked to cede control during the negotiation process.

In the case of Honest Tea, finding the right chemistry with its investing partners was more important than obtaining a large amount of capital. Honest Tea turned down a $5 million equity investment from a venture capital group when the investor demanded significant control over the company. Instead, the founders settled for a much smaller investment by its customers and fans of the products, even though this decision meant that the company would grow more slowly.

Considering their limited business experience, many of our entrepreneurs may not have qualified for institutional equity investment, i.e., venture capital or private equity. Also, as discussed at the beginning of the chapter, attracting institutional investors would have been difficult given their unconventional views of business and their interest in sharing profits with their employees and communities. Conversely, it probably would have been unwise for our values-centered entrepreneurs to accept financing from professional investors with traditional views about business because of the strings (controls) attached. That said, the investment community in recent years has become more open to the prospect of investing in socially oriented ventures. In fact, an increasing number of venture capital and lending organizations have been established specifically to finance socially focused ventures. Table 4.2 lists a sample of these organizations. Note that they range from a private equity firm offering equity capital to a regulated bank providing loans. They also include an angel group committed to funding responsible ventures, a non-profit foundation offering micro-financing to the Developing World entrepreneurs, and a venture division of a mutual fund company.

Landing Institutional Investors—Be Strategic and Resilient

Landing financing from venture capital or private equity firms is not easy but certainly possible and several of our values-centered companies have done so. Revolution Foods, a newly formed company dedicated to bringing healthy meals to school children, for instance, has successfully raised multiple rounds of venture capital investments. Its two founders attribute their success to four factors:

1. **Implementing a Pilot Program.** Revolution Foods began with a pilot program, partnering with a single school in Oakland and the local Whole Foods store. The pilot program was able to show clearly that the company's business model would work. It also showcased the founders' operational capability. Thus, the pilot program reduced much of the uncertainty and risk for the investors and increased the venture's likelihood of getting funded.
2. **Befriending Investors with Similar Values.** The founders were fortunate to identify several professional investors who embraced the company's mission. Consequently, the founders and the investors were able to work together effectively.

Table 4.2 Samples of Socially Focused Investment Entities

Entity	Type	Profile
Pacific Community Ventures	Private Equity Investment Firm	PCV manages over $60 million in private equity funds. Headquartered in San Francisco, PCV concentrates on investing in small, high-growth California businesses, with a focus on businesses in the state's underserved communities.
RSF Social Finance	Aggregates Investors to Provide Loans	Located in San Francisco, RSF partners with investors, donors, and social enterprises to realize financial transactions that enliven consciousness and enhance quality of life.
Gray Matters Capital Foundation	Non-profit Organization Offering Microfinance for the Third World	Gray co-creates initiatives with partners world-wide and researches sustainable, replicable business models in developing countries, for the benefit of underserved populations.
Shorebank	Regulated Bank Offering Loans	A pioneer in community revitalization, Shorebank provides financial products and assistance to businesses focused on achieving prosperity while also attaining community revitalization and environmental well-being.
Investors' Circle	Angel Group Providing Equity	A network of over 200 angel investors, professional venture capitalists, foundations, family offices and others who are using private capital to promote the transition to a sustainable economy. Since 1992, Investors' Circle has facilitated the flow of over $130 million into 200 companies and small funds addressing social and environmental issues.
The Calvert Special Equities Program	Venture Capital Part of Calvert Funds	Venture capital to generate a greater return not only for its investors but for future generations as well. Invests in higher-risk, socially and environmentally responsible enterprises. These companies provide market-based solutions to some of the more difficult social, environmental, and health problems facing society today.
Investeco	Canadian Sustainability-Oriented Venture Fund	Located in Canada, Investeco acquires interest in promising North American companies specializing in alternative power, water technologies, organic and natural foods, and environmental technologies. It focuses primarily on high-growth private companies with lasting competitive advantages and over $2 million in revenues.

3. **Constructing an Accurate and Detailed Financial Model.** With backgrounds in investment banking, the founders developed a very sophisticated financial model to demonstrate the company's profitability and forecast growth. The effort comforted investors, knowing that the managers had tight grip on the numbers.

4. **Maintaining a Balanced Capital Structure.** Revolution Foods worked to establish a reasonable balance between debt and equity. The company did not want to raise too much external equity, because it would dilute the founders' ownership equity and could also endanger their control. Conversely, over-emphasis on debt would result in high interest expenses and increase financial risk during business downturns.

Targeting institutions sympathetic to mission can be very helpful. In fact, many of our values-centered companies have been successful in raising funds by finding institutional investors that were aligned with their mission. One such company, Pacific Community Ventures (PCV), manages a private equity fund to finance and cultivate businesses typically underserved by conventional investment funds. It typically invests in the growth of companies with a large number of employees classified as low to moderate income, frequently in manufacturing or distribution industries. Its goal is to improve the economic status of lower income workers. PCV has received financial assets from three distinct sources: private investors, other operating enterprises, and institutions. It has successfully raised three investment funds (PCV Fund I, II, and III), all of which have had significant institutional investment. Institutional investors in these PCV funds have included: Provenex (The Rockefeller Foundation), California Public Employees Retirement System (CalPERS), the Community Development Financial Institutions Fund of the U.S. Treasury, Wells Fargo Bank, and Citigroup. Institutions that have invested in PCV have done so to earn a return but also because they wanted to generate a positive impact on communities.

Similarly, the founders of Novica, the online marketplace featuring Developing World artisans, sought out investment partners, such as National Geographic Ventures and Foursome Investments, which shared the goal of preserving indigenous culture and slowing migration from villages to cities. In addition to the needed cash, these investors have brought credibility in the marketplace to Novica through co-branding activities and a variety of innovative ideas.

In general, entrepreneurs should seek out investors who are enthusiastic about or at least accepting of the firm's mission. They should openly discuss questions and concerns that investors have about the company and, conversely, investors should be made aware of any apprehensions that the entrepreneurs might have about being controlled or constricted in fulfilling their mission. Theoretically, there should be sufficient room for agreement between the parties if and as long as the venture is profitable and growing.

Having a good financing strategy as in the case of Revolution Foods, Pacific Community Ventures or Novica is very helpful, but old-fashioned persistence and resilience is equally important. While some of the entrepreneurs we have observed give up too early, others are relentless in their pursuit of financial resources and eventually are successful. Howard Schultz of Starbucks is a good example of the latter.

Starting in the fall of 1985 when Schultz left Starbucks to found Il Giornale, he was constantly raising capital. He spoke to dozens of potential funding sources, explaining his plan to transform coffee from a commodity into a branded offering that consumers would associate with quality, service, and community. Most were not interested in funding the venture citing a variety of reasons: Coffee sales were stagnant if not decreasing. Retail establishments, especially restaurants, were notoriously precarious endeavors, particularly vulnerable to poor management and downturns in the business cycle. Some potential backers questioned whether in the absence of a proprietary technology, Schultz could establish a sustainable competitive advantage. Undeterred, the energetic and resilient Schultz approached a grand total of 242 institutional and individual investors. Of the 242 people to whom Schultz made pitches, well over 200 decided against investing in his venture.[13]

A few brave souls, however, did purchase equity in the young company. In the first round of financing, Schultz raised $1.65 million. He earmarked the funds for Il Giornale's growth, opening a second store in downtown Seattle and a third in Vancouver, British Columbia. In early 1987, Schultz saw an opportunity to expand the business even faster. The two remaining founders of Starbucks were thinking about selling the Seattle coffee business in order to pursue other opportunities. Schultz learned that he might be able to acquire Starbucks, which included the company's six retail stores and roasting plant in Seattle as well as the Starbucks name. All he had to do was raise more money! In August 1987, Il Giornale bought the Seattle assets of Starbucks for $3.8 million. Shultz financed the purchase by selling equity to private investors, most of whom already owned stock in his business. It seemed that Schultz was always fundraising.

Don't Ignore the Public Markets

Companies typically go public, i.e., raise capital in the public markets through IPOs to attain growth capital. An IPO, however, is not for everyone, especially small firms not well-positioned for fast growth. The vast majority of our values-centered firms are not public companies, and some that were found the experience challenging. Most of our entrepreneurs feared that being public would threaten their control and interfere with their firm's social mission. Nonetheless, the prevailing assumption that ethical or values-centered firms cannot be public companies is not an iron-clad law.

Five of our values-centered companies have taken the IPO route to become publicly traded entities: Interface Carpets, Whole Foods, The Body Shop, Starbucks, and EV Rental. For each of these companies, it made good business sense, at the time, to go public, and for Interface Carpets, Whole Foods, and Starbucks, their public company status has not prevented them from pursuing vigorous social/environmental agenda.

In Howard Schultz's mind, becoming a public company was necessary for Starbucks to achieve both its business and social missions. From early on, Schultz believed that Starbucks stores had to be managed as part of a corporate entity and not as franchises. He described franchising as "nothing more than a cheap source of capital."[14] Moreover, Schultz reasoned that only a company-owned system could offer its front-line "partners" (employees) health benefits, stock options, and career development opportunities. Such policies, he believed, would help Starbucks build a customer-oriented organizational culture that, in return, would enhance customer experiences and strengthen the Starbucks brand. Hence, to finance the rapid growth Schultz wanted without franchising, Starbucks had little choice but to go public to raise the required capital.

Being public has not changed Schultz's or Starbucks's commitment to its social mission. The company, in fact, has become more vocal in recent years. As Schultz travels around the world, he has been vociferous in making the case that social responsibility is good for business. He talks about how today's consumers have started conducting a "values audit" of the companies whose products they are asked to buy, and that they prefer buying from companies that treat their employees well and serve their communities. He argues that,

> Long term value for our shareholders cannot be achieved in an enduring and sustaining way unless the management of the company is completely, comprehensively committed to creating long term value for the employees. The two are directly linked together. Any company or any management team that turns its back on its employees and does not share the success of the company with people who do the work will not finish the race.[15]

EV Rental Cars went public in 2008 by merging with a small publicly traded company to raise financing and grow faster. By completing the merger, EV Rental Cars, which maintained its name and its mission, was able to attract both investment capital and a strong management team, neither of which it could have done otherwise. Heading the new management team was William N. Plamondon, former senior executive with Budget Rent a Car, Alamo Rent a Car, and National Car Rental, as Chairman and CEO. Plamondon and his team brought a proven record of success in turnaround, growth, and acquisition situations. They also brought credibility with the financial community, as well as extensive relationships with suppliers, customers, and channel intermediaries. As of late 2008, the biggest obstacle to the company's expansion was the scarcity of hybrid vehicles following from the dramatic rise in gasoline prices.

The Body Shop's experience in the public markets was decidedly mixed. In 1984, when the company boasted 138 stores, Anita Roddick decided that to continue its fast growth, and thereby do even greater good in the world, the company should go public by floating shares on London's Unlisted Securities Market. By early 1986, The Body Shop International's stock attained full listing on the London Stock Exchange and had risen from an opening price of 95 pence (1984) to 820 pence. Over the next eight years, as growth accelerated the firm's stock split five times and its price rose 10,944 percent. The stock became known in financial circles and beyond as "the shares that defy gravity." During this period, Anita Roddick as Managing Director, had essentially free rein to pursue whatever social causes she wanted. But, by the mid-nineties, with increased competition in natural body care products, revenues and profits slowed and the company's stock price started a precipitous downward trend. Facing enormous competitive and financial pressure, Roddick ceded her managing directorship of The Body Shop. Although she continued her association with the company in various capacities, from this point on her influence receded. In a 2001 interview, she described the company as a "dysfunctional coffin." She complained that her dream of "ethical capitalism" began to fade after the company went public in

1984. The drive to earn stockholder dividends, she explained had destroyed the company's spirit and blunted its celebrated "political edge."[16] Although Roddick obviously was venting, she was also expressing an important reality lesson for values-centered entrepreneurs. Raising capital in the public markets is a two-edged sword. It can provide the funding for greater growth than otherwise and, concomitantly, the opportunity to do greater good. But, on the other side, should financial results decline, the entrepreneur's degree of control is likely to wane, endangering her vision for the company.

Make the Case to Wary Investors

It seems that no matter what entrepreneurs say, many investors are uneasy about investing in socially conscious firms. They fear that values-centered firms will fail to control costs or to compete aggressively against other companies, and most importantly, that they will not make sufficient profits. In some cases, it is just a matter of providing the right information. From our research, we learned that the approach outlined in Table 4.3 will work with quite a few (but not all) investors wary of investing in social ventures.

As expressed in Table 4.3, we find that being open and upfront is the right thing to do, especially as investors are becoming increasingly aware of and are somewhat more open to socially responsible businesses. To illustrate, there is no need to hide the fact that one wants to treat employees well, if that is a goal. Companies like Starbucks and Whole Foods have been consistently ranked among the best companies to work for—and clearly have been very profitable, too. Most entrepreneurs on our list have found that treating employees well is good for both business and their mission.

Table 4.3 Dealing with Wary Investors

Show that you are determined to make profits. Many traditional investors don't know what to expect from values-centered or triple bottom-line companies. Show them your history and how you have made money. Telling investors that you want to make money can be reassuring.

Show that you are serious about a lean operation. Tell the investors that you will be, like most other values-centered entrepreneurs, disciplined in terms of cutting and controlling costs to survive and enhance profitability. You might remind them that most of the salaries of values-centered entrepreneurs, even the CEOs running public companies, are below their respective industry standard.

Be committed to growth. Show investors that you and the majority of the values-centered companies pursue aggressive growth to increase profits, taking market share away from both large and small competitors.

Be open about your non-financial mission. Don't hide your mission and don't surprise them with it late in the process. The fact that an entrepreneur has goals other than the bottom-line should not necessarily in itself scare away most investors. Entrepreneurial dedication toward innovation, quality, or "changing the world" has often resulted in strong and enduring companies. Also, remind wary investors that a firm's social mission can strengthen its brand image. Furthermore, remember that some investors specifically look for companies with social missions. When it comes to these investors, you may even need a way to quantify your social impact.

Watch Out For Questionable Investors

We feel that some of the concerns that values-centered entrepreneurs have about investors are overblown. Our results tell us that, in many cases, as long as the vision of the company is spelled out upfront and the appropriate expectations set beforehand, responsible entrepreneurs and profit-minded investors usually can work together. But of course, there must be a meeting of the minds and sometimes that just doesn't happen.

Douglas Hyde, founder of Vermont-based Green Mountain Energy, a pioneering supplier of cleaner electricity made from less-polluting sources like wind, water, solar, biomass, geothermal, and natural gas experienced the worst case scenario. Hyde, formerly an attorney for the poor, was so taken with Green Mountain Energy's potential that he quit his post as CEO of Green Mountain Power Corporation (the mother company) to start this "green" start-up. Lining up financing, however, turned out to be much more troublesome and ominous than he had expected. Hyde eventually decided to take in $30 million in seed capital from Sam Wyly, a high-profile investor who in return received 67 percent ownership and majority control of the venture. Green Mountain Power Corporation kept the remaining 33 percent stake.

A Dallas-based entrepreneur, Sam Wyly had founded and helped build several publicly traded companies, such as Sterling Commerce, Sterling Software, and Michaels Stores, a retail chain with more than 450 stores nationwide. He also ran Maverick Capital, a private hedge fund. Wyly had a reputation for being a hard negotiator, someone who liked to be in control, and sometimes pushed the boundaries of the law. Wyly later invested another $10 million, upping his share to 74.3 percent. In January 1999, the Wyly family bought out the final portion of Green Mountain Power's shares. Seeking someone with better Wall Street ties in preparation for a public offering, Wyly eased Hyde from the CEO post in October 1999 in favor of David White, then a 37-year-old investment banker with Donaldson, Lufkin & Jenrette. White was gone in a few months, and Dennis Kelly, a former Coca-Cola executive, stepped in. Then, in July 2000 Wyly moved the company from Vermont to his home state Texas. Wyly had brought the needed financing to kick-start the business, but founder Douglas Hyde, in the end, lost control and was unable to fully achieve his dream as a green entrepreneur.

Others among our values-centered entrepreneurs were more circumspect about involving outside equity, believing that it would be too risky for a company trying to pursue a social mission. Igor and Ludmilla of Iggy's Bread, for example, were told by a business advisor that a proper business strategy would be to raise money, expand their business, go public, and then sell the company to enjoy all the money they would make. "I would never sell out because it's everything I don't believe in," responded Ludmilla.[17] Iggy's founders, instead, took out loans rather than pursue equity for expansion. This more conservative strategy has allowed Igor and Ludmilla to maintain sole control of the company and run it according to their somewhat unconventional business philosophy.

Chapter Takeaways

As a consequence of their social and environmental commitment, many of our values-centered companies faced greater financial hardship and were forced to grow more slowly then they might have liked. But, by staying focused on their mission and selectively choosing the right financing options, our entrepreneurs have been able to build more authentic, purpose-oriented companies that have been effective and resilient in the long run. Below are the chapter takeaways for aspiring values-centered entrepreneurs.

- Do not be afraid to start small and bootstrap—this process will make you better.
- Put your own skin in the game, if possible, before raising capital from others.
- Raise early stage financing from friends or angels with shared values—be resourceful.
- Be open and explicit about your objectives when approaching institutional investors.
- Do not count out the possibility of raising capital from the public markets but be cognizant of the risk of losing control.

5

Hire Talented Employees with Shared Values

Although technical and professional competency are important, we feel that their personal values, the way they interact with others personally, and their willingness to go the "extra mile" every day, are far more important attributes.
—Timothy Haahs, founder of Timothy Haahs & Associates, Inc.[1]

If we don't feel like there is a synergy with the mission, we will not hire that person.
—Robert Milk, co-founder of Novica[2]

Hire People with Compatible Personal Values

Hiring is an important function in any growing business but it has been particularly critical for our values-centered firms. Conventional companies hire new employees based on a range of criteria such as professional competency, personal connection, and shared interest, among others,[3] but our entrepreneurs have added an additional gauge—kindred personal values. Our research indicates that this criterion, while it may pose a challenge at times, seems to have served as a sound strategy for our values-centered companies.

In several instances, our entrepreneurs have readily admitted to giving greater weight to job candidates' personal values than to their professional competencies. Skeptical of "business types," Patagonia's Yvon Chouinard has always preferred to hire "dirt bags" who can learn the business to professionally trained business people and trying to convert them to Patagonia's values.[4] Similarly, Anita Roddick of The Body Shop, who distrusted traditional business people, was known for hiring employees for their heart and spirit over their professional background. Iggy's Bread of the World liked to hire high-character kitchen workers with no previous baking experience so they could be trained to bake bread "the Iggy's way."[5] These entrepreneurs seem to have been of the opinion that business and technical skills were more easily taught than personal beliefs and values. They may have been right.

As one might guess, we did find instances when our entrepreneurs were able to hire individuals with both exceptional professional expertise and kindred personal values. A case in point is Jeff Pink, founder of EV Rentals (car rental company specializing in rentals of electronic and low-emission vehicles), who was fortunate enough to secure both qualities in hiring his first employee, Terry O'Dea, out of Southern California Edison's Electric Vehicle program. Pink, who had been a real estate professional, had neither fleet management experience nor connections in the environmental community. O'Dea, an environmentalist who shared Pink's values, brought the needed experience and connections.

Hiring new employees with values and personal goals akin to the others in the company tends to build a mutual fit between the new employee and the organization. Newman's Own, a leading sauce and salad dressing company, for this reason, specifically looks for both job skills and ethical values in considering a job candidate. Similarly, Pamela Marrone of AgraQuest, maker of natural pest control solutions, has preferred employees who are both entrepreneurial and enthusiastically supportive of the company's vision for a better environment. Rhythm and Hues, a leading special effects company in Los Angeles, not only looks at how talented its candidates are but also tries to get a fix on how likely they are to fit in with the firm's unique culture.

While trying to find the right personality/values match may be difficult, it may pay dividends later. Employees with kindred personal values can make it easier for a company to maintain a consistent corporate culture which in turn buttresses the company's mission. Tim Haahs, of Timothy Haahs and Associates, explains how the fit of personal and organizational values can give the company an extra edge:

> We look at every candidate who walks through our door looking for a job—at how we feel they would fit in with our corporate culture, as well as in implementing our mission statement. Although technical and professional competency are important, we feel that their personal values, the way they interact with others personally, and their willingness to go the "extra mile" every day, are far more important attributes.[6]

There are exceptions to every rule, however. Gottlieb Duttweiler, Migros's founder, was a clear exception to the pattern we detected among values-centered entrepreneurs of hiring employees with beliefs and values similar to theirs. Duttweiler was known for hiring people whose views differed from his. In fact, in several instances he hired political enemies. He claimed to be guarding against the danger of being surrounded by "yes men." But he may have had an additional motive. Duttweiler had a huge ego and believed so strongly in the rectitude and virtue of his core philosophy that he was confident that others, once exposed, would quickly see the light. Thus, he could accept criticism and even encourage it at first but he also expected those newcomers around him to assimilate fairly quickly into the Migros culture and whole-heartedly adopt his values and philosophy. Recognition and advancement at Migros depended on it. Executives who did not fit in were replaced although they typically were let down easily by being helped to find suitable employment elsewhere. In the final analysis, Duttweiler was perhaps not so different from others in our example. He, too, wanted an organization composed of people with strongly held, shared values who were motivated to work toward the accomplishment of his mission.[7]

Tom Chappell of Tom's of Maine is another counter-example but his story also illustrates the problems created for a values-centered entrepreneur by not hiring for mission in the first place. By 1981 his company had passed through the take-off stage and sales had plateaued. Chappell wanted to take his products into the mainstream market and get on a new growth path. To accomplish this he knew that he needed to add professional talent to manage the growth of new accounts, more complex distribution channels, burgeoning advertising budget, etc. Hence, he hired several experienced marketing executives along with some young MBAs. The company grew at a 25 percent rate over the ensuing two years. But the rapid growth exposed an underlying conflict in values between Chappell and his new professionals. For example, they tried to convince him to add saccharin to Tom's toothpaste to sweeten it and thereby make it more palatable to the mainstream market. As Chappell perceived it, they were promoting a course of action based on bottom-line considerations rather than adhering to his commitment to natural products. As a consequence of such tensions, Chappell found his company less and less personally fulfilling. Recalling this period in company history, he recounted, "our values were pushed to the margin, growth and profit dominated business planning."[8]

Several years later, he enrolled part-time in Harvard Divinity School where for the next three years he studied toward a master's degree. When he returned to Tom's of Maine on a full-time basis, he had new inspiration and a "language" that would allow him to debate what he called his "beancounters." His first priority was to codify the company's mission and values. Over an intense three-month period with the participation of his board of directors and his entire staff, mission and beliefs statements were drafted and approved by all participants. Then, over time, through his leadership by example, a series of seminars and workshops, and rewarding those who "lived the mission," he was able to engrain the codified values as the nucleus of the company's culture.[9] Like Gottlieb Duttweiler, he found an alternative route to developing an organization that ardently shared his values.

Make the Effort to Find Those with Shared Values

It's not just enough that candidates claim to be interested in the company's mission. They should be examined to understand their level of commitment.

Many of our values-centered companies take advantage of the interview process to understand the candidates' values. Robert Milk, co-founder of Novica, has found that the best and most committed employees are those who are motivated by the company's mission. Thus, Novica tries to identify those candidates in the hiring process. Novica has found it useful to ask candidates in detail what they like the most about the Novica mission. Milk explains, "If we don't feel like there is a synergy with the mission, we will not hire that person."[10] Similarly, while Working Assets does not specifically inquire about candidates' values, they are typically asked if they feel comfortable with the organizations the company supports, such as Planned Parenthood.

To identify employees who will fit best with the company's culture, Rhythm & Hues typically selects from a pool of freelance artists with whom it has worked intimately. During any busy month, the company employs some 350 full-time artists and about 300 additional freelance artists—a situation not atypical of other special effects firms. Recently, foreseeing that more work was ahead, Rhythm & Hues assessed the freelancers on its payroll, and made permanent job offers to ones already known to be a good fit with the company. Freelancers who have worked with Rhythm & Hues before are generally very pleased to join the company on a full-time basis. They already know the people at the firm and its employee-friendly policies and environment. At Rhythm & Hues, even freelancers receive the company's extravagant health benefits and holidays (see discussion below)—a practice almost unheard of in the harsh entertainment industry.

Revolution Foods, which supplies healthy meals to school children, realized that anyone could claim to believe in the company's mission. Consequently, it began looking for specific evidence that demonstrates candidates' commitment to the company's cause, e.g., work experience as former teacher or nutritionist, etc. A perfect example is the company's executive chef, Amy Klein, who formerly was director of operations for Teach For America before she attended culinary school and became a chef. Revolution Foods sometimes hires the parents of kids at schools that the company is serving. Few employees have shown more devotion to the company or motivation to perform than these parents. The company's mission and the parents' interest are perfectly aligned.

When Chris King realized that he simply could not find the right machinists for his manufacturing operation, he made a pointed capital investment in the interest of building a more positive, harmonious organizational culture. King was intimately aware that in most machine shops, including his, the skilled and highly paid machinists were "prima donnas" and consequently disruptive to organizational harmony. Realizing that in all likelihood he would constantly have personality problems with machinists, he invested money and time in developing computer numerical control (CNC) machines to simplify the machining task. Since then, instead of hiring machinists, King has hired less skilled operators with good attitudes and has trained them on the use the CNC equipment. In this way, King was able to create a more congenial and productive machine shop while also lowering labor costs.

Finding employees with shared values can become more difficult as companies grow. With growth, companies usually need to hire special skill sets, e.g., machining, employee benefits, and financial control, and they often don't have a wide pool of talents to draw from. Our firms are no exception. For example, Working Assets used to hire interns and generalists with values similar to its permanent employees, but as the company grew in the very competitive telecommunications industry, it had difficulty finding people with the desired combination of skills and personal values. As a consequence, Working Assets and other values-centered firms have had to get creative to maximize their chance of landing top talent with similar values—such as finding "Diamonds in the Rough."

Find Diamonds in the Rough

Our entrepreneurs' heavy emphasis on personal values, even at the expense of professional qualifications in some cases, makes sense also for a not-so-obvious reason. For conventional businesses, a predominant consideration in hiring is where the potential employee worked before or what he or she has or has not accomplished before. But a values-centered employee might not have performed well in a conventional work environment because he or she was never motivated! Perhaps not fitting in at a typical corporation means that the person has yet to find meaning and passion in the workplace and may be in search of an environment where these needs can be satisfied. Or, maybe idealistic employees, like many entrepreneurs, are simply ignored, out of hand, in the business world and are really "the hidden gems" or "diamonds in the rough." For this reason, taking chances on people who have not thrived in the conventional business world might make much sense. Our values-based entrepreneurs would be the first to understand that there are many extraordinary people (like themselves) who don't "get" capitalism the way it is typically practiced. Given the proper context, some people may surprise themselves and their employers with their productivity and loyalty. An example is Kris McDivitt, the general manager of Lost Arrow, the parent company of Patagonia and the other companies owned by Yvon Chouinard. The woman Chouinard describes as his "bombproof belay" (a mountaineering term that refers to rope holding fast and means the strongest support in the world) began working for him in 1972 as an assistant packer in the shipping department. She has since held every job in the company with the exception of blacksmith and RURP (a form of piton) grinder.

As educators, we have advised hundreds of students over the years, and we are familiar with professionals who don't give their best at work because they can't find the purpose or meaning in their work. Thus, identifying underperformers who can excel in a more meaningful work environment may be a big win for values-centered entrepreneurial companies. For these individuals, the company mission and the job itself can provide all the motivation needed. This is important because not all values-centered entrepreneurs have patience with employees lacking motivation or dedication. As Magic Johnson clearly articulated in an interview, "I try to hire people I don't have to motivate."[11]

The Benefits of Hiring People with Similar Values

- Easier to teach skills than values
- Better chemistry with others in the organization
- More passionate and dedicated—willing to go the extra mile
- May find "diamonds in the rough"

Attract Top Talents

Some of our savvy values-centered companies have successfully taken advantage of their inspiring mission, employee-oriented organizational culture, and/or extraordinary benefits to attract top talents in their respective organizations—sometimes even at lower than market salaries.

Take the example of Rhythm & Hues, a leading special effects company in an industry known for fierce competition for talented artists. The company has had to compete for talent with some of the biggest names in entertainment, such as Dream-works and International Light and Magic (George Lucas's company that produced *Star Wars*) without having the financial resources of these firms. Salaries for artists at Rhythm & Hues can be as much as 20 percent lower for top artists. So, outstanding artists who can demand high salaries always go to the competitors? Not always!

Ken Roupenian, director of digital production, explains what attracts people to Rhythm & Hues:

> A lot of people do not come here for money reasons. It is not all about the money. We feed people every day, there is always something for breakfast; people bring their dogs to work; financial information is shared with employees every week so that they actually know what is going on whereas many other companies work a lot under rumors.[12]

Indeed, Rhythm & Hues is known for having a great kitchen, where its entire staff spends a good amount of time. It offers two large kitchen rooms, one for coffee and reading, and another for food.

Another big benefit of working at Rhythm & Hues is its incredibly long vacations. The average vacation time for full-time artists at Rhythm ranges from 9 to 12 weeks which is about 6 to 9 weeks above the industry standard. Although it is not likely that artists will actually take off this much time, the firm's hard-working employees appreciate having the option. This vacation policy, moreover, is not as costly to the company as it might at first seem because downtime is common in the industry. Also, legendary at Rhythm & Hues are the health benefits provided to employees. Instead of paying an insurance company for heath coverage, the company manages its own medical benefits program and pays bills directly to doctors and hospitals. This self-managed insurance program covers a wide range of procedures and medications, some of which are not covered by conventional company-sponsored insurance programs. Clearly, Rhythm & Hues' vacation and benefits programs create the kind of atmosphere that can be persuasive in attracting and retaining top artists.

Albeit Rhythm & Hues is a generous and kind employer, it is also fiercely competitive when it comes to competing for talent. One year, company representatives made a trip to San Francisco where Industrial Light & Magic was located and held a series of recruiting events at a nearby hotel featuring 20-minute presentations on the advantages of working at Rhythm & Hues. Senior managers knew that it was going to be a busy year and that they needed to hire additional experienced artists. They went right to the location of their arch rival knowing that there was no better place for attracting top talent because the contracts of many of its rival's employees were about to expire.[13]

Working Assets has also benefited from having a reputation for offering an employee-friendly work environment and benefits package. Co-founder Laura Scher explained in an interview, "We would never run a business without offering the basic benefits. Even when we had 3 employees we offered health benefits. When you run a socially responsible company, employees have to be taken care of."[14] In addition, at Working Assets, employees are intimately involved in making key decisions related to the company's mission. For example, once customers nominate the slate of charities for consideration, the next step is for employees to do the necessary research and due diligence on these organizations. Employees make their recommendations to the company's board, which then picks the final donation list. Working Assets employees are also encouraged to take part in protest and advocate marches on company time and have even taken a trip to Washington DC to do so. Further, employees are kept aware of what is happening in the world of charities through regularly scheduled brown bag lunches where representatives from various non-profit organizations make presentations.

Innocent Drinks, the leading maker of smoothies in the U.K., also boasts an organizational culture that attracts talented employees. The company has been voted a "top employer" in the U.K. by the *Guardian,* one of the country's leading newspapers. Its policies and culture reflects the founders' belief that it is not so much what they do but who they employ that makes their company successful. Employees are respected, their opinions are heard, and they are empowered to make a difference. It also helps that the company's culture eschews the traditional formalities of corporate life in favor of a more informal, natural progression of ideas, experience, and learning.

Innocent Drinks has a somewhat unconventional hiring philosophy. The company follows a policy of picking talented people over filling specific gaps in its business operation (the best-athlete approach). Head of Creative, Dan German explains, "We hire as many smart, clever people as we can find room for."[15] In doing this, Innocent Drinks has been able to recruit talent that can benefit the company for the long run. German adds, "If you have truly inspiring and motivated people around you, you can do anything—learn to be better managers, learn to be better at business. We have an ambition to be Europe's most talent rich company, and as long as we keep trying to achieve that, we'll be ok."[16]

While compensation and benefits are important, nothing excites a values-centered employee like a cause or mission. To that end, our companies make their mission and values very public to their prospective employees. Chris King's employment website begins with this statement: "If you are passionate about what you do and are interested in working hard for a progressive company that you can believe in, we just might have something for you."[17] Most, if not all, of Working Asset's job candidates, whom co-founder Laura Scher calls "corporate refugees," are conversant with the company's mission. She notes, "Everybody who comes to join us does so because of our social mission."[18] Scher adds, "It is very difficult for a new job applicant not to know what we stand for. We make it very explicit."[19]

What attracts top talent to Salesforce.com, a leading technology company in Silicon Valley, is, of course, its business model and financial success. The career section of the company's website shown in Figure 5.1 informs visitors that it is the second fastest growing technology company in a very hot ("software as service") market. But it also helps that the website's benefits section lists such programs as yoga classes, healthy snacks, paid time off for community service work, pre-tax commuter benefits, paid maternity/paternity programs, and takeout meals for new moms and dads. Whatever these benefits amount to in dollar terms, they are attractive to prospective employees and in combination with the company's progressive culture and fun working environment have played a big role in attracting and also retaining the firm's many talented programmers and managers.

Build your career at the global leader in software as a service. With over 40,000 global customers, 1,000,000 subscribers, and huge growth momentum, the opportunities are unlimited. Recognized by Forbes magazine in January 2008 as the 2nd-fastest-growing tech company, salesforce.com is dominating the SaaS (software as a service) and PaaS (platform as a service) markets, revolutionizing the software industry and The Business Web™.

Why do you want a career at salesforce.com?

• Join top talent from across the world who share a "change the world" mentality

• Surround yourself by peers and leaders who inspire, motivate, and innovate

• Enjoy a performance-based, meritocracy culture

Figure 5.1 Careers Page of the Website of Salesforce.com

The company's "change-the-world" attitude, coupled with the opportunity to work in an environment populated by inspired and motivated people also plays a big role. Salesforce.com's recruitment process is enhanced because employees enthusiastically describe the company atmosphere as exciting and innovative. It also helps that prospective employees know that Salesforce.com is more than an industry leader with committed people and enormous potential for growth; it is also a company with a soul. The company has received countless awards and accolades, including the number-seven spot on *Business Ethics'* list of most ethical companies. Finally, Salesforce.com's policies on volunteerism seem to have had a positive impact on the recruitment process. In fact, Suzanne DiBianca, executive director of the Salesforce Foundation, believes that these policies have been a crucial differentiator for recruitment. For example, Chris Sommers joined Salesforce.com three years ago in large part because of the company's integrated approach to volunteerism. "I'm not teaching children to read for a living, but I am doing good," he says about his volunteer activity. "It's redeeming for me and for the company as well."[20] Other employees we have talked to also seem to be proud of their company's volunteerism policy.

Keep Your Talented, Committed Employees

Retaining employees may be thought of as the best form of hiring because it lowers recruitment needs and costs. But it can also deliver the additional benefit of preserving a committed and valued staff. Grameen Bank's Muhammad Yunus notes, "Although we pay the salary of an entry level government worker, we find that privately owned commercial banks that offer much higher wages can rarely entice our workers away from us."[21] Yunus explains that his employees do more than fulfill their basic role as bankers. "Unlike other commercial bank workers, our staff members grow to consider themselves as teachers. They are teachers in the sense that they help their borrowers to explore their full potential, to discover their strengths, to extend their capabilities further than ever before."[22]

Although employees who share the firm's values are less likely to leave, many of our values-centered companies took no chances in that regard. As discussed earlier, they designed policies and offered attractive benefits that encouraged employees to be content and stay with their respective companies. Going even further, some of our companies have elevated employee retention to the level of a formal goal. For instance, given the competition for talent in the entertainment industry, a specific Rhythm & Hues objective is to keep as many talented artists as possible. The company does this by showing employees that they are willing to go the extra mile to minimize mistakes in the evaluation process. To this end, Rhythm & Hues is very cautious about laying off or firing employees based on a single supervisor's review. Ken Roupenian, who as director of digital production assigns artists to projects, knows that an artist may be evaluated very differently by different supervisors. He has seen circumstances where one supervisor gives a poor review to an artist while another supervisor thinks the same person is outstanding. He explains the subjective nature of artistic work, "We deal in shades of grey; if life were about black and white everything would be very easy . . . A lot of times, it has nothing to do with the quality of the work but their personalities and perception."[23] Roupenian has come to understand that making a layoff decision based on one supervisor's opinion would neither be productive for the company nor fair to the employee. He says, "Supervisors usually don't have the global issue in mind. As a corporate manager I look at the longevity of the business as a whole whereas production supervisors are usually focused on the short term goals of their department."[24] Going the extra mile to evaluate talents fairly gives employees additional motivation to stay with the company.

By emphasizing shared values and providing above-norm benefits, Patricia Karter and Suzanne Lombardi, founders of Dancing Deer, maker of all-natural, gourmet cookies, cakes, and brownies, have prioritized the retention of employees and consequently have been able to retain the majority of their workforce—most of whom are inner-city immigrants. The company offers perks uncommon in small businesses of its type: All of its 60 employees receive stock options and free lunches as well. By offering stock options, Dancing Deer encourages employee ownership, which in turn fosters greater employee commitment and responsibility. Health insurance and paid overtime are also benefits the company offers, somewhat of a rarity in inner cities where labor is abundant.[25] Dancing Deer's website proclaims, "All Dancing Deer employees are stakeholders in its profitability and share in the rewards of a well run, growing company. We believe that if people love what they're doing, it shows in the food."[26]

Karter, speaking about her full-time employees, says that when most of them started, they barely spoke English. Today, however, many serve in management positions. She sincerely appreciates the employees whom she and Lombardi trained and developed over the years. In 1998, when the company outgrew its space, the founders decided that instead of moving to a bigger and cheaper location in the suburbs, they would stay in Roxbury (Massachusetts) so as not to lose their loyal staff, many of whom lived in the area. "We had built this workforce," Karter said, "and they are a big part of why we were successful. We needed to hang onto them."[27] Indeed, employees may be our values-centered companies' greatest assets.

Chapter Takeaways

- Hiring employees with similar values can be smart strategy as they will be more dedicated in their effort toward the company's mission.
- Recruit talented employees by publicizing your company's values and exciting them about the opportunity to make a difference.
- Entice talented employees to join the firm with a progressive organizational culture, generous benefits and other smart policies appropriate for your industry and company.
- Make efforts to retain talented employees through benefits and policies that build a loyal base of employees.

6

Promote Your Company's Values

We had to make everything explicit from ingredients to values so that customers made informed choices—informed decisions as to whether they wanted to do business with us, and I believe customers crave knowledge, and they want it honest. They don't want psycho-babble, they don't want psycho-anything, they just want truths . . . they want to feel sympathy not only with the product but with the company making the product.
—Anita Roddick, founder of The Body Shop[1]

If it comes from the heart, it goes to the heart.
—Ludwig von Beethoven[2]

A Different Approach toward Marketing

Our research into the marketing and promotion strategies of values-centered entrepreneurs has led to one unequivocal finding: The vast majority of our entrepreneurs use their values orientation to promote their products and companies. Overall, they seem less obsessed with conventional marketing techniques such as in-store promotion, product branding, price cutting, flashy advertising, or catchy slogans, but more concerned about being authentic, informative, and appealing to customers' intelligence. This difference in approach is both distinct and refreshing. The principal contrasts are displayed in Table 6.1.

Connect with Customers' Hearts and Sense of Values

Entrepreneurs have long been credited with bringing to market new products or services with superior features and attributes that benefit customers.[3] Some have been successful also in making emotional connections with their customers: Well-known examples of such companies include Nike, Harley Davidson, BMW, Apple, and McDonald's. They have created "brands" that appeal to certain basic human emotions, e.g., the need to feel young, free, or respected.

For the most part, our values-centered entrepreneurs have brought to market high-end products and services with superior features and attributes. They typically have

Table 6.1 Contrasts in Marketing Approach

Conventional Marketing	Values-Centered Marketing
Connect with people's emotions	Connect with people's sense of values
Promote your product's functions and benefits	Promote your values (as point of differentiation) too
Develop a good marketing slogan	Appeal to customers' common sense and intelligence
Present select information strategically (e.g., about product, ingredients)	Offer full disclosure
The right positioning is key to success	Authenticity is key to success
Build a brand	Build a soul
Spread the company's message to customers	Engage in an open dialogue with customers

used high-quality ingredients, instituted sound and safe processes, and offered first-rate customer service. Moreover, like some of the above-named brands, many of our values-centered companies have been successful in connecting with their customers' emotions—but with a unique twist: Rather than appealing only to superficial emotions, our values-centered companies are using their marketing message to stir and engage customers' moral sense.

After all, the brands our entrepreneurs have created stand for a cause. Their brands mean something ethical or benevolent. Their marketing messages attempt to appeal to the best of human nature. They ask customers to care for the environment and people in and outside of their communities. They also ask their customers to make a social statement by buying their products. In return, customers receive not only a high-quality product but also an intangible benefit—a sense of satisfaction from knowing that they are supporting an ethical company and/or a benevolent cause.

One such company whose mission has ignited a passionate response from its customers is Revolution Foods. Who can disagree with Revolution Foods' goal to serve nutritious and tasty meals to school children? But many of its customers and constituents, i.e., school teachers, administrators and parents, are excited beyond measure. Here are testimonials by a parent and an administrator:[4]

> My daughter, Isabella, a first grader attends school there and she ABSOLUTELY hated eating lunch at school last year. . . . The menus were full of processed foods, fats, and sugar. . . . Thank you so much for providing a healthy and tasty alternative to standard (or should I say "sub-standard"?) school lunch fare.
>
> (Parent, 8/10/2006)

> I just wanted to let you know that the kids have LOVED the new menu changes. Today's tamales were a total hit along with the chicken noodle soup and the lasagna last week. . . . Many (of our kids) are excited to tell you about how much they are enjoying the food and how much they appreciate you listening to their comments! :) Again thank you so much for making our kids really enjoy lunch!
>
> (1/15/2008, School Staff Member)

It's not just that students are eating healthier. The company has collected anecdotal evidence from schools reporting higher attention levels in class, fewer disciplinary problems, an increased interest in healthy food, and weight loss amongst their students. Thus, it is not surprising that Revolution Foods has a close relationship with schools, which more resembles a true partnership than the typical vendor–buyer relationship.

Promote Values as a Means of Differentiation

As mentioned above, our values-centered entrepreneurs do not shy away from publicizing their message. Why should they? They are passionate about their values and want to share their beliefs with the world. But there is another motive behind their promotional efforts. In the world of hyper-competition and parity, their values and sustainable business practice are a way of creating a meaningful differentiation. Moreover, increasingly more customers welcome the opportunity of knowing what they are supporting beyond the physical product they are purchasing, i.e., are they supporting a corporation whose CEO will make $200 million from a golden parachute (like the former Home Depot CEO) or small family farms in Vermont that take care of the environment even at the cost of lower short-run profit (as Stonyfield Farm does)? Many of our entrepreneurial firms have been able to stand out among their peers, jumpstart sales, and capture a niche early on by publicly advocating their respective values and causes. Often, for an entrepreneurial company, a small yet solid niche is all that is needed to get through the risky start-up period.

Thanks to most conventional companies that focus on "business as usual," authentic values-centered firms that promote their socially responsive positions and practices tend to receive a disproportionate amount of media attention. Consider Anita Roddick of The Body Shop who may have been the queen of free advertising. Because of her infectious personality and anti-establishment philosophy, she garnered an astonishing amount of free positive media coverage. Being both provocative and entertaining, she had the rare ability to embody her company's entire advertising program. Through most of its growth, The Body Shop spent zero money on advertising.

For the media and many consumers, values-centered entrepreneurs and companies, with their sincerity and passion for their principles, are highly worthy of news coverage. Take a more current example. While most beer companies in the U.S. in recent years have experienced difficulty in the slowly declining and highly competitive beer market, New Belgium, the maker of the Fat Tire brand, has been able to attract consumer dollars with a combination of good beer and strong environmental values. Fat Tire has become a fresh alternative for those beer drinkers who have grown tired of the common American beers and the corporate giants that supply them. New Belgium's sustainable business practices that use wind-powered electricity, minimize the use of water, and run a philanthropic program are helping to attract a growing cadre of loyal customers. In 2006, the company gained an invaluable public relations opportunity when NBC Nightly News produced a special segment on sustainable business practices where Fat Tire was featured. By promoting its core values rather than simply pushing beer sales, New Belgium has grown rapidly to become the eighth largest brewer in the U.S.

Appeal to Customers' Intelligence

Values-based entrepreneurs tend to shy away from conventional marketing trickery. They try to appeal to customers' common sense and intelligence, rather than confuse or misinform customers with what Anita Roddick called "psycho-babble." Unbeknownst, apparently, to many marketers, a growing segment of consumers yearn for more information and accurate information—rather than the selective omissions and calculated misinformation that so many corporations seem to be putting out. Consumers are becoming tired of it. Think about it: They are forced to read the label carefully just to make sure that a drink that claims to be "juice" is indeed more than 10 percent pure juice; that an ice cream that claims to contain "chunks of fruit" actually has any fruit at all; or that a skin care product that claims to be natural has indeed no strange chemicals. It's certainly no stretch to say that consumers do not like being manipulated and want good, accurate information.

Seventh Generation, an innovative company that offers natural, environmentally safe household products, is betting on the intelligence and environmental concern of consumers, believing that smart, well-informed consumers will choose its products. To help consumers appreciate its products' healthy environmental benefits, Seventh Generation provides educational information about the harmful effects of traditional household products as well as the advantages of using natural alternatives. The company delivers this information on its product packaging, corporate website, and e-newsletters, as well as through a book by its founder and CEO, Jeffrey Hollender.[5]

In similar fashion, Tom's of Maine, a personal care product maker, features full disclosure of product information and open dialogue with its customers. From the beginning, Tom and Kate Chappell have listed all ingredients used in their products on the packaging along with the source of the ingredients and an explanation of their purpose. They believe that this policy builds customer confidence and loyalty. A related trust-building measure is the signature of Kate and Tom on all company products. Additionally, it is the company policy to answer every letter from customers with a personalized return letter. Organizationally, this is the responsibility of the company's Consumer Dialogue Team, which has no small task since the firm receives some 10,000 letters per year (the team estimates that about 80 percent of them represent positive consumer feedback). Tom's established a factory tour in 1993 as still another avenue for providing information and connecting with its customers. The tour is normally led by one of the Chappell children. There is also a virtual tour on the company's website for those who can't travel to Kennebunk, Maine.

Our values-centered entrepreneurs posit that well-informed customers will make the "right" choices, which in return will benefit their companies as well as society. Eric Henry, President of T.S. Designs expresses his view in the following manner:

> Ultimately, it's about educating the consumer, and turning them from consumer, to citizen. We vote with our dollars so we have a responsibility how we spend those dollars in determining the community we want. If we can raise awareness of the problems, get consumers to ask questions, offer solutions and to demand answers, then businesses will be forced to respond. So the power does not really lie with legislation, or with business, it's the consumer who will decide what kind of business model will thrive in the future.[6]

Be Authentic!

Values-based companies are often authentic in how they present themselves to the market. Authenticity or plain honesty can come across as a refreshing change in a world where misinformation and manipulation are the norm.

Consider the case of Ben & Jerry's and one of its chief competitors in the premium ice cream segment, Häagen-Dazs, now owned by the Pillsbury Company. Häagen-Dazs is undoubtedly a successful brand with superb products, but its approach to marketing is vastly different from that of Ben & Jerry's. We tried this exercise in class a few times. We played a word association game with "Ben & Jerry's," i.e., we asked our students what words they thought of when they heard "Ben & Jerry's"? We repeated the same exercise for Häagen-Dazs. Some of the common answers are listed in Table 6.2.

Table 6.2 makes it apparent that these are both great products with strong brand identities—but with a fundamental twist. Everything about Ben & Jerry's is authentic while almost everything about Häagen-Dazs (other than high quality) is made up. "Ben" and "Jerry" are the real first names of the firm's quirky, hippie-style founders. They are as American as pie: The company has for years presented its products in hand-lettered containers with the founders' pictures on top, a cow on the side, and Vermont-made ice cream inside. The founders have for years expressed their political views on their ice cream containers. Its products are made with all-natural ingredients. In comparison, the word Häagen-Dazs is a meaningless term in a nonexistent language, made-up presumably to imply that the product is from Scandinavia although the ice-cream is made in New Jersey. Häagen-Dazs has no political opinion but has positioned itself as a high quality product that is rich in taste and sexually appealing. Although both brands are successful, one fact is clear: In one case, the founders were authentic while in the other case, the company fabricated a whole false identity.

Similarly, Innocent Drinks' fun and non-corporate brand image has been effective in attracting customers. From the outset, Innocent has presented itself with its straightforward, almost irreverent approach to business, using a simple, down-to-earth communication technique that mirrors the no-nonsense honesty of the Innocent brand and its products. The packaging and logo designs were created by the founders, not a high-priced identity consulting firm. Richard Reed, one of the three co-founders, recalls,

Table 6.2 Terms Associated with Brands

Ben & Jerry's	Häagen-Dazs
Quirky	Elegant
American	European
High quality	High quality
Political	Apolitical
Opinionated	Sexy
Natural	Rich

We didn't have any sophisticated marketing plan, we just wanted the way it looked and tasted and for it to stand out on café shelves. After consultation with members of Innocent's core target market—young, urban professionals—the apple with halo logo was chosen as the one that most clearly illustrated Innocent's core values.[7]

Interestingly, most entrepreneurs in our sample, from Anita Roddick to Howard Schultz to Chris King have, to varying degrees, not been staunch advocates of advertising. They maintain that the superior quality of their products and the enthusiasm of customers will drive their sales. Starbucks, for example, has almost never spent money on conventional advertising. Founder Schultz believes strongly that outstanding in-store customer service is the best form of advertising.

Honest Tea is a great name for what the company stands for. Early on, co-founders Barry Nalebuff and Seth Goldman discovered that most of the tea purchased for bottling by American companies was the lower quality dust and fannings left after quality tea had been produced. Nalebuff looked for a name to accurately describe the firm's bottled tea which was made with real tea leaves, and came up with Honest Tea. Goldman concurred, believing that it was the perfect descriptor for their all-natural brand. The partners wanted their company to be known for the authenticity, integrity, and purity of its products. Befitting its name, Honest Tea also seeks to create honest relationships with its employees, suppliers, customers, and with the communities where it has facilities.

Do Names Matter?
Some names do seem to sound more <u>authentic</u>

- Ben & Jerry's
- The Body Shop
- Honest Tea
- Innocent
- Seventh Generation
- Whole Foods

Build a Soul, Not a Brand

A number of our values-centered companies, particularly those in consumer goods industries, have created valuable, widely recognizable brands. In doing so, they have, for the most part, focused more on substance than style, believing that authenticity trumps manipulated perception. Their implementation philosophy is to engage in honest, open relationships with their customers rather than use sophisticated branding techniques.

Sarah Endline of Sweet Riot, an up-and-coming brand in consumer sweets, does not even like the word "brand."[8] She prefers to use the word "soul" believing that "the soul inside will radiate on the outside."[9] To this end she is trying to build her socially conscious brand without resorting to traditional advertising. Table 6.3 profiles her thinking.[10]

Table 6.3 Building a Brand Without an Advertising Budget: Sweet Riot's Approach

---

1. **Start by building an internal soul**. As a means of building the brand on the outside, Endline has tried to develop a strong culture and operation inside. This includes everything from the way it sources its supplies from Latin America to implementing open-book management. The company's goals and agenda are clearly communicated and its people are expected to act accordingly.

2. **Be authentic by being yourself**. Authenticity is important since less sincere companies have jumped on the sustainability bandwagon as a marketing ploy. Given that so many companies claim to be or are great at what they make, the values-centered firm needs to tell consumers what it does differently. The best way to do it is to be honest about who you are and what you stand for. Let the company be a reflection of the entrepreneur.

3. **Educate customers about your company**. Sweet Riot tries to educate customers about social and environmental issues as well as sell its products. It puts much information about the company on its website. It provides anecdotes and stories that can help form and perpetuate reputation for the organization. The company also replies to virtually all customer inquiries.

4. **Get distribution.** Being on shelf space is not just important financially but actually a great way to build brand awareness. Landing a retail chain like Whole Foods, which has a national distribution network as well as similar brand identity, can be ideal.

5. **Get free publicity.** Since most entrepreneurial firms have no advertising budget, create news! Sweet Riot has lobbied to be covered by the leading health, lifestyle, and business magazines.

6. **Outreach.** Get in front of people's faces. Sweet Riot found offering samples was one of the most powerful ways to attract customers and build brand awareness. Its website, blogs, and monthly newsletters also seem effective, cheap ways to communicate with customers.

7. **Don't get defensive.** Endline warns that there will always be critics. Consumers and media do not necessarily cut a company slack because it is socially responsible. She believes in embracing the critics' comments to make improvements. She suggests not being defensive, but rather to admit, "Wow, sorry, we are doing our best." And then find ways to turn the situation around.

Publicize through Advocacy

Some of our values-centered companies have engaged in advocacy programs that not only serve to promote their causes but also help raise their brand recognition and strengthen their customer base. Calvert's advocacy for its ideals, for instance, has been integral to the success of this investment management group. The company's investment standards regarding labor relations, corporate governance, product safety, community relations, human rights, and other social issues have helped to attract over 400,000 investors who have placed some $16 billion of assets with the firm.

Throughout its history, Calvert has, on numerous occasions, exercised its right as an institutional shareholder to voice social/political concern. In 1982, Calvert was the first U.S. mutual fund to explicitly prohibit investment in South Africa. This initiative increased the spotlight of international attention on apartheid and helped bring down this oppressive policy along with the government that enforced it. More recently, the firm has used a similar approach to try to alter the political oppression and economic deprivation in Sudan. Calvert's advocacy has seldom gotten in the way of its business. In fact, it may have enhanced the company's reputation as a trustworthy steward of people's money.

Over the years, Stonyfield Farm has also engaged in a variety of advocacy programs. The purpose of its longest-running program has been to educate customers on the value of small family farms, to garner further support for such farms, and to build awareness for and commitment to sustainable farming practices. Its programs, in addition to building support for important causes, have also served to attract customers with shared beliefs.

While most of our values-centered entrepreneurs have championed relatively non-sensitive issues, e.g., children's health or voter registration, thereby not limiting their potential customer base, some firms in our sample have deliberately taken highly controversial stances. A classic example is Ben & Jerry's which has proudly promoted its founders' political views on its products and through advertisements. In 1990, for instance, the firm protested New Hampshire's Seabrook nuclear power plant with a Boston billboard campaign declaring, "Stop Seabrook. Keep our customers alive and licking."[11]

Working Assets, the wholesale phone service provider, which now boasts a loyal customer base of some 400,000, has never shied away from controversial issues that it believes in. In fact, the company's management believes that its argumentative positions on social issues, e.g., its pro-choice stance, has given the business a competitive advantage. "The lion's shares of people who sign up with us are people who support our mission. Very few people would not know about our mission. We are always very explicit about what we do," Laura Scher, co-founder of Working Assets, explained. "We distinguish ourselves by being willing to tackle the hard issues."[12]

Since 1991, Working Assets has operated its Citizen Action program to provide customers with timely information and easy ways to speak out on important public issues. It has turned its monthly bill into a combination political hot sheet, call-to-arms, and fundraiser. Each month customers get the usual phone charge listings along with information on timely public issues, such as an upcoming vote in Congress or a new EPA policy. The information sheet typically outlines the issues in question, explaining what is at stake, Working Assets' position, and who to contact (to protest or support)—names and telephone numbers. Customers also have the option of using a free three-minute call on any Monday to phone in their protest. Or, alternatively they can check a box and for $3 Working Assets will send a letter in their name.

Created in 1995, Working Assets' Flash Activist Network (FAN) is a rapid response program designed to give customers a chance to speak out on fast-moving issues before all is said and done. Throughout the year FAN monitors critical events as they unfold and notifies members by phone, fax or email when it is time for action. Members can call a toll-free number for details on the issues at hand, then be transferred directly to the targeted decision-maker, or they can send a personalized fax. Working Assets provides this timely service for a low monthly fee.

Today, Working Assets is one of the most powerful and progressive citizen-action groups in the U.S. Each month its customers generate approximately 80,000 calls and letters to public officials and corporate leaders on important issues of public concern. Recent political victories include helping save the Arctic National Wildlife Refuge from oil drilling, defeating certain judicial appointments, standing up for strict organic food labeling standards, and thwarting the Pentagon's intrusion on the civil rights of citizens by rejecting the Total Information Awareness Project.

Of course, many people disagree with Working Assets' position on many issues and even its basic approach. But there is little doubt that the company's political activism is the consolidating force that attracts and retains a loyal activist customer base.

Promotion as a Challenge to Oneself

Federal Express, in the 1980s, had one of the most famous slogans in advertising history, "When it absolutely, positively has to get there overnight." Fed-Ex founder Fred Smith contended that this slogan was a message not only to its customers but also a challenge to its employees. That is, it was not used just as an advertising tool but also as an aspirational goal for the company to meet. But, "the problem with good advertising," Smith often recounted, "is that it can destroy a bad company (that cannot fulfill its promise)."[13]

Similarly some of our values-centered entrepreneurs have promoted their values to others in part as a challenge to themselves to deliver on what they stand for. Tim Haahs of Timothy Haahs & Associate explains: "Our mission and core values are an extremely important part of our company and the way we do business. We do promote our values widely so that we can try to serve as a model for others. This helps not only our clients know what to expect when they have us serving them, but it also helps to keep us accountable to ourselves."[14] Haahs, like most of our other entrepreneurs, understands that if the company fails to deliver on what it claims to stand for, it will be viewed as disingenuous and deceitful.

Some readers may be wary of companies touting their values as a marketing tool. After all, aren't you supposed to be humble about your good deeds? Maybe. But recall it is important to our values-centered entrepreneurs to be role models and share their values and goals with the public. Moreover, in the competitive (some say, cutthroat) marketplace, it appears to make good business sense to use values as a means of differentiation and brand building.

If any firm is going to promote its "pure heart" and good deeds as a competitive lever, however, it had better be what it preaches. All of our entrepreneurs understand that they must live up to their avowed standards to be credible in the eyes of their customers, employees, and other stakeholders. Otherwise, they run the grave risk of being exposed as hypocritical with potentially devastating consequences.

Chapter Takeaways

- Don't be shy about promoting your values to connect with customers.
- Treat customers as intelligent individuals, using good and honest information.
- Be honest and authentic—be yourself.
- Build a soul first, then the brand.
- Don't be afraid to advocate your case or even take a controversial stance.

7

Build a Cohesive, Dedicated Organization

Long term value for our shareholders cannot be achieved in an enduring sustaining way unless the management of the company is completely comprehensively committed to creating long term value for the employees. The two are directly linked together. Any company or any management team that turns its back on its employees and does not share in the success of the company with people who do the work will not finish the race. . . . You certainly will not achieve the aspirational dreams you have for your business.
—Howard Schultz, CEO, Starbucks[1]

Our values-centered entrepreneurs make unusual efforts to build organizations that foster satisfied and proud employees, who, in return, reward their employers with a higher retention rate, higher-quality products and services, and strong financial performance.

These entrepreneurs sincerely seem to be proud of the organizations they have built. By and large, they have established more cohesive organizations and dedicated workforces than are typically found in conventional companies. To earn employee loyalty and strengthen commitment, they have utilized generous, innovative, and sometimes highly unconventional methods. In return, their loyal and committed employees have made noteworthy contributions to the company mission and viability. As Howard Schultz of Starbucks has asserted, treating employees well can indeed be good for business and for mission.

A Fundamentally Different View toward Employees

Our values-centered entrepreneurs demonstrate genuine concern for the well-being of their employees and tend to provide excellent benefits. But then, so do many conventional companies. The noteworthy difference between values-centered and conventional entrepreneurs, however, is not found in their individual employee benefits programs but, rather, in their fundamentally different attitudes about employees—whom many of our values-centered entrepreneurs refer to as "associates," "co-workers," "partners," or even "family." For our entrepreneurs, people are not just a means to achieving their mission; they are the means and the end, i.e., they are part of a triple bottom-line mission.

How often have we seen business owners who view employees as something they "have to put up with" to operate their businesses? Most large corporations perceive their employees as (human) "resources," or, in some cases, as "liabilities" on the balance sheet—especially the moment business results turn sour.

Over the years, we have often wondered why so many businesses, small or large, have such poor relationships with their employees. We have been curious about the hideous lack of effort on the part of many employers to create more employee-oriented organizations, when a modest effort and a more positive attitude could make a huge difference in employee moral, productivity, and contribution.

The following are some of the educated guesses we have come up with over the years: First, a common reason among many employers appears to be that employee well-being is nowhere on their minds. It never occurs to them that people who work for them deserve respect; they see them as merely "factors of production" or "cogs in a wheel." Some employers seem to operate on the assumption that they are doing their employees a big favor simply by employing them. Many conventional e.ntrepreneurs assume that they can't afford to be generous considering their tight financial position. Some of the entrepreneurs that we have met with worry that they will be taken advantage of by their employees if they are too good to them. We have also encountered employers who give lip service to concepts such as "employee empowerment" and the like, but with little sincerity. In general, conventional employers just don't seem to have the same respect and positive attitude toward their employees that our values-centered entrepreneurs do. In Table 7.1 below, we have listed some of the most common reasons or excuses as to why so many conventional entrepreneurs don't put in much effort to enhance the work environment.

In contrast, most of our values-centered entrepreneurs see employee well-being and motivation as an integral part of their mission. For these entrepreneurs, having satisfied, inspired employees is one of their key organizational goals. Clif Bar founder Gary Erickson says it best with the simple statement, "People are the company, and not just a means to an end."[2] Many of the values-centered CEOs seem to worry less about whether they are being overly generous or whether they will be taken advantage of, but try to find an effective (and economic) way to build the organization that will fulfill the mission of the company. Table 7.2 summarizes some of the fundamental differences between conventional and values-centered entrepreneurs in attitudes about employees.

Consider the case of Starbucks CEO Howard Schultz, who always wanted to create the kind of company where there was "respect and dignity for all people, old and

Table 7.1 Common Excuses Why Conventional Entrepreneurs Do Not Make the Effort to Become Excellent Employers

- "These employee programs consume too much effort and time."
- "The various employee benefits and 'feel-good' programs will cost a lot of money."
- "We can't measure the ROI (return on investment) of these feel-good programs."
- "Our employees will take advantage of me if I am too nice to them."
- "My employees won't really appreciate it."

Table 7.2 Fundamentally Different Approach Toward Employees

Common View	*Values-Centered View*
■ "Employees."	■ "Partners," "Associates," "Family."
■ People are an important resource.	■ People are the company.
■ Having happy employees can increase productivity for the company.	■ Having satisfied employees is an important part of the mission of our company.
■ Employees will take advantage of me if I am too nice.	■ Inspired employees will fulfill the company's mission.
■ Programs to make employees happy cost too much money.	■ There are many things we can do that are inexpensive and effective.
■ Employees don't really care about the feel-good meetings and stuff.	■ We need to make efforts to build a strong community.
■ People work simply for a paycheck.	■ People also work for self-fulfillment and for a "cause."

young, educated, non-educated, black or white." He was determined to create the kind of company that his father, a blue collar worker, never had a chance to work for. Schultz's concern for employees came from his life-changing experience when he was seven years old: One day, when Schultz came back from school, he saw his father lying on a sofa with a cast from hip to ankle, after having fallen from his job as a truck driver. Bedridden for the next several months without medical insurance or workers' compensation, Schultz's father was unable to provide for the family. Schultz later said that he witnessed the "fracturing of the American dream and what could happen to a working class family when their dreams and aspirations are left behind." Years later, in 1987, when he acquired Starbucks and started growing the company, he was determined to "build a different kind of a company," one that could "achieve a delicate balance of profitability and benevolence."

As Schultz was growing the business, he came to the realization that he was not in the "coffee business serving people, but in the people business serving coffee."[3] He followed with the strategic decision that because franchising would likely dilute the company's culture and values, Starbucks should continue to develop as a company-owned system. In 1990, Starbucks became the first coffee retailer in the U.S. to offer comprehensive medical benefits and stock options to its part-time employees—whom he calls "partners." Paying these benefits increased the company's costs but also helped build competitive advantage by attracting strong, committed partners who provided superior service quality—Schultz often argued.[4] Starbucks's employee attrition rate shrank to one-fifth of the average of the North American restaurants and retailers. Schultz believes that in taking care of his people he has created long-term financial value for the company's shareholders.

Far Above the Standard

Not all of our values-centered companies offer (or can afford to offer) exceptionally generous compensation or benefit packages. But some do. One could criticize these firms as being paternalistic, but they don't see it that way. They see it as an investment in their people that will pay them back manifold. They have little concern for what the industry standard is or what minimal benefits they can get away with. In fact, some of our values-centered companies offer benefits and compensation schemes that far exceed the industry standards.

Examples are plentiful. Eileen Fisher Clothing, in an industry (apparel) with a reputation for exploiting workers, provides each of its 400-plus employees a $1,000 education benefit and a $1,000 wellness benefit, to be spent on rejuvenators such as massages, spa visits, and gym equipment.[5] Clif Bar, in addition to many of its extremely generous benefits and programs, offers a three-month paid sabbatical program for employees every seven years. To ease the burden of working parents, Patagonia pioneered corporate on-site childcare programs in the U.S. with its Great Pacific Child Development Center.[6] Calvert, a financial services company in an industry known for being hypercompetitive and unconcerned about job demands on family, provides "family-friendly benefits" that include a new baby bonus, flexible work scheduling, and a sport and health club subsidy, among others. Calvert also offers what it calls a transportation and parking subsidy, which includes walking shoes if employees hoof it to work! As these examples demonstrate, a number of our values-centered entrepreneurs are highly concerned about employee well-being and go to great lengths to meet their needs.

Some of our companies offer ownership shares to their employees. Starbucks, as mentioned, became the first coffee retailer in the U.S. to offer not only comprehensive medical benefits but also stock options to its part-time employees. All of Dancing Deer's employees, many of whom are recent immigrants and don't even understand stock options plans, are enrolled in them. At Stonyfield Farm, all employees participate in company profits through bonus and stock option programs, which come out of the first 15 percent of the company's yearly profits. Pacific Community Ventures, a values-centered venture capital firm, even requires its portfolio businesses (as part of the deal) to structure equity-sharing programs for employees to allow them to participate in the financial upside that Pacific hopes to help create.

New Belgium Brewery's founders are also ardent believers in employee ownership. From the beginning, Jeff and Kim Jordan knew that it would take more than the two of them to accomplish their vision. When Brian Callahan, an aspiring brewer, came knocking at the door, they had their first employee-owner. To the Jordans, it seemed natural to bring in people and give them a vested interest in the company. "It's important that we share in all the benefit," says Kim "and, frankly, in the risk too."[7] Today, stock ownership is awarded after one year's employment (along with a one-year, commemorative gift—a neat-o cruiser bike!). The employee stock ownership plan currently amounts to 32 percent of company equity. After five years with the company, employees are awarded a trip to Belgium. In 2008, two groups of nearly 25 employees took the two-week trip. These rewards are part of the plan to achieve and maintain what CEO Kim Jordan calls New Belgium's "high involvement culture."[8]

While equally committed to sharing success with employees, Clif Bar follows a different path. Founder and CEO Gary Erickson decided against stock options in favor of cash bonuses. Erickson believes that the only time the company's stock will have significant value is during an IPO or acquisition—neither of which he is willing to pursue. Consequently, he felt it would be misleading and not financially beneficial to give employees company stock. Instead, Erickson provides an annual cash bonus based on the company's overall financial performance.

As one might expect, many of our values-centered companies are considered among the best companies to work for. Several of them, including Starbucks and Whole Foods, are consistently ranked in *Fortune* magazine's annual listing of the best employers in the U.S. Whole Foods has been recognized by *Fortune* as one of the "100 Best Companies to Work For" for eleven consecutive years (1998–2008), ever since the rankings began.[9] *Health* magazine in 2003 named Clif Bar the Healthiest Workplace for Women in America. The same year, *Fortune Small Business* magazine named Clif Bar founder Gary Erickson one of the six best bosses in America. Calvert, another of our values-centered firms, earns a spot on the "100 Best Companies in America for Working Mothers" almost every year. It achieved this award in 2000, 2001 and 2003 through 2005. The company has consistently scored in the near top of its class in the categories of pay scale, opportunities for advancement, support for childcare, and the availability of family-friendly benefits.

Establish a Tight-Knit Community

Almost without exception, our values-centered entrepreneurs endeavor to build a work environment that is pleasant, cooperative, and productive. Their admirable treatment of employees and community-building efforts have successfully built strong, cohesive cultures that unite around their missions and bring demonstrable results. Their practices are not necessarily extravagant or expensive. In fact, most of them appear to be quite reasonable and often inexpensive to the company. But they do exhibit thoughtfulness and concern for the well-being of their employees which, quite naturally, is reciprocated.

Consider the case of Timothy Haahs, whose successful architectural firm, Timothy Haahs & Associates, has averaged 20 to 30 percent growth in annual gross revenue over the past three years. But the achievement that Haahs is most proud of, however, is not the firm's remarkable growth rate but rather the family atmosphere that he has created in the workplace which keeps stress levels low, and employees loyal and motivated. Moreover, he has built his family-style work environment without spending an exorbitant amount of money.

His company has adopted a number of traditions which have helped not only promote its values, but also strengthen the close-knit, family atmosphere. For instance, every morning a different employee is scheduled to provide breakfast for the rest of the firm. Each person is only scheduled about once every two months or so, and thus the ritual is not overly burdensome. It costs the company nothing, but has the benefit of getting employees together every morning before starting the work day. In addition, on Mondays and Fridays the company purchases lunch for the entire staff. These company-sponsored meals help employees enjoy each other's company and create community amongst them.

Timothy Haahs & Associates also sponsors a number of get-togethers throughout the year outside of work hours. Its annual employee retreat is an opportunity to bring everyone together, in a relaxing and fun environment, to both reminisce and look to the future. After the retreat, families are invited to join in various social activities, such as picnics and games. The company's annual Christmas party is yet another community-building event. Here, Haahs invites not only the employees' families but also close clients and friends of the firm to come together to reflect on the year and celebrate the holiday season.

Clif Bar maintains that employees thrive in a work environment that promotes health and sense of community. To this end, the company has promoted a unique work environment that values its employees and puts emphasis on what its founder, Gary Erickson, cares most about—health and well-being. Often, first-time visitors to the Clif Bar headquarters are confused as to whether it is an office or a gym. The company is known for its climbing walls, dogs, yoga classes, and playrooms. Employees can hop on a two-story rock-climbing wall in the office or use the company gym. Approximately 80 percent of the company's employees take advantage of the company gym and its professional trainers who offer more than 20 fitness classes per week, during work hours. The company also has a dance studio that employees can use. Clif Bar, furthermore, employs a wellness manager who is fondly referred to as the Wellness Diva. Erickson sees the several wellness activities as addressing employees' physical, emotional, and spiritual needs.

To help shorten its employees' days and alleviate stress (if there is any left), Clif Bar has instituted a Concierge Service. The program provides laundry and dry-cleaning services at a low cost. Additionally, the company provides a car-wash service, on-site masseuses twice a week, and a hair stylist who comes by once a week. Further, the company has what it calls a 9/80 Program where employees work 9 rather than 10 days during a two-week period. This creates a three-day weekend every two weeks for workers to spend with their families and re-energize. And lastly, Clif Bar employees are encouraged to volunteer for community service on company time.

New Belgium Brewery hosts relatively inexpensive programs yearly such as retreats, bike races, and other outings for employees that are believed to be highly effective in fostering teamwork and community. Recently, employees' sense of community and commitment to the company became evident when the company decided to take a fun trip to Mexico. When it came time for the trip, some people volunteered to stay behind and work for the company. "There was a lot of work that needed to be done while we were gone," recalls one of the workers. "Several employees volunteered to stay behind, and they worked long hours. That's an example of a staff that cares about the work."[10]

Small Dog Electronics illustrates what a tiny company with 27 employees can do to create a tight-knit culture. Don Mayer, the founder, considers all of his employees as members of his "family" and goes out of his way to provide attractive benefits and programs. Somewhat unusual for a company of its size, Small Dog offers flex-time schedules and paid time off for employees to donate their time to local organizations. Other unorthodox activities and benefits include bocce ball and badminton tournaments, pet insurance, and the option of employees bringing their pets to work.

Thanks to the tight-knit culture that these policies have created, the company maintains a motivated and productive staff with virtually no turnover.[11] In Table 7.3, we have listed some of the innovative, yet inexpensive activities that a sample of our values-centered companies offer to establish a tight-knit community.

Develop Thoughtful Policies that Empower Workers (and Obtain Results)

Many of our values-centered entrepreneurs have organizational policies and processes designed to empower their workers in hopes of gaining greater creativity, initiative, commitment, and the like from them. The thoughts and efforts they have put into these policies and processes far exceed those of most conventional companies.

To illustrate, Tom Chappell of Tom's of Maine, has made conscious organizational design choices that he describes in geometric imagery, namely, "a triangle inside a circle." The circle represents the team that is the basic unit of organization. Teams meet in circles to emphasize equality and encourage everyone to contribute ideas. To support this notion, Chappell has removed all elongated tables from his facilities in favor of round tables. He wanted to make clear that no one is superior when it comes to creative ideas. Chappell credits the circle concept with the generation of many of the innovative ideas and solutions that have helped the company grow and prosper in recent years. He asserts, "The power of the circle is in its openness; it is the place where you are willing to open up and listen."[12] He also credits the circle with improving employee moral.

The triangle, on the other hand, symbolizes the company's authority structure. As Chappell sees it, Tom's is not a consensus organization. There is a leader on each team who is accountable to a higher manager and there is a clear chain of command. Ideally, the two systems—circle and triangle—work in harmony. The circle encourages participation and creativity. The triangle provides an apparatus for decision making and accountability. Like many of our values-centered entrepreneurs, Chappell has thoughtfully fine-tuned the organizational structure and policies to empower workers and deliver results.

Table 7.3 Inexpensive Ways to Form a Tight Community
(Based on Timothy Haahs, Clif Bar, New Belgium Brewery, and Small Dog Electronics)

Office Programs/Services	Budget/Expense
■ Have employees bring breakfast for others.	None
■ Offer concierge service in conjunction with a local car wash service and/or dry-cleaning company.	None/Small
■ Buy lunch or breakfast on a regular basis (e.g., on Fridays).	Small
■ Sponsor employee outings monthly or quarterly.	Small
■ Sponsor a bicycle race, or bocce ball or badminton tournament for employees.	Small/Medium
■ Offer flex-time.	Small/Medium
■ Sponsor an annual retreat.	Small/Medium
■ Sponsor a Christmas party.	Medium/High

Several of our other values-centered entrepreneurs have made similar conscious decisions to reduce barriers between management and employees. A few have even begun to employ "open-book management," i.e., the practice of sharing their financial information with employees. Stonyfield Farm for example, has been one of a growing number of privately held firms that exercises this policy. The company initiated its open-book policy in the late 1980s after experiencing major financial losses. As a central component of the policy, semi-annual, company-wide meetings are held to review financial performance. Co-founders Kaymen and Hirshberg firmly believe that being completely open with employees promotes loyalty and committed employees. This open-book policy has worked hand in hand with Stonyfield's culture of encouraging input at all levels. For example, teams with colorful appellations such as the "Cream Team" and "Where's the Milk" have developed significant recommendations that have resulted in more efficient operations. Furthermore, Stonyfield employees have participated in plant expansion decisions, including specific design suggestions. The company offers both individual and team awards to stimulate input and creativity. Each year, one employee receives the "President's Cash Award" for his or her waste reduction efforts. Financial incentives are also extended to departments and teams that develop environmentally sound programs. Moreover, Stonyfield's open-book policy and open culture have encouraged employees to participate in the company's key business decisions.[13]

New Belgium Brewery also practices open-book management and trains all employees in financial literacy to make the policy even more meaningful. Further, the company involves its financially literate and informed "co-workers" in strategy development, budgeting, and departmental planning. The process starts with the management team sitting down and deciding on big-picture issues, such as long-term goals and strategic direction. Then the management team takes the overall strategy back to its co-workers during an annual retreat. Next, each department, using the strategy as a guideline, develops departmental plans. During this process, all co-workers have the opportunity to review the financial status of the company, assess its present and future business prospects, and offer input. Co-founder Kim Jordan believes that the company's ownership and open-book policies encourage a community of trust and mutual responsibility. "We have tried to make our relationship with our co-workers—in terms of running the business—very transparent," Kim explains, "and I think that's a foundational piece of who we are."[14]

At Chris King Precision Components, the company's empowered workers have taken ownership of its high-quality manufacturing process. From the beginning, founder Chris King worked hard to create the kind of work environment and culture that would be compatible with his mission of producing functionally and environmentally superior products. Believing that "happier employees make better products,"[15] King has worked to provide the policies and create a culture that would make employees content. He has also made efforts to be a "nice" boss. King admits that it is easier to be a mean boss and much more challenging to be a kind, inspiring boss when you want to get things done quickly. But he believes that there is only one way to create quality products consistently. King explains, "If you want quality, you will have to make them want to produce quality."[16]

Consequently, employees at Chris King have sincerely bought into the company's mission of making the world's best bicycle components while minimizing environmental damage. King recalls occasions when he wanted to say to his employees working on a component, "Don't you think this is good enough?" But he couldn't utter those words because he worried that they might get offended. King's workers have become so committed to quality that their standards at times exceed even his expectations.

In most cases, empowering employees and treating them well has proven to be good both for business and mission. Table 7.4 lists some of the commonly acknowledged benefits of having appreciated and inspired employees (that our entrepreneurs as well as others have mentioned). However, it should be emphasized that actually being successful in building an inspired workforce that delivers measurable results is much easier said than done. Our values-centered entrepreneurs not only had an enlightened approach to employee motivation but also have expended a lot of effort over many years to make their "people" ideas work in practice.

Encourage Employees in Giving Back (to Strengthen Organizational Unity)

Many of our values-centered companies encourage their employees to give back on (and off) company time. Our interviews suggest that this policy is an effective means for getting employees to share in the company's mission and further strengthen the organizational unity.

As should be clear from our earlier discussion, Tom Chappell has devoted much time and thought to formulating Tom's of Maine's mission and beliefs, and has tried to mold a corporate culture that personifies those tenets. Commenting on one of his bigger mistakes, Chappell said that simply "handing down the company's mission and beliefs is not enough, that it is important for the staff to see the company mission in action and that you have to do the training."[17] In practice, this meant setting an example through his own behavior and decisions, as well as encouraging and rewarding the people who "live the mission," and are proactive in their volunteer work.

Tom's of Maine's policy on volunteerism has been a prominent way by which the company encourages its employees to live its mission. Under this policy, employees are encouraged to spend five percent of their paid work time (two hours per week or 2.5 weeks per year) performing volunteer work for non-profit organizations of their choosing. The policy was instituted in 1989 and has proved to be popular with

Table 7.4 Benefits of Appreciated and Inspired Employees

- Happy employees who are proud of their company and promote its products/services.
- Higher employee retention rates (and lower training costs).
- Higher quality products and services.
- Stronger financial viability/performance.
- Attainment of company's aspirational goals.

employees as well as helpful to the beneficiaries. Moreover, the company occasionally organizes day-long projects that may include as much as one-third of its workforce. In one instance, 14 employees, including Tom Chappell, drove to Rhode Island and spent the day helping clean up an oil spill. One of the participating employees commented afterwards that the venture was not only helpful to the people of Rhode Island but also was a bonding and team-building experience for the participating employees.[18]

Calvert has also instituted a policy where its employees are encouraged to become involved in good deeds. Through Calvert Community Partners, employees are granted up to 12 days of paid leave each year to participate in community service activities which have included tutoring, organizing charity fundraising events, and participating in the Greater DC Cares Servathons.[19] As Calvert sees it, reaching out to the community is not only a morally responsible policy, but it serves to create a better working environment for its employees. Employees engaging in community service feel a sense of accomplishment. This translates into greater job satisfaction and ultimately happier, more productive employees.

At Tom's Shoes, employees regardless of their functional role in the company (e.g., marketing or accounting) are encouraged to participate in the companies "shoe drops" in various locations. There, employees get to see first-hand the fruit of their labour as they personally hand out shoes to barefooted kids in developing countries. When employees return to their Los Angeles headquarters, they often talk about being proud of their company and being more determined to make a difference.

Salesforce.com is a Silicon Valley-based high-tech company that encourages its employees to give back. Since the inception of the Salesforce.com Foundation and its "1/1/1 Philanthropic Model" in 2000, Salesforce.com has given employees an average of six days of paid time off each year to participate in volunteer opportunities. Under this 1/1/1 model, Salesforce.com encourages its workers to give 1 percent of their time to community engagement; the company gives 1 percent of its equity and 1 percent of its products to non-profit organizations. By 2008, nearly 85 percent of the firm's employees had participated in the program, donating more than 77,000 hours to help feed the hungry, combat homelessness, teach children to read, and improve the environment among other activities. The company had also donated in excess of $12 million to non-profit organizations, and supplied Salesforce licenses to more than 3,500 nonprofits in 56 countries around the world. The combination of time, money, and product helped numerous nonprofits run their operations more efficiently and increase the effectiveness of their programs.[20] Moreover, there was another significant beneficiary—the company itself—its employees became more motivated and committed to its triple bottom-line mission.

Chapter Takeaways

- For values-centered entrepreneurs, creating an employee-oriented organization is an important component of their core mission.
- Many of our values-centered organizations go out of their way to offer benefits and compensation packages that far exceed the industry standard.
- Values-centered entrepreneurs make efforts to build a work environment that is pleasant and cooperative. They sponsor (often inexpensive) activities and events that help foster a sense of community.
- Values-centered entrepreneurs are thoughtful about designing organizational policies that empower their employees and deliver results.
- Values-centered entrepreneurs encourage their employees to give back, which gets employees involved in practicing the company's mission and strengthening its organizational culture.

8

Maximize Profits . . . With Some Exceptions

> A person's treatment of money is the most decisive test of his character, how they make it and how they spend it.
>
> —James Moffatt, biblical scholar, 1870–1944[1]

Plan for Difficult Financial Choices

Although there are a fair number of books and articles that profile the works of various values-centered entrepreneurs, few if any have carefully examined their financial practices. After reading these works, the uninitiated might conclude that profit is the simple by-product of good ethical, and socially responsive business decisions. But the reality is to the contrary: as any businessperson knows, financial performance is the result of sound financial planning and decision making.

From the outset, our entrepreneurs, who by their nature are sensitive to social issues, have some key decisions to make. Should they, for instance, price their products low such that the vast majority of consumers can purchase them? Or maybe they should give their products to people who can't afford them? Should they pay their employees above-market wages? Should they eschew trying to take customers away from competitors who, after all, are members of the community and have families to feed? What about assiduously cutting costs at every opportunity in hopes of maximizing short-term profits? Under what circumstances should they sacrifice profit to exercise their social/environmental beliefs? Is it possible to create win-win situations where the company both makes money and helps society? These are very real questions that face principled entrepreneurs. In some cases the answers are straightforward. In other instances decisions are difficult, even daunting. In this chapter we look to our pioneers to gain insight as to how they dealt with these kinds of issues and what aspiring entrepreneurs should do.

To find answers to the above questions, we conducted a three-part analysis. First, we looked into the strategies through which our sample companies pursue profits. In particular, we examined their policies in the areas of (1) pricing, (2) cost control, and (3) growth, all of which impact profitability directly. The second part of our analysis identified specific examples of how our sample entrepreneurs and their companies sacrifice profits to accommodate their social and/or environmental causes. We looked at whether and to what extent our entrepreneurial firms purposely (1) acquire particular supplies at above-market prices for certain resources, (2) pass up profitable opportunities, and (3) take on non-profitable projects.

Lastly, we sought out examples of win-win situations, i.e., programs and policies that benefit both the companies' financials *and* their social/environmental objectives. We learned that our values-centered entrepreneurs are particularly good at exploiting such opportunities by (1) developing or modifying their business model, (2) doing business with struggling communities, and (3) treating employees well to obtain results, among others. We describe the most prominent of these strategies, listed in Table 8.1, in this chapter.

Pursue Profits

Through Premium Positioning

Product positioning and pricing are the core elements of any business strategy. They delimit the firm's target market and define its projected profit margin. The pricing/positioning strategies of the vast majority of our companies became obvious early in our analysis. Interestingly, more than 80 percent of our sample companies positioned their offerings at the high end of the market and charged premium prices. This finding was surprising to us because we expected our entrepreneurs to be more concerned about the affordability of their products, especially to lower income groups.

Examples of the premium pricing strategy abound. For instance, a reputation for high quality along with an unprecedented 10-year warranty allows Chris King Precision Components, a bicycle component manufacturer, to set the highest prices in its industry. Similarly, the quality of its craftsmanship allows Berkeley Mills to charge a heftier price than other comparable furniture designers. Stonyfield Farm's organic yogurt sells at a premium at retailers such as Whole Foods, which, in turn, demands above-average margins for its healthier and safer product offerings. (By the way, some of our students call Whole Foods "whole wallet.") Patagonia prices its "ridiculously overbuilt" (term used by the founder) outdoor clothing at a premium and sells it to a loyal customer base. Starbucks provides a variety of premium coffee products and a

Table 8.1 Financial Strategies for Values-Centered Entrepreneurs

Pursue Profits	*Give Up Profits*	*Achieve Win-Win*
Premium positioning/pricing	Paying above-market prices for some inputs	Through the business model
Controlling costs	Passing on profitable opportunities	Making investments that pay for themselves
Aggressive growth	Undertaking non-profitable projects	Business with struggling communities
		Treating employees well to get results

pleasant environment to validate its $3–5 coffee prices. Magic Johnson Enterprises charges the same prices at its theaters and coffee houses in the inner-cities as those in more affluent communities.

We discovered that some of our sample companies are able to apply premium pricing at least partially *because* of their environmental or social positioning. By offering safer and more environmentally friendly pesticides, AgraQuest can charge a higher price than its competitors. Similarly, Interface Carpets, one of the leading floor covering companies in the U.S., can set prices at a higher rate than others in the industry because of its reputation for sustainable products and manufacturing processes.

Our findings clearly show that while the majority of our values-centered firms are socially responsible in many regards, making their products affordable to all people is not a goal. They appear to have set prices at or close to profit maximizing levels. This high-end pricing strategy may appear misguided to some readers. How can values-driven businesses charge premium prices making it difficult for lower-middle class people to afford their products or services? How can they consider themselves to be socially responsible?

One explanation for the high-end positioning strategy is economic reality, i.e., the existence of large competitors with powerful economies of scale. Our start-ups needed to find a niche and, given their higher cost structure and focus on quality (e.g., the use of natural ingredients), they need to position their offerings at the high end of the market to assure profits. Remember, our values-centered entrepreneurs build "triple bottom-line" companies, not non-profit organizations, and one of the bottom-lines is profitability.

Consider Grameen Bank, founded by Nobel Prize winner Muhammad Yunus, the world's pioneer and leader in offering micro-loans to the poor. Although Grameen charges interest rates that are dramatically lower than those offered by the loan sharks in developing economies, its loans are not cheap. For the bank's "income generating loans" (business loans), the usual interest rate is 20 percent—almost double those of most industrialized countries. Of course, Grameen has justifiable reasons: the high cost of operation due to its larger number of small loans and its high-interest savings accounts that yield 8 to 12 percent. The basic point here is that even Grameen charges adequate rates to remain profitable and finance its growth—to serve more people.

One might think that a company could be *more* socially responsible if it were in the business of offering their *superior* products or services at prices that are more affordable than those of its competitors. This strategy, however, is not feasible for many of our companies such as Stonyfield Farm, whose cost of doing business (e.g., using organic ingredients) is higher than that of conventional yogurt manufacturers. Beyond this, even if a low price strategy theoretically might have been financially feasible, it is clear that the vast majority of our entrepreneurs do not view product affordability as a prerequisite for serving society. Pricing is just not perceived as an essential lever for serving society or protecting the environment. Most seem to look to other ways to serve.

We should note that a few of the companies in our sample are exceptions to our general observation. For instance, Migros offers its products at among the lowest prices in the industry. Migros, one of Switzerland's largest retailers, follows a low margin/volume strategy offering quality products priced at 10–20 percent below its competitors. Low-end positioning is integral to the company's original social purpose of serving a community (Switzerland) with historically little price competition. It also has been a sound business strategy that has resulted in phenomenal growth and profitability over many decades. Similarly, Iggy's Bread of the World, a prominent Massachusetts bakery, is more concerned about making its breads affordable than making high margins. Consequently, Iggy's sets its prices below those of similar products in other bakeries to ensure that members of its community can afford its famous breads.

Diligently Control Costs

Cost control is an essential component of our values-centered entrepreneurs' strategy. Cost cutting efforts are a reflection of any business's level of resolve for creating a "lean and mean" organization. Our analysis indicates that most of the companies in our sample, like most successful conventional businesses, are highly disciplined in controlling costs as part of their ongoing struggle to survive and enhance profitability.

Our companies follow a variety of approaches in controlling their expenses. Migros, for instance, produces about 25 percent of its merchandise internally (private label) to better hold down its costs. Conversely, Seventh Generation, maker of safe and environmentally friendly household cleaning products, credits its effective control of costs to outsourcing many of its functions, including product development, marketing, and distribution. Patagonia has held down operating expenses, among other ways, by paying salaries that were somewhat below the industry standard and concomitantly maintaining low employee turnover (through its employee-friendly environment). Novica, the online retailer of Third World artisans, makes no secret of its cost consciousness. Co-founder Robert Milk remarked in an interview:

> We've had to monitor cash tightly in our quest to build a sustainable company. We negotiate hard with vendors and take a tough stance when it comes to costs and extraneous expenses, particularly with shipping and marketing vendors, where you have to take a very proactive approach to rate negotiation and results.[2]

Rhythm & Hues, one of the leading special effects companies for the movie industry, has developed unusually creative cost control measures that are in line with its mission of establishing an artist-friendly work environment. For Rhythm & Hues, employee compensation is by far its largest cost item and the slight mismanagement of this element on a large project could result in significant financial loss. Thus, to control costs, Rhythm & Hues has been highly disciplined with respect to the salary range that it offers to prospective employees, even when it has just landed a large movie project and needs people quickly. In fact, there have been times when prospective employees were offered salaries 20 percent higher by competitor companies. Rhythm & Hues, nevertheless, has been successful in recruiting talented artists *because* of its artist-friendly work environment. "Our salary and pay scale is very consistent," confirms Ken Roupenian, Director of Digital Production. He adds,

> Many people come here for many reasons other than money; it is not about the money. We feed people every day; there is always something for breakfast; people bring their dogs to work; financials are shared with employees every week, and people actually know what is going on whereas our friends in other companies depend on rumors.[3]

It helps that Rhythm & Hues is known for having one of the best kitchens in the industry, where all of its employees spend a good amount of time munching away.

Rhythm & Hues is also innovative in controlling the burgeoning costs of its employee medical benefits. While it provides health benefits for all regular full-time employees and even many contractors (highly unusual), it does not utilize a third-party insurance company as most firms do. Company executives have concluded that it is cheaper to manage medical benefits directly by enrolling employees under its own program and paying bills directly to doctors. By running an in-house medical coverage program, Rhythm & Hues has been successful in lowering the overall costs to the company even though its health plan actually covers a wide range of elective procedures and treatments that most companies' health plans do not offer. Needless to say, not all companies should manage their own health benefits. This approach works for Rhythm & Hues because, in part, it is fortunate enough to have a young, healthy workforce. However, we cannot help but applaud this firm for its out-of-box approach to cost control—that goes hand in hand with its mission. To generalize, it appears that our companies have undertaken cost saving measures that are sensible for their respective situations.

Pursue Aggressive Growth

Growth can impact profitability both by increasing revenue and reducing costs through the economies of scale. But growth can also mean drawing customers away from other companies including fragile family businesses. Does this present our entrepreneurs with an ethical dilemma?

Our analysis suggests that most of our companies, like conventional firms, pursue aggressive growth to increase profits by expanding the total market and by taking market share away from their large and small competitors. For instance, aggressive geographical expansion in the U.S. and internationally with little concern for the fate of local coffee shops has been a trademark of the Starbucks Corporation. Switzerland-based Migros has diversified beyond grocery stores and supermarkets into travel, restaurants, banking, insurance, gasoline, marketing, and publishing to continue its astonishing growth. Currently, Migros accounts for about 25 percent of the supermarket industry in Switzerland while being a major player in the other above-mentioned industries. Magic Johnson Enterprises has aggressively established new retail outlets in the inner cities, often crushing incumbent family businesses in the process.

Most of the entrepreneurs in our sample do not appear overly sympathetic about the fate of their competition. Jeff Hollender, CEO of Seventh Generation, explains his position: "We have tended to regard every unit of our products sold as a victory against the monolithic corporations that made the petroleum-derived, hyper-synthetic, chemically ridden products that our products were created to displace."[4] Hollender feels that the greater the demand becomes for healthier products, the better off everybody will be, especially future generations. Furthermore, as his logic goes, the stronger the public support for businesses committed to social responsiveness, the more likely it will be that responsible business will become larger and more influential. Dancing Deer's founder, Patricia Karter, also recognizes the importance of size and financial stability in becoming a social force. She says, ". . . Dancing Deer is not big enough to make an impact now . . . to be a social or economic force. If I hit $50 million in sales, it can be."[5]

Ben Cohen and Jerry Greenfield, the founders of Ben & Jerry's, see it in similar fashion. "We believed that the best way to make Ben & Jerry's a force for progressive social change," they have written "was to grow bigger so we could make more profits and give more money away." Sarah Endline of Sweet Riot, a relative newcomer compared to Ben & Jerry's, agrees. She stated in an interview, "If you want your company to make an impact, you have to get your revenues to grow."[6] Interestingly, she adds "I welcome this conflict between making money and making a difference. It's a 'lovely creative tension'—we need to make money but also have social impact." There isn't much "tension" in the mind of Novica CEO Robert Milk who believes that growth is perfectly in line with his company's mission. He explains that his artists who live mostly in the Third World want Novica to sell more and more of their goods and that his Western customers want him to help more artists. Whether the logic is sound or not, the founders of Ben & Jerry's, Seventh Generation, Dancing Deer, Sweet Riot, Novica and numerous others in our sample believe that their cause-orientations validate their growth objectives and justify taking market share away from competition.

There are always exceptions to the rule, however. A handful of the values-centered companies on our list reject the endless pursuit of aggressive growth. Some are concerned for reasons related to quality control or risk management. Berkeley Mills, for instance, refuses to grow at the expense of its excellent craftsmanship which is consistent with its strategy of producing high-quality furniture products. Explore Inc., an after-school program, used to follow a strict policy of only partnering with what it saw as quality schools which potentially restricted its growth. Clif Bar executives talk about a certain "natural demand," and that it should not try to create an artificial demand.

But more importantly, there are those who are opposed to aggressive growth for fundamental philosophical reasons. The founders of both White Dog Café, a widely known restaurant in Philadelphia, and Iggy's Bread of the World categorically reject the conventional concept of growth. White Dog's Judy Wicks views growth as a "reflection of greed and a systematic problem with business."[7] Igor and Ludmilla of Iggy's Bread want everyone to "open their own version of Iggy's and make their own dreams come true."[8] Thus, while most entrepreneurs in our sample feel that aggressive growth is justified, there are a few who feel that they can better serve the society as a small company.

Give Up Profits

Pay Above-Market Prices for Some Inputs

The previous section illustrates some of the various ways our values-centered entrepreneurs pursue profitability. The second part of our analysis identifies specific examples of how our values-centered entrepreneurs and their companies sacrifice profits to accommodate their social and/or environmental causes. Examining the trade-off between profit and supporting a cause in an entrepreneurial context versus the milieu of a large public corporation is especially revealing because of two critical factors: (1) financial resources are significantly more constrained for entrepreneurial firms and (2) the chief executive officer has more latitude in the choice and is likely to be directly and personally affected by the decisions.

Our analysis demonstrates that our entrepreneurs deliberately undertake certain actions that reduce their profit—a noteworthy departure from conventional business practice! A good number of them incur higher than necessary input costs. They intentionally use more expensive materials, methods, or energy sources in their production processes to accommodate their social and environmental goals. Patagonia, for instance, has for many years used more costly post-consumer recycled (PCR) fleece and organic cotton in its products because of their environmental advantages. Similarly, Tom's of Maine's toothpaste is packaged in aluminum tubes that can be recycled when empty rather than the non-recyclable plastic laminates used by most other manufacturers. The aluminum tubes are significantly more expensive, but Tom's of Maine feels that it is important to use recyclable material to protect the planet. Historically, about 75 percent of the lumber Berkeley Mills purchased was Forest Stewardship Council certified, which significantly increased the company's material costs.

Similar logic has been applied in choosing energy sources. Chris King and Patagonia use higher-priced renewable energy to power their offices. New Belgium Brewery also pays a premium to be a 100 percent wind-powered company. New Belgium has invested heavily in R&D aimed at developing new ecologically sustainable systems and processes. Being ecologically sound does not always come cheap, but many of our values-centered entrepreneurs choose to incur these higher input costs.

Whole Foods Market offers another instructive example. The supermarket chain has decided to engage in the sale of sustainable seafood, which requires fisheries to remove fish at a rate equal to or lower than the rate at which they reproduce. Considering that the majority of the world's fisheries are in danger of collapse, John Mackey and his management team have concluded that supporting this sustainable fishing philosophy makes sense for the company even if it means paying higher prices for fish from small, independent, sustainable fishermen. This policy has direct financial consequences by putting Whole Foods at somewhat of a competitive disadvantage because in addition to paying a higher price for seafood, the time and efforts spent to create the new policy, processes, and the certification procedure have resulted in additional expenses. These elevated costs, naturally, have necessitated charging higher retail prices for fish and other seafood than its less-principled competitors do.

Of course, Whole Foods' stance attracts environmentally concerned consumers and may well provide the company with a future competitive advantage as the demand for sustainable seafood increases.

Some of our values-centered companies, rather than choosing more expensive inputs, select the more expensive suppliers for essentially equivalent goods, in support of their localities, employees, or Third World suppliers. For example, although Stonyfield Farm could easily buy cheaper milk from corporate dairies, its policy has been to purchase strictly from family farms in New England. Stonyfield follows this policy because it is essential to the firm's mission. It pays a premium to farmers to help offset the added expense of producing milk without using hormones, chemical fertilizers, or pesticides. Similarly, Ben & Jerry's supports Vermont-based dairies by continuing to pay above-market prices. Chris King, in an effort to purchase the highest-quality parts and concomitantly bolster domestic manufacturing, sources principally from U.S. suppliers.

Several of the entrepreneurs on our list go to great lengths to pay "fair prices" to their Third World suppliers. The late Anita Roddick of The Body Shop instated an official policy ensuring that its small producer communities around the world receive fair prices. The purpose of the policy was to assure that these suppliers are paid sufficiently to feed, clothe, and educate their families. Roddick once explained, "We go in and have a relationship with the communities . . . When they say yes, we buy above market price." The Body Shop policy required that the CEO, not some middle manager, be responsible for ensuring that it was properly executed. In the case of Novica, which sells Third World artisan artwork through its website, the firm has chosen not to negotiate with its artisans; instead, it allows them to set the final consumer price. In this way the artisans can receive what they perceive as fair prices for their works.

A discerning (perhaps cynical) reader may feel that there isn't anything particularly admirable or interesting about our firms choosing the more expensive, sustainable materials or energy sources. After all, they have branded themselves as green companies and expect to attract environmentally conscious customers. Nonetheless, it is important to realize that (1) they are incurring costs on activities and inputs that are not absolutely necessary and in doing so (2) they are taking significant risks that may not pay back in form of new revenues. Given uncertainty about the level of consumer support for their sustainable products and processes, these higher-cost policies could easily backfire on them.

Pass on (Certain) Profitable Opportunities

A good number of our values-centered companies have demonstrated that they are willing to pass up profitable opportunities if that means they would have to bend their beliefs. Consider Dancing Deer Bakery, an inner-city Boston company that sells baked goods both online and through major retail outlets such as Whole Foods, Williams-Sonoma, and Wild Oats Markets. The company was founded in 1994 by Patricia Karter, an idealist with strong convictions about using all-natural ingredients, participating in philanthropy, and taking good care of her employees.[9] Having opened its doors at a former pizza restaurant, the company quickly earned accolades for its creative cakes and cookies and found a huge demand for them.[10] In the midst of the company's rapid growth, however, Karter nixed a deal to sell molasses clove cookies to Williams-Sonoma—a move that would have doubled sales—because it would have required the use of preservatives. Her steadfastness impressed the Williams-Sonoma people who later asked her to make dry batter mixes. "They are a wonderful company," said Sally Geller, divisional manager of Williams-Sonoma's retail food division. "I have great respect and admiration for Trish and what she has done in providing high-quality products with natural ingredients."[11] By sticking to its values and mission, Dancing Deer has built an enviable reputation in the baking industry.

Another great (and perhaps, *extreme*) example is Craigslist, a community website with all kinds of job, rental, service, and sales listings. The site has incredible traffic but many observers are nonplussed by the fact that the company does not try to maximize its income potential. Jim Buckmaster, the CEO of Craigslist, caused lots of head-scratching when he tried to explain to a bunch of Wall Street types why his company was not interested in "monetizing" his ridiculously popular Web operation. Appearing at the UBS global media conference in New York in December 2006, Buckmaster was asked by UBS analyst Ben Schachter about how Craigslist planned to maximize revenue. "It doesn't," Buckmaster replied. "That definitely is not part of the equation," he said, "It's not part of the goal."[12] Indeed, the company charges money for job listings, but only in seven of the cities it serves ($75 in San Francisco; $25 in the others) and $10 a pop for apartment listings in New York City—but just to pay expenses. The analyst then suggested: How about running AdSense ads from Google? Buckmaster responded the company had considered that option. He mentioned that the company even crunched the numbers, which were "quite staggering," but decided against it because users hadn't expressed an interest in seeing ads, and hence it was not going to happen. Craigslist, a small organization, feels that it has all the money it needs and finds no reason to "intrude on its customers" by selling things to them. See Table 8.2 below for more detailed exchange between Buckmaster and the UBS analyst.[13] Careful—you may fall off your chair reading Buckmaster's statements.

Undertake Non-Economic Projects

Several of our values-centered entrepreneurs have shown that while they are aggressively pursuing profits and growth, to exercise their beliefs they are willing to take on special projects or tasks that are not financially beneficial.

Judy Wicks of White Dog Café, for example, sacrificed some of White Dog's volume when she initiated a campaign to spotlight the economic and ethnic diversity of Philadelphia by encouraging her own affluent, suburban dining clientele to sample inner-city neighborhood restaurants. Explore Inc., the high-quality after-school center, had a policy of offering its program for free to every 10th student as a way to help those who could not afford it. Patagonia makes highly durable ("ridiculously overbuilt") clothes believing that buyers will need fewer replacement items and thereby produce less environmental waste.

Table 8.2 Exchange between Craigslist CEO Jim Buckmaster and UBS Analyst Ben Schachter[14]

UBS analyst Ben Schachter: Craigslist ranks 47th in terms of number of monthly unique visitors among U.S. Internet properties. But because the average user spends so much time on the site—about five days a month, 20 minutes per day—the site ranks a startling seventh in terms of monthly page views. Its 3.35 billion page views in October were more than double that of Amazon.com . . . So how exactly does Craigslist make money?

Buckmaster: We make money by charging $25 for job postings in six of its largest U.S. markets and $75 for job listings in San Francisco and by assessing a $10 fee for brokered apartment listings in New York City. All other listings in those markets are free, as are all listings in the more than 100 other markets the company serves in the U.S. and overseas . . .

Schachter: Is maximizing profit not part of the equation?"

Buckmaster: That's definitely not part of the equation. That's never been a goal . . . We have been fortunate to do well by doing good, whatever phrase you want to use, by focusing only on improving the service for users.

Schachter: How, then, does Craigslist determine how much to charge for the few listings that carry a fee?

Buckmaster: Like a lot of things, we mostly look to user input for making decisions like pricing . . . Before we started charging for brokered apartment listings in New York, we put up a public discussion board I think almost two and a half years before we started charging to discuss the idea of charging, whether we should charge and if so, how we should charge, etc. So the pricing decision in large part came out of that.

Schachter: By simply running text ads on Craigslist as a Google AdSense partner, clearly the site could be monetized to an incredible extent due to the massive amount of traffic it draws.

Buckmaster: We certainly have been approached about putting text ads on the site quite a few times . . . The numbers are quite staggering, the amount of revenue that could be added.

Schachter: So why not add them to the site?

Buckmaster: No users have been requesting that we run text ads. [As if that were a perfectly sensible answer.]

Schachter: OK, so Craigslist boasts a huge potential to make money, but isn't really interested in generating big profits. Given that combination, why not raise funds through equity investments or advertising and then give the money away to charity?

Buckmaster: I think it's a valid argument and one that we don't necessarily have a persuasive answer for. That is a proven model for doing good in the world. It just doesn't happen to be our model. Ours is to try to be as philanthropic in our core business as we can be and leave all the money out there in the hands of users.

Tom's of Maine in a couple of situations has made decisions that clearly reduced potential profits. In one instance, during the formulation of plans for a new wellness line, the company realized that it could save $250,000 if it located the entire production and packaging operation for the product line in Vermont as opposed to the original plan of extracting the herbs in Vermont and shipping them back to Maine for packaging. Disregarding financial rationality, co-founder Tom Chappell adhered to the company's commitment to the Kennebunk community in Maine and split the work between the two locales.

Tom's of Maine also made a significant financial sacrifice to obtain the American Dental Association (ADA) Seal of Approval for three of its fluoride toothpaste flavors without conducting the conventional animal tests. The ADA required a standard efficacy protocol that was lethal to rats. Rather than compromise its stated values,

Tom's worked with the ADA to develop a new test that could be conducted safely on human subjects which eventually received the Association's coveted seal. Because of the cumbersome process of developing the new protocol, approval for the new flavors took several years longer than normal and cost approximately ten times as much as it would have otherwise. Tom's later strenuously lobbied the Federal Drug Administration (FDA) to modify its rules and eventually identified a non-animal protocol that was acceptable to this regulatory agency. Again, this initiative unnecessarily increased the firm's costs.

The above examples demonstrate the willingness of values-centered entrepreneurs to make calculated financial sacrifices in balancing their non-economic mission with the profit objectives of their firms. None of the sacrifices were huge and none was large enough to put the companies at significant financial risk, but they do illustrate that these are not strictly profit-maximizing organizations.

Win-Win

Through the Business Model

In our analysis we looked for win-win strategies. We found that our values-centered entrepreneurs are particularly good at identifying such opportunities and make extra efforts to make them work.

Some entrepreneurs in our sample have created win-win propositions through their business models. Several of our companies, such as AgraQuest, Green Mountain Energy, Sterling Planet, Novica and EV Rental, market products that are environmentally or socially superior to those of their competitors. For these entrepreneurs, it is clear that for each unit of product they sell, they are in fact helping the environment or disadvantaged people. To illustrate, AgraQuest develops and markets natural pesticides that are environmentally superior to the conventional chemical pesticides offered by most of its competitors. The greater the firm's sales, the greater the use of its natural pesticides in place of chemicals, the greater the benefits to the environment. Similarly, Sterling Planet markets renewable energy that is better for the planet than the fossil fuel alternatives offered by conventional utilities. In fact, with its mission, "to lead the migration to sustainable energy that is good for the environment, the economy, and all current and future generations," Sterling's founders and employees believe that they are improving the environment with each dollar of sales they are generating.[15] Recently, Sterling created another win-win proposition by partnering with a prominent legal firm and an investment firm to develop the company's Renewable Energy Fund. The fund's resources are earmarked for the development of renewable energy projects and provide investors with a mechanism for seeking "excellent returns from socially responsible, economically sound investments."[16]

Most of our values-centered entrepreneurs, not just those with socially or environmentally oriented products, believe that the mere existence of their business is a win-win situation. Even when their products do not directly cure a social ill (e.g., apparel or coffee), our entrepreneurs typically use healthier ingredients, treat employees better, deal more fairly with their suppliers, and proportionately give more money to charity.

There are also those who find ways to creatively modify or even completely transform their business models to concurrently improve their business and better serve their cause. Interface's Evergreen Lease™ is one such example. The program allows customers to purchase a carpeting service, rather than buy carpet—thereby eliminating a large one-time investment and providing for convenient maintenance. Under this program, Interface produces, installs, cleans, maintains, and replaces carpet for customers and recycles the old carpet into new carpet—making sure that nothing goes to the landfill. Interface's novel business model has not only been popular but also enabled Interface to be a better steward of the environment.

Judy Wicks of White Dog Café, in another example, has incorporated into her restaurant business a steady flow of events, speakers, and special programs that address a wide range of social and environmental issues. These events and programs not only render a public service, but also attract new customers to the restaurant. Through the strategic timing of these special events, Wicks has been able to revive business on the typically slow restaurant nights of Monday and Tuesday. White Dog's unique program and involvement in local issues have proven to be a robust business proposition for the restaurant. For the first five years of its existence, White Dog's revenues doubled each year, and their local restaurant developed a national reputation.[17]

T.S. Designs offers a unique example of a company that has created a truly transformational win-win business model. For most of its history, T.S. Designs was a conventional screen-printing contractor using an environmentally unsound printing process that required plastisol ink which contains highly toxic chemicals. After a severe downturn in business in the 1990s due to the migration of much of its business overseas (following the exodus of apparel manufacturers) the company reinvented itself. It redefined its business model and market niche. Under the new model, it uses a sustainable, nano-technology-based printing process called REHANCE. It also promotes the use of organically grown cotton T-shirts, purchases locally when possible, and emphasizes rapid customer response and superior quality. The new strategy has enabled the company to survive and even grow in a highly competitive market as well as become a paragon of sustainable industry.

Do Business with Struggling Communities

Most of the entrepreneurs on our list understand the positive social and economic impact that business and trade can have in impoverished communities, particularly in the developing economies. In 1987, Anita Roddick began The Body Shop's Trade Not Aid program, with the objective of using trade to help people in the Third World utilize their resources sustainably to meet their own needs. Roddick firmly believed that government aid programs were not the answer. Combining the company's need for exotic natural ingredients with its social/environmental mission, the Trade Not Aid program established business partnerships with struggling communities. Under the program, The Body Shop purchased such ingredients as blue corn from the Pueblo

Indians in New Mexico and Brazil nut oil from the Kayapo Indians of the Amazon River Basin, while being extra cautious not to exploit the native peoples in any way. The Body Shop in fact, often paid above market prices for these inputs. The program operated in 23 countries with 36 different suppliers. By supplying The Body Shop with sustainable, natural raw materials, the supplier communities have been able to earn money selling renewable resources rather than by depleting their habitat. Honest Tea has had a similar Fair Trade program with the Guatemalan farming cooperative, El Limon. By purchasing chamomile tea bags at a fair price from the cooperative Honest Tea concomitantly increased the employment rate in a desperately poor community.

In the U.S., Magic Johnson Enterprises has helped revive several neglected communities by investing in real estate projects in inner-city areas that other businesses scrupulously avoided. Johnson, not unlike Anita Roddick, believes that jobs are a better solution for poor communities than social programs. Johnson, moreover, has been able to show that there is money to be made in the inner cities and that mainstream businesses can locate there. Interestingly, it has been rumored that Johnson's Starbucks franchise store in Harlem generates as much revenue (nearly $5 million) as its counterparts in upper Manhattan. Companies like The Body Shop, Honest Tea and Magic Johnson Enterprises have found profitable opportunities in impoverished communities by simply doing business with them.

Make Pro-Environmental Investments Pay for Themselves

Most investments designed to protect the environment do not result in clear savings or profit, but some do and several of our entrepreneurs have creatively found such situations. Frog's Leap Winery, a small sustainable Napa Valley winery with an annual 60,000 case output, for instance, has been successful in demonstrating how a company can save money and protect the planet at the same time by being innovative and risk taking. In 2005, Frog's Leap became a pioneer in its industry by installing 1,020 PV solar panels on a half acre of its 130-acre vineyard. General Manager Jonah Beer explained adamantly that the winery installed the panels for "financial benefit" and that the installation has been one of the "biggest financial successes" of the winery.[18]

The total bill for the solar panel system was $1.2 million, a rather hefty investment for a small winery. However, PG&E (the major utility company in the area) was willing to subsidize half of the bill, $600,000. Then, Frog's Leap went to the bank and negotiated a loan for the remaining $600,000 at terms such that the monthly loan payment was less than the company's electricity bill. Sounding almost too good to be true, the investment was cash-flow positive from the start and is on track to pay for itself completely in 6.5 years. Considering that the panels are warranted for 25 years and inverters for 30 years, the winery will get 18–20 years of free electricity. During the life of the system, the panels are projected to save 1,600 tons of CO_2, the equivalent of not driving 4 million miles on an average car or planting 480 acres of trees. "We are doing what we have always believed: You can do right by the bottom-line, right by the environment and right by the people, all at the same time," said Beer.[19]

Consider also the example of Gaia Napa Valley Hotel and Spa. It may be the greenest hotel in the U.S. and currently is the only Gold LEED Certified hotel.[20] Earning this certification required a good deal of investment. On the roof alone, Gaia founder Wen Chang has installed Solatube Tubular skylights, photovoltaic solar panels, and cool reflective roof materials. The skylights magnify the sun's rays to deliver light to the property's interior space during the day, thereby saving electricity. The photo-voltaic thin-film solar panels collectively produce about 12 percent (30 KW) of the hotel's electricity needs; the roof's reflective materials deflect the suns rays thereby reducing heat absorption.

Wen Chang acknowledges that it cost more to start such an environmentally sound hotel. He says that his investments will pay off in about eight years, versus six years for a typical hotel. Nevertheless, he thinks that he made a smart decision since he will save money for the subsequent 30 years, considering that the life of a hotel is about 40 years. Between solar panels, solar tubing, and water reduction, Wen Chang believes that he is saving $50,000–75,000 a year, which will pay off over time. Moreover, the hotel has received a Transit Occupancy Tax credit from the city, which can provide the hotel with up to a million dollars in tax savings in the future.

Treat Employees Well to Obtain Results

We discussed this topic in much broader terms in an earlier chapter but here we want to stress specifically that some of our values-centered entrepreneurs look for win-win situations through their employees. Eileen Fisher of Eileen Fisher Clothing, for example, offers employee benefits that are extravagant by retail clothing and apparel manufacturing industry standards. She gives her 400-plus employees a sense of ownership by sharing at least 10 percent of pre-tax profits with them each year. In addition, everyone receives a $1,000 education benefit, and a $1,000 wellness benefit to be spent on rejuvenators such as massages, nutritional consultations, reflexology, spa visits, and gym equipment. After ten years on the job, her employees receive $5,000 toward a vacation trip. They also receive anywhere from $500 to $2,500 a year to spend on Eileen Fisher clothing at wholesale prices. She justifies these lavish programs, claiming that the firm actually benefits from them financially. She points to the turnover rate at her retail stores which is around 19 percent—far lower than the retail industry's 51 percent—resulting in a saving of $325,000 a year in recruitment and training costs. She also argues that satisfied workers are more productive.

Eileen Fisher is not alone among our companies in treating employees well. Some have been true pioneers in providing employee benefits. Patagonia, for instance, was the first U.S. corporation to establish an on-site childcare service, an atypical perquis-ite for its 55–60 percent female staff. Starbucks was the first major coffee retailer in the U.S. to provide comprehensive medical benefits and stock options for part-time employees. Iggy's Bread of the World generously provides language training for its immigrant employees. Rhythm and Hues offers its artists an unheard-of 9-week paid vacation per year.

Although treating employees especially well may be part of the mission for these firms, they also believe that their employee relations programs and policies produce financially beneficial results. Eileen Fisher, as mentioned, stresses that treating employees well means that they are less likely to leave, which saves the company money. Patagonia believes that its childcare service saves money by significantly lowering absenteeism and turnover, among its majority female staff. Starbucks CEO Howard Schultz credits his company's employee benefits with attracting and retaining committed "associates" who provide superior service quality.[21] Iggy's Bread of the World's language training not only aids in its immigrant employees' assimilation into American culture, but also makes them more productive on the job.

Being good to your employees and getting better performance in return may seem like a no brainer at first thought but it's not that simple. There is no unequivocal evidence that superior or more attractive employee benefit packages lead to either improved employee productivity or enhanced profitability. Nonetheless, the majority of our entrepreneurs are firmly committed to their employee-friendly programs and policies. Obviously, one reason is that these policies reflect their triple bottom-line mission. But, as discussed above, most of these entrepreneurs also believe that they pay off operationally and financially. And, indeed they may be right, but we strongly suspect that there are other factors at work here. We think that our firms' attractive, socially responsible missions along with the enthusiasm of their founders/leaders also are important ingredients of mix. These factors, in combination with their appealing employee relations' policies, we postulate, attract and motivate top-notch employees resulting in a highly committed and productive workforce.

In general, creating win-win situations is far more challenging and risky in practice than it may appear at first, especially for companies strapped for cash. Consider that these firms are investing in an expensive employee benefits package or environmentally sound technology that incurs known upfront costs while the correlating financial benefits are uncertain, difficult to predict, and in some instances difficult to measure (e.g., employee morale). Moreover, while certain win-win strategies seem logical or obvious after the fact, they can be challenging to implement. Working with Third World communities, for instance, can be a genuine learning process that requires special management attention and commitment. In sum, it takes uncommon dedication, discipline, and even faith to identify win-win opportunities and make them work in practice. It is an effort and a risk that most conventional firms are unwilling to undertake—just consider the fact that most firms (and individuals) have not even replaced their old incandescent light bulbs with the new energy saving bulbs.

Chapter Takeaways

- Plan to make difficult choices that will positively and negatively impact the profitability of your business.
- Maximize profits whenever possible, e.g., through premium positioning, cost control and aggressive growth.
- Make exceptions to the above to exercise values/mission, e.g., by buying goods at above-market prices, passing on certain profitable opportunities, and undertaking non-profitable projects.
- Seek and achieve win-win situations, e.g., by having a win-win business model, doing business with struggling communities, and treating employees especially well.

9

Minimize Your Environmental and Social Footprint

The first industrial revolution, of which we are still beneficiaries, is flawed; it is not working; it is unsustainable; it is a mistake. And we must move on to another and better industrial revolution and get it right this time.
—Ray Anderson, chairman of the board, Interface Carpets[1]

No business can be done on a dead planet. A company that is taking the long view must accept that it has an obligation to minimize its impact on the natural environment.
—Yvon Chouinard, founder of Patagonia[2]

Our values-centered entrepreneurs have taken meaningful, proactive, and in some cases extraordinary steps to minimize the harm their companies inflict on the environment and society at large. Some of these steps have been financially beneficial, some have not, but all have evolved from a sense of duty to the environment and society.

Set Clear Environmental/Social Objectives for the Company

All our values-centered companies have been exemplary in their efforts to protect the environment and contribute to society at large. But the companies that have had the greatest impact for the good seem to be those that have clearly defined and articulated their environmental and social goals. They have formulated a sound basis for their priorities and communicated them effectively throughout the organization.

To illustrate, Gary Erickson has set clear environmental and social goals for his company, Clif Bar. Erickson has stressed throughout the organization that all of its five bottom-lines, "sustaining our planet," "sustaining our brands," "sustaining our people," "sustaining our community," and "sustaining our business,"[3] are equally important for maintaining a prosperous and responsible company. The five bottom-lines or "Five Aspirations" are promoted internally and furnish a definitive decision-making framework for all employees. Before anyone at Clif Bar makes a business decision, he/she is expected to think about how the decision will affect the five goals. Moreover, during annual reviews, employees receive feedback and bonuses based on their contributions to each of the five aspirations and their ability to *balance* their responsibilities. Clif Bar has both articulated its goals and has effectively operational-ized them through its performance appraisal system.

Akin to Clif Bar's "Five Aspirations," Broad, China's leading non-electric (and less polluting) air-conditioner manufacturer has formulated its "8 No Principles" in an effort to set clear environmental and social objectives. These are: No pollution, no technology infringement, no cheating of the customers, no involvement in debt cir-cles, no vicious competition, no tax violations, no bribery, and no activities that contradict "organizational consciousness."[4] These principles, widely promoted inside and outside the company, have made Broad the gold standard for ethics and environmental protection in China.

True to its own principles, Broad has over the years remained in its core busi-ness of engineering and selling only non-electric absorption chillers. The company continues to eschew electric cooling systems because of the series of energy con-versions required and the environmental damage they create. Technically speaking, conventional electric cooling systems require fossil fuel conversion into heat, heat into mechanical energy, mechanical into power, power back into mechanical energy and finally mechanical energy into chilled water—with each conversion resulting in energy loss. Conversely, Broad's air-conditioning units burn cleaner fossil fuels, can utilize solar energy, and can recycle waste heat above 90°C. Its technology works by using heat to cool water in a continuously renewable chemical process called the absorption cycle, thereby making it more energy efficient.[5] Although Broad has lost market share to manufacturers of electrical systems (that have become the norm), it remains committed to its principles and its non-electric method.

Interface Carpets, the world's largest commercial floor coverings manufacturer with more than $1 billion in revenue, has announced that it plans to be the world's first "truly sustainable and restorative company." Ray Anderson, the company's foun-der, envisions, by 2020, a corporation "that exists in harmony with the environment, consuming no more resources than it restores."[6]

While this vision is admirable and even seems plausible today, Anderson struggled at first to develop it and sought his answers in nature. He explains:

> There was no blueprint for this kind of organization in business . . . Nature has some fundamental operating principles . . . Our job was to translate these principles into a new model for business. To begin with, it meant that we would become a business that runs on renewable energy. We would carefully eliminate waste from all areas of our operations and recycle and then reuse the materials from our products and those that support our business. We would find a use for everything we use and waste nothing. And finally, we, too, would reward cooperation—with suppliers, customers, investors and our communities.[7]

Anderson determined that a company that is aligned with these principles will be the prototypical sustainable enterprise of the next industrial revolution. Figure 9.1,[8] from his book *Mid-Course Correction*, illustrates the depth and complexity of his thinking of this subject so near and dear to his heart. Sparing the reader excruciating detail, suffice it to say that he has come to view his company as part of the larger ecosystem. With this paradigm clearly in mind, he then took the next step of designing

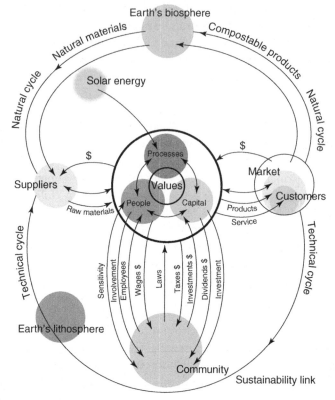

Figure 9.1 The Next Industrial Revolution: Model for the Prototypical Company of the Twenty-First Century

Source: Anderson, *Mid-Course Correction.*

internal systems for his company that would be as compatible as possible with the physical environment.

Formalize Objectives into Concrete Policies and Actions

With overall corporate objectives and priorities in mind, our values-centered entrepreneurs can move forward to design concrete policies and action plans. For example, Ecover, the world's largest producer of ecological detergents and cleansing agents, and a trendsetter in the industry, has developed a comprehensive policy for minimizing its environmental damage. As shown in Figure 9.2, the company's progressive environmental efforts are not just found in its greener products, but in every facet of business operation. These include such disparate activities as purchasing, water treatment, and energy management. Perhaps the firm's most conspicuous achievement to date is its ISO 14001 certified manufacturing facility—what it calls "the world's first ecological factory."[9] The facility has a "green roof" covered with grass extending over more than 6000m² that keeps the factory cool in the summer and warm in winter. The facility's

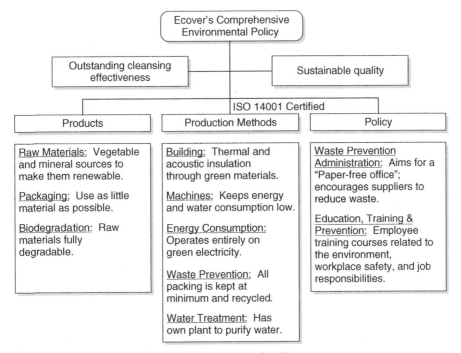

Figure 9.2 Ecover's Comprehensive Environmental Policy

Source: Company website (http://www.ecover.com/us/en/about)

water treatment system runs on wind and solar energy and its brick walls are made of recycled clay from coal mines.[10]

Predictably, Ecover has not gone unrecognized for its efforts. It has received major international awards such as Best Eco Cleaning Product from the U.K.; Gold Environment Medal from Belgium; Corporate Conscience Award from the U.S.A.; Global 500 Roll of Honour from the United Nations; and Prize for the Most Innovative Products in the U.K.

Returning to our Interface example, to achieve its goal of becoming a truly "restorative" company, it has developed a set of guidelines called the "Seven Concrete Steps to Sustainability" which it tries to practice on a daily basis. These are:[11]

1. *Eliminate waste* (all forms including financial and environmental).
2. *Benign emissions* (e.g., eliminate molecular waste emitted with negative or toxic impact into the natural systems).
3. *Renewable energy* (i.e., reduce the energy used by its processes while replacing non-renewable sources with sustainable ones).
4. *Close the loop* (i.e., redesign its processes and products to create cyclical material flows).
5. *Resource efficient transportation* (i.e., reduce the transportation of molecules (products and people) in favor of moving information).
6. *Sensitivity hookup* (create a community within and around the company that understands the functioning of natural systems and its impact on them).

7. *Redesign commerce* (focus on the delivery of service and value instead of the delivery of material).

Today, about a decade after these plans were first enunciated, Interface has made significant progress. Particularly noteworthy is the impact of 7: Redesign Commerce. This guideline along with 1: Eliminate Waste and 4: Close the Loop has furnished the impetus for Interface's Evergreen Lease™ program mentioned in an earlier chapter. To reiterate, customers lease the service of keeping a space carpeted, rather than buying carpet—thereby eliminating a large one-time investment and benefiting from easier maintenance. Under this program, Interface produces, installs, cleans, maintains, and replaces carpet typically in the modules for customers. Interface owns the carpet and ensures proper disposal, i.e., recycles it, thus bringing the company a step closer to "eliminating waste" and "closing the loop," as well as "redesigning commerce."

Employ (Old and New) Technology

It is inspiring to see that our values-centered companies don't just settle for existing methods in their attempt to minimize waste or reduce resource consumption. Many of them have experimented with innovative methods to achieve their objectives.

One of the best ways to minimize waste is to make products that do not need to be replaced and thereby do not use up more of nature's resources. Chris King for example, after much experimentation, now makes bicycle components that seldom need replacement. Chris DiStefano, marketing manager, explains how quality goes hand in hand with environmental benefits at Chris King: "One of Chris' (King) fundamental issues is that we do make things, so we use energy and use resources, which we try to minimize. And the products we make, like our headsets, never need to be replaced, so they can occupy a useful place and stay there."[12] Similarly, as mentioned in an earlier chapter, Patagonia makes its high-quality, "ridiculously overbuilt" outdoor clothing for the same reason—so that customers would not need to buy replacement items.

Frog's Leap Winery engages in a century-old, yet innovative, process that it calls "dry farming" on its 200-acre certified organic vineyard. Dry farming essentially means farming without the use of an irrigation system, which saves a tremendous amount of water and is especially laudable for a winery based in Napa Valley—a region that gets almost no rain during the grapes' growth season. By employing the right natural micro-organisms, deep-rooted vines, and other agricultural techniques, the dry farming process increases the soil's capacity to hold water and preserve moisture. In essence, the soil acts like a sponge when there is rain in the winter and releases the moisture to the grapevines slowly over the summer season. The process is also said to create grapes with balanced flavors that arise from vines "drinking from the earth, not from an irrigation system."[13]

T.S. Designs, a screenprinting company (specializing in T-shirts) in North Carolina, employs a patented technology to not only reduce environmental damage but also to redefine its market niche and implement a unique new business model. The new model emphasizes high-quality, rapid-response, inventorying organic T-shirt blanks, and domestic sourcing, as well as utilizing the nano-technology-based printing process called REHANCE.

Conventional screenprinting places a surface coating on an already dyed and finished garment. The ink typically used for the coating is plastisol which contains polyvinyl chloride (PVC) and phthalates. PVC presents a serious health risk because it releases dangerous dioxins during both manufacturing and disposal. Dioxins are highly toxic and phthalates, although not as well researched as PVC, are also considered to be toxic. Using its REHANCE technology, T.S. Designs can print an undyed T-shirt and then garment-dye it to a specified color. This eliminates the need for the company to invest in a color inventory and allows for a rapid response to a variety of color requests. The REHANCE method also eliminates the plastic surface coating of the T-shirt, eliminating abrading of the printed surface and allowing the material to breath. The process also produces a garment that will not shrink.[14] T.S. Designs, further, uses the lowest impact reactive dyes consistent with its quality standards. Its dyes require less salt and result in no heavy metals; consequently they leave a smaller environmental footprint than the conventional industry dyes. In summary, T.S. Designs has designed a seemingly successful business strategy around a sustainable technology.

Few firms have been more proactive in their pro-environmental efforts than Colorado-based New Belgium Brewery. Founded by an electrical engineer and a social worker, this company has embraced state-of-the-art technologies to find ways to reduce waste and utilize alternative forms of energy. As early as 1999, the company subscribed to 100 percent wind power. It has installed throughout its facilities compact fluorescent lighting, which consumes 75 percent less electricity than the widely used incandescent bulbs.[15] The company's brewhouse has an innovative heat-exchange system that remains hot for the next batch of beer, thereby reducing energy consumption. The brewhouse also has sensors that automatically open windows when the temperature reaches a predetermined point. This helps reduce the need for air conditioning. Perhaps the most technologically advanced innovation is New Belgium's wastewater treatment plant. Here, anaerobic bacteria digest leftover nutrients in the wastewater. This process creates methane gas which is captured in a sealed bubble and piped to a methane-powered generator to produce enough electricity to meet 15 percent of the brewery's needs.[16] Overall, the company boasts a 98 percent diversion rate which means that only 2 percent of the waste produced goes to a landfill. The diverted 98 percent is either recycled or reused in some way. See Table 9.1 for a summary of New Belgium's innovative pro-environmental methods.

Minimize Any Direct (Social or Environmental) Harm

One commonality among most, if not all, our values-centered firms may be their dedicated efforts toward reducing any direct environmental or social harm their business operation may cause. Gaia Napa Valley Hotel and Spa, for instance, has made

Table 9.1 New Belgium's Process Innovations

Greenhouse Gas Emissions Reduction. In 1998, New Belgium took an employee vote and became the country's first brewery to subscribe to wind-powered electricity. Employee owners voted to dip into their bonus pool to help finance the conversion.

Economical Water Use. Water is a key ingredient of beer. Through process efficiencies, New Belgium uses less than four barrels of water to produce one barrel of beer, significantly less than the industry average.

Healthy Watersheds. New Belgium partners with local advocates to maintain a healthy watershed along the Poudre River.

Green Building. From sun tubes and de-lighting throughout the facility to reusing heat in the brewhouse, the company has found new ways to close loops and conserve resources.

Reduce, Reuse, Recycle. Reduction program involves motion sensors on the lights throughout the building to evaporative cooling in the new packaging hall. New Belgium's reuse program includes heat for the brewing process, cleaning chemicals, water, and much more. Recycling at New Belgium takes on many forms, from turning "waste" products into something new and useful (like spent grain to cattle feed), to supporting the recycling market in creative ways (like turning its keg caps into table surfaces).

Living Sustainably. Having its own Sustainability Specialist has given the firm access to all sorts of great information. New Belgium shares some of its wisdom on its company website with its customers so that they can use it in their own homes.

Source: www.newbelgium.com.

conscientious efforts to minimize pollution through its choice of materials and hotel operations. It uses low VOC (volatile organic compound) paints, including coatings, adhesives, and sealants, throughout the hotel. All of the fertilizers used for landscaping are 100 percent natural and chemical free. Every piece of lumber used for the hotel, including for walls and chairs, is Forest Stewardship Council (FSC) certified.[17] Carpets are also made with natural fibers that contain post-consumer recycled material. The hotel also uses small HVAC air conditioning units which both are more efficient and use a more environmentally friendly refrigerant than standard units.

Gaia has also been successful in reducing its water use by about an impressive 40 percent! This has been achieved in part through the hotel's low flush toilets and low flow showerheads. Gaia's toilets use 1 gpf (gallon per flush), whereas standard toilets expend 1.6 gallons per flush. All guestrooms are equipped with low flow shower-heads which emit only 1 gallon per minute. Additionally, all soap and shampoo is released from a dispenser in the bathrooms rather than from the conventional small plastic bottles that end up in landfills. The koi pond in front of the hotel uses recycled water from the site which is filtered and cleaned prior to entering the pond.

At Clif Bar, maker of bestselling energy bars, reducing waste from packaging materials has been a principal focus of its internal environmental efforts. The company has eliminated 90 percent of its shrink-wrap usage, a total of about 90,000 lbs per year. Almost 100 percent of the 10 million caddies (the cartons that hold the energy bars) are now made from recycled paperboards. Using recycled paperboard, the company estimates, saves each year 7,700 trees, 3.3 million gallons of water, 4 billion BTUs of energy, and 660,000 lbs of greenhouse gases. The company, moreover, uses

87,250 lbs of recycled paper, saving another 570 trees, 151,300 gallons of water, and avoiding another 47,800 lbs of greenhouse gases.[18] Beyond packaging, the snacks inside the boxes consist of 70 percent organic ingredients, including honey, rolled oats, and roasted soybeans. Furthermore, the firm's promotional T-shirts are 100 percent certified organic cotton.

Clif Bar, in addition to significantly greening its packaging and products, has committed to "offsetting" its greenhouse gas emissions. In 2003, the company added up all the energy used in its offices, bakeries, and air travel to estimate its "carbon footprint." Subsequently, through Native Energy's Wind Builders program the company purchased enough renewable energy credits to offset 2,000 tons of CO_2 emissions. Clif Bar's investment has helped to build the Rosebud Sioux Tribe Wind Turbine Project in South Dakota, a wind farm that generates electricity without producing CO_2 and other pollutants. Clif Bar, furthermore, has partnered with American Forests' Global ReLeaf's tree planting program to offset the impact of the carbon emissions arising from its employees' daily commutes. According to company founder Gary Erickson, this "Cool Commute" program "recognizes the importance of trees to our ecosystem and is another way that Clif Bar can reduce its own ecological footprint."[19] So far, the joint effort has planted some 8,000 trees. Also, as part of the Cool Commute program, the company provides $5,000 subsidies to employees who purchase biodiesel or hybrid vehicles.[20]

The Body Shop, Eileen Fisher, and Tom's Shoes are among the companies focused on minimizing any harm they might inflict on their Third World suppliers. These firms stress both treating suppliers equitably and protecting their natural environments. Eileen Fisher is one of only three U.S. companies to comply with a strict set of workplace standards, SA8000, administered by the non-profit watchdog group, Social Accountability International (SAI).[21][22] SA8000 is a voluntary code with eight human rights components: child labor, forced labor, health and safety, freedom of association, discrimination, discipline, working hours, and remuneration. Certified companies like Eileen Fisher must adhere to these standards in their supply chains.

Similarly, Tom's Shoes, the company that gives away a pair of shoes to kids in underdeveloped countries for every pair sold in the United States, makes products in Argentina and Ethiopia under very strict material and labor guidelines. The company boasts a "no sweatshop" manufacturing policy. Founder Blake Mycoskie makes perfect sense when he says, "If we are going to have a company geared towards helping people, we don't want to hurt one person to help another."[23]

Measure Your Environmental and Social Achievements

Recall the old accounting axiom, "Never measured, never managed." While all of our values-centered companies are effective in their environmental and social endeavors, some have made special effort to develop clear standards for their work. These metrics, usually custom-developed for each situation, are seldom used to brag or even to compare with other companies. In most cases, they are used as internal performance measures for monitoring performance and motivating their employees.

Consider Pacific Community Ventures (PCV), a venture capital firm based in Silicon Valley that aims to create wealth for its investors while improving the living standards of workers in the state of California. PCV focuses its investments on companies with a large base of low-wage employees so that these firms can grow larger and more profitable—and subsequently provide better salaries and benefits for their employees. Although PCV has been successful in delivering an acceptable Internal Rate of Return (IRR) for its investors, it also measures its success in terms of its unique Social Return on Income (SROI) metric. Specifically, SROI tracks:

- Number of jobs created in low-income zip-codes associated with a company that received PCV funds (including those for people previously unemployed or underemployed).
- Number of jobs with salaries above a living wage level and extent of benefits offered.
- Career mobility: Turnover information and surveys of why employees leave the targeted companies.

Some of the reported impacts of PCV's investments are as follows: PCV-financed companies have created hundreds of jobs and pay an average wage of $13.56 per hour (nearly double the California minimum wage of $7.50 per hour and a "living wage"). All of them (100 percent) offer health benefits to their employees. Many of the employees who have left the companies over time, have done so to land even better and higher-paying positions. These SROI measures plainly show that PCV has made a positive impact on the lives of hundreds of workers and their families.

Magic Johnson also keeps track of his company's social impact. In a recent interview, he recounted how his redevelopment projects have put more than 30,000 people to work and helped drive up property values in inner cities, such as Harlem and South Central Los Angeles. He also disclosed that his business has facilitated $4 billion in urban revitalization. "That has changed the face of urban America,"[24] said Johnson proudly.

The venerable Interface Carpets, a leading force in sustainable manufacturing, is also a leader in measuring its environmental and social impacts. Each Interface plant tracks and reports on hundreds of metrics quarterly. Noteworthy here is EcoMetrics™, a measurement system that founder Ray Anderson and his employees developed to track the company's progress toward its Mission Zero™ goal. EcoMetrics™, initiated in 1994, quantifies the company's "metabolism," measuring mass and energy flow through the company's operations. The system tracks how much material and energy the company takes in and what goes out in the form of products and waste. Key metrics are: waste elimination, cumulative avoided costs, solid waste generated, non-renewable energy use, raw materials, greenhouse gas emissions, and water intake. The company's website reports these metrics for each individual plant to allow all stakeholders to track them. The information is presented in easy-to-understand charts such as Figure 9.3

Analogously, Interface Carpets also measures the company's employee-oriented contributions through its SocioMetrics™. For example, it keeps records through

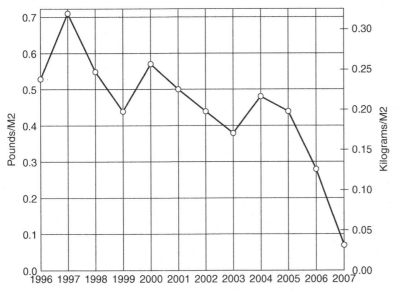

Figure 9.3 Solid Waste Generation per Unit of Product, LaGrange and West Point, Georgia (Weight per Square Meter)

Source: Company website (http://www.interfaceglobal.com/Sustainability/Progress-to-Zero.aspx).

the number of company-sponsored family social events held and average hours of training per employee. Additionally, the company measures its external social impact via the dollar amounts and volunteer hours contributed to outside organizations.

Patagonia recently launched perhaps the most adventurous and ambitious measurement program of all. This initiative, called Footprint Chronicles, is an effort to document and share with customers and others the environmental impacts of every link in its production chain. The program began in May of 2007 when Yvon Chouinard challenged a group of ten employees to track five products through their life-cycles—from initial design through yarn spinning and fiber manufacturing all the way to the company's Nevada distribution center. Later, ten more products were added to the list. All that was learned, both good and bad, was made available through short videos on Patagonia's website. One big surprise was the low energy expenditure of shipping by sea which turned out to be under 1 percent of total energy utilization. Manufacturing, on the other hand, consumed more energy than expected and in some cases produced toxic by-products. For instance, the team discovered perfluoro-octanic acid (PFOA), a highly suspect chemical, in the water-repellent membranes and coatings of the firm's Eco-Rain Shell jackets. Upon learning this, several customers complained bitterly, with one demanding that "eco" be removed from the name of the jacket. Patagonia executives were reluctant to sacrifice product quality. They eventually were able to replace the PFOA membranes but have yet to find a viable substitute for the prevailing coatings. Jill Dumain, the Company's Director of Environmental Analysis, in commenting on their thinking, said, "We don't want to sacrifice quality for environmental reasons. If a garment is thrown away sooner due to lack of durability, we haven't solved any environmental problem."[25]

Patagonia admits that, in this ground-breaking experiment, it is merely scratching the surface. Currently, it is only tracing some primary materials and no packaging has been put under the microscope. Moreover, by putting production information in the public domain, it is providing competitors with access to it. But Dumain argued that transparency outweighs the risk because the company hopes to prod other companies to action.

Minimize Your Company's Financial Burden

Many of the comprehensive environmental plans implemented by our values-centered firms have involved making costly investments in new processes, equipment, or energy sources that are less harmful to the environment. Several of our companies including Frog's Leap Winery, Gaia Napa Valley Hotel and Spa, and New Belgium Brewery have been resourceful in concocting ways to minimize such cash expenditures and, in some cases, even make positive financial returns. For example, as described in an earlier chapter, Frog's Leap Winery installed 1,020 PV solar panels at a total bill of $1.2 million, but has been able to realize a positive cash flow from the start. Take also the example of Gaia Napa Valley Hotel and Spa, perhaps the greenest hotel in the U.S. and the world's first and to date, only, Gold LEED-certified hotel.[26] Between solar panels, solar tubing and water reduction, founder Wen Chang believes that he saves annually $50,000–$75,000. Moreover, the hotel has received a million dollar Transit Occupancy Tax (TOT) credit from the city which potentially increases its future cash flow by up to a million dollars.

Of course, not all pro-environmental investments result in measurable cost savings. Such measures can, however, provide intangible benefits. For example, sustainable investments by values-centered companies can demonstrate that they are operationalizing their values, thereby burnishing their brand image. They can also be motivating for employees. For instance, New Belgium Brewery's green production system is consistent with and supports the company's brand image of providing quality beer for environmentally conscientious consumers. This posture is rooted in the belief that its target consumers want to identify with the companies behind the products they consume and that employees prefer to work for socially responsible companies.

Interface Carpets operates under a similar philosophy. Ray Anderson and the senior management of Interface are betting that through sustainability leadership, the company can achieve competitive advantage vis-à-vis less proactive rivals. One obvious but difficult to quantify benefit is that Interface has been included in the portfolios of numerous socially responsible investment funds including Calvert, Sustainable Assets Management, and Zuricher Kantonalbank. On occasion, the company's positive reputation has also yielded some very tangible benefits. In several instances, the company won large carpet contracts because the customer supported its corporate identity. The U.S. Department of Energy, for example, installed Interface carpeting at its headquarters office specifically because Interface was the kind of forward-thinking company with which it wanted to do business.[27]

Of course, many of our entrepreneurs have made investments in processes knowing fully well that the financial returns would be negative and promotional value minimal or nonexistent. As one example, Chris King Precision Equipment invested in a new anodizing process that completely recycled all of the water it used and produced minimal solid waste. Chris King and his employees agreed to make this relatively sizable investment, in terms of both money and time, because they felt that the positive environmental impact simply outweighed making more money. King along with other values-centered entrepreneurs who have made such investments, we surmise, can readily identify with the following Wen Chang quote: "I try to make the numbers work, but if they don't, then I listen to my heart."[28]

Spread the Message

There is a limit to what any company, much less a small firm, can do on its own. Understanding this limitation and to multiply their positive impact, a good number of our values-centered entrepreneurs have engaged and educated their customers and suppliers. Consider Small Dog Electronics, a relatively small online store for computer products with its own eWaste Program. The program's objectives are three-fold: (1) to help give people a place to recycle their electronic waste, (2) to spread the word to individuals and businesses about the harmful effects of electronic waste if not recycled or properly disposed of, and (3) to help prevent the dumping of toxic wastes at home and abroad. In particular, the company recognizes that it cannot get far without enlisting its customers. Consequently, the focus of its program has been to "educate consumers and to help reduce the amount of computer and electronic waste being improperly discarded."[29] The company's website plays a central role in spreading the word:

> . . . Improperly disposed electronics can end up being shipped to Third World countries where [they are] broken down for parts to sell. The toxins from these electronics can cause harmful effects on the workers who are typically not equipped with safety gear. Harmful effects on the environment from lead, mercury and hexavalent chromium can be found in the millions of tons of electronics that end up in landfills every year . . .[30]

Gaia Valley Hotel's Wen Chang says that the educational program his hotel offers to customers is the "most important" part of his work in that he can "influence people in the right way."[31] In that effort, he places a copy of Al Gore's *An Inconvenient Truth* in every room, right next to the Bible. He has also installed in the main lobby a four-panel kiosk that displays the hotel's energy usage minute by minute. The first three "touch screens" show CO_2 emissions, electricity use, and water use. The fourth panel on the bottom compares Gaia's environmental performance to that of other hotels. Chang explains the significance of these panels: "We wanted to make sure all of our guests see this, so they can see how much we are doing, and they can interact with the system as an education center."[32]

Some of our companies have been successful in requiring responsible practices from their business partners. Following an internal study in 2003, Aveda, a leading sustainability-oriented cosmetics company, began requiring that magazines, to qualify for carrying its advertisements, have a minimum of 10 percent post-consumer recycled content. Subsequently, *Natural Health*, a magazine where Aveda advertises, went from 100 percent virgin paper usage to 40 percent recycled content in less than five months.[33] In another example, T.S. Designs requires that its apparel suppliers adhere to sustainable manufacturing practices and monitors them to this end.

Calvert Funds has been successful in exercising influence over a wide range of companies and industries. Utilizing a multifaceted approach to socially responsible investing, it employs seven investment criteria: Corporate governance and ethics, environment, workplace, product and safety impact, international operations and human rights, indigenous people's rights, and community relations. Companies are screened as potential investments and if a candidate firm is found deficient in any of these areas, it will not be included in Calvert's investment portfolio.

The lure of Calvert's seal of approval has frequently propelled companies to change their ways. Numerous companies have had to make significant improvements in their operations to pass Calvert's tough environmental screens which, for example, require that their air, water, and soil practices be equal to or better than the average of the industry.[34] Calvert also uses its power as a large shareholder in corporations to influence their environmental policies. For instance, only after pressure from Calvert did computer maker Dell switch from cathode ray tube monitors to liquid crystal displays which contain less lead. Moreover, Calvert's scrutiny has helped motivate Dell to redesign both its portable and desktop computer packaging which purportedly saves 400 tons of lead and 1,000 tons of waste each year.[35]

Chapter Takeaways

- Determine and articulate objectives/priorities clearly.
- Develop concrete policies and action plans.
- Experiment with and pursue new technology and innovative methods to reduce harm.
- Minimize any direct damage your company may cause to the environment by minimizing waste and offsetting pollution.
- Measure (quantify) your achievements.
- Find ways to minimize the financial burden associated with pro-environmental or pro-social investments.
- Spread the message to customers and business partners to maximize impact.

10

Stay With It for the Long Haul

Work is not, primarily, something one does to live, but the thing one lives to do.
—Dorothy Sayers, British author and Christian humanist, 1893–1957[1]

Think Long Term

Paul Hawken, in his book *Growing a Business*, said something very inspiring. He proposed that as an initiator of a new business, one should "plan to be around a hundred years or longer."[2] He observed "If you are planning to be here ten, thirty, seventy years from now, you have to conduct your business as if the world around you will remember everything you have done to date." He recalls that when he started his company, he set out to create a company that would "peak in the next century." While a century may be too long for today's entrepreneurs, we think that extending one's time frame out beyond the conventional five-year financial projections may be a healthy exercise. To paraphrase Dorothy Sayers, a business shouldn't be something you do to live, but something you live to do.

Our values-centered entrepreneurs seem to share similar views about business as Hawken and Sayers. They expect their businesses to last and prosper for decades. They couldn't care less about the "quick flip" or the expeditious IPO (initial public offering). After all, these values-centered entrepreneurs have dreams and goals that go beyond personal financial gain—an attitude that tends to extend their time frame and reduce the attraction of selling the business for a profit. In fact, many of our values-centered firms, even though they may look new and trendy, have been around a long time. As Table 10.1 shows, many of our values-centered companies have been in existence for 30, 40, or even 80 years, even though most of the world has just begun to recognize their exemplary business practices. In large part, it appears that building a company for the long haul and building a successful values-centered, triple bottom-line company go hand in hand.

Consider, for instance, Chris King, who envisions his company, King Cycle Group, living out its mission as long as possible. He explains, "I don't need my business to survive me, but I would like it to carry forward the philosophy that the company is founded upon."[3] King is in no rush to sell his business for profit like most other

Table 10.1 Year of Company Founding: Sample List

Company	Year Founded
Migros	1925
Interface Carpets	1973
Shorebank	1973
Calvert Group of Mutual Funds	1976
Chris King Cycle Group	1977
Patagonia (Clothing)	1979
Whole Foods	1980
Newman's Own	1982
White Dog Café	1983
Working Assets	1985
Clif Bar	1986

entrepreneurs. He asks, "What do you do with a company that has your name?"[4] Moreover, he would like to see his company be a self-sustaining company that can "run itself"—a goal that he has been working toward for the last 30 years. In fact, the goal of building a self-sustaining company is the reason King has put most of the earnings back into the business every year. King displays his dedication to the company's longevity when he says, "I don't need a lot of money. I have always viewed that profit is something that benefits the company not me . . . Company is a livelihood to your small society, so it is important to ensure its health."[5]

Gottlieb Duttweiler found a unique way to perpetuate Migros, the large Swiss retailer, and its special culture for generations to come. He and his wife, Adele, with no children to leave their legacy to, decided in 1941 to convert the company into a cooperative. In other words, the Duttweilers relinquished their ownership and let its customers become its legal owners. With its new structure, the company's "service to the Swiss people/customer" mission was further strengthened. Customers could now influence the organization for an indefinite period of time through their ballots as well as their purchases. The cooperative structure also protected the organization to a large degree from acquisition.

Duttweiler, in addition to radically altering the governance structure, infused his colleagues with his philosophy and vision for Migros. Several of these colleagues became the senior management team at Migros after his death in 1962. They perpetuated Duttweiler's policies and ideology and, in turn, passed them on to the next generation of management. Today, Migros continues to stand out as an exemplar for those entrepreneurs who hope to "make a difference" through a long-lived company.[6]

Magic Johnson contemplates about times long after he is "dead and gone" when he is asked about his business. In an interview with *LA Times Magazine* in 2008, he shared how the rewards of running his business have exceeded those of five NBA Championships he won because of the long-term effect of his business enterprise:[7]

> Oh, yeah, they have passed it, because long after I'm dead and gone, the brand will still be living and people will still be going in those buildings and enjoying themselves or in those different companies and having a good time. You have to remember that when you put more

than 20,000 people to work, that means some of their kids, and then some of their kids' kids, they work for me, and they have a job because of me.

Exercise Patience

Our values-centered entrepreneurs are patient business people. They do not mind starting small and growing their businesses at a steady, sustainable pace—something that many of today's entrepreneurs find unappealing. Unfortunately, much of today's entrepreneurship is about raising enormous amounts of capital and scaling hastily. However, it is easier for our values-centered entrepreneurs to be more patient as they are focused on their mission and thus have a longer-term horizon.

As discussed in Chapter 4 (Raise Capital with Mission in Mind), many of our entrepreneurs did not raise or borrow capital from institutions such as venture capital firms or banks in the early days of their companies. Of course, some of them may not have qualified for such investments since they did not have the right background or experience and, in addition, their vision of a socially responsible company would have turned off most traditional investors. The majority of our entrepreneurs began with the capital they were able to amass on their own or from close friends, which typically was very little. Since growth in the early years was limited by the lack of financial resources, our values-centered entrepreneurs had to build their companies more slowly through "sweat equity" (i.e., value created by hard work versus capital). Although being short on financial resources is relatively common among conventional entrepreneurs as well, it appears to be especially prevalent among values-centered entrepreneurs.

Craigslist is an excellent example of a firm that started small, took time to grow, and has been fabulously successful. The company began in early 1995 when Craig Newmark sent out an email promoting a local technology and arts event to about 12 friends. The mailing was basically an endeavor by Newmark to spice up his social life. The idea caught on and his list grew slowly from there. By the end of the year, he created a corresponding website to better facilitate the growing phenomenon of connecting people within a geographic region. Viewing itself as a "mom and pop" business and not overly concerned with rapid growth or making a lot of money, Craigslist started offering for free the services that other websites were charging for, e.g., job listing. On Craigslist, visitors could buy and sell motorcycles, futons, and mobile phones. They could also find apartments, blind dates, child care, and rides across the country—and the list of services continued to grow. No money was spent on design. Everything was automated to reduce overhead. Craglist was a lean operation that basically operated on its own.

It took seven years, until January 2002, to reach 768,000 visitors per month, mostly in three locales, San Francisco Bay Area, Los Angeles, and New York.[8] The company did not pursue venture capital and did not use traditional advertising. Its offices took up two floors of a house in San Francisco's Inner Sunset district. Newmark saved money by renting out one of the floors to a group of graduate students.

By 2008, Craigslist had established itself in over 450 cities in 50 countries. The site served over nine billion page views per month, putting it in 56th place overall among websites world wide, and ninth place overall among websites in the U.S. (per Alexa.com on January 10, 2008). With over thirty million new classified advertisements each month, Craigslist has become the leading classified services provider in any medium. The site receives over two million new job listings each month, making it one of the top job boards in the world. Today, Craigslist is a solid operation that many venture capitalists would love to get a stake in—although it is highly doubtful that Craig Newmark would welcome outside investment.

To a certain extent, as was suggested in an earlier chapter, the humble beginnings and the hardships that our values-centered entrepreneurs have endured from being strapped for cash may have helped their businesses survive and prosper in the long run. Studies have shown that bootstrapping can provide tremendous advantage by "revealing the strengths and weaknesses in one's business."[9] Having little money can expose what may otherwise be hidden problems and force the company to solve them before they become major concerns. Rather than simply throw money at a problem, the company has little choice but to fix the problem, often innovatively, and thereby strengthen its operations. In other words, the company is forced to develop sound habits that can help sustain it in the long run.

Think Twice Before Selling

Because of their long-term view, our values-centered entrepreneurs tend not to be preoccupied with an exit plan, i.e., the prospect of selling a company or taking it public. To the contrary, they are often reluctant to put their companies up for sale even if it means immediate personal wealth. In fact, our research indicates that many of our values-centered entrepreneurs' exit options have often been constrained as a consequence of their *self-imposed* social and environmental goals. Our entrepreneurs' social/environmental values tend to not only dictate how they operate their companies, but also limit their alternatives in terms of pursuing investors, sell-off, or pursuing an IPO.

This hesitance to sell is understandable considering how committed our entrepreneurs are to their causes and missions. Working Assets' Laura Sher, for example, shared her thinking with us about exiting the business. She explained, "We are a social change organization that happens to be inside a phone company or credit card company. How could we exit our cause for social change?"[10] She makes an important point: For idealists sincerely committed to changing the world through their companies, exit probably makes little sense.

Craig Newmark of Craigslist continues to be enthusiastic about maintaining control of his company knowing that he is providing valuable (mostly free) service to people in hundreds of communities. Newmark has repeatedly been asked to relinquish his ownership or to sell the entire firm to the likes of eBay. Any such transaction would make him a millionaire many times over. But he explains that "it just didn't feel right" considering that his business was never so much about making money and more about providing a useful service to communities.[11] Newmark believes that he has to retain control of the company to assure that his vision of helping communities will endure.

In 1991, Yvon and Melinda Chouinard of Patagonia met with a consultant who suggested that they sell their company and use the proceeds to establish a foundation to fund the environmental causes so dear to their hearts.[12] Upon reflection, Chouinard reasoned that the money generated by the foundation would barely make a dent in the world's environmental problems. He concluded that the best way to make a difference would be to maintain ownership of Patagonia and make it an example of how all businesses should be managed.[13] Chouinard still owns the company and guides it toward his vision of sustainability—an unachievable goal, in his view, but one worthy of pursuit.

In a very similar scenario, one spring day in 2000, Gary Erickson, co-founder and wife Kit Crawford, and their former business partner were minutes away from selling their fast-growing nutrition bar company, Clif Bar to Quaker Oats for $120 million. At about the same time, Balance Bar was being sold to Kraft and PowerBar was cashing out to Nestlé. Convinced that selling the company was the only way Clif Bar could compete, Erickson prepared employees for the sale by asking them to work harder than ever. He hired an investment banker. He traveled the country, wining and dining with the potential suitors. But minutes away from signing on the bottom line and becoming a very rich man, Erickson started to shake and couldn't breathe. He took a walk around the block. He wept. Seconds later, he had a revelation, an epiphany. "I don't have to do this," he said to himself.[14] And, as he vividly describes in his recently published book, *Raising the Bar*, he instantly felt free.[15] Most importantly, Erickson reports, he felt happy from knowing that, after a critical moment of confusion, he followed his passion and his gut. Later he said that not selling the company when he was within hours of doing so was the best business decision he has ever made. "I still think about that as something that changed my life forever," says Erickson.[16]

Tim Haahs has received multiple inquiries from agents and corporations interested in acquiring his company. But selling the business makes little sense to him. Instead, he wants to strengthen the organization to fulfill its mission far in the future. Haahs explains,

> I often receive inquiries from outside about purchasing the firm. However, because the firm is cause-driven rather than profit-driven, it is hard to even think about selling the firm. The minute the firm is sold we would no longer be able to promote our mission statement of "helping those in need" because that would officially make us profit-driven.[17]

He continued,

> In terms of my exit strategy, if I didn't care so much about our corporate mission it would be easy to just sell the firm. However, instead, we are working on training and grooming the next generation of leaders within the firm who have the same passion for what we do; leaders who get up in the morning not thinking about how to make more money, but rather thinking about how we can continue to fulfill our mission. These are the leaders who I am confident will continue to lead our firm long after I have stepped away.

Take Time to Find the Right Buyer

Several of our other values-centered companies were eventually acquired and became subsidiaries of larger, in some cases, public corporations (see Table 10.2 below). These values-centered firms attracted strong interest from large corporations because of the strength of their brands, their ability to generate profit, and, in some cases, their reputation for being socially responsible. For example, Aveda was bought for about $300 million by Estee Lauder in 1997 because Estee Lauder wanted to boost its environmental reputation. One commonality in all the cases we reviewed is that our values-centered entrepreneurs were very thoughtful about their sell-off decision and took time to find the right buyer that would carry on (at least some parts of) the mission of the company.

Tom and Kate Chappell of Tom's of Maine, in 1996, seriously considered selling the company to achieve financial freedom and pursue personal interests. Working with their investment banker, they established specific criteria for the acquirer based on the company's beliefs and mission. They insisted that the controlling factor in the sale decision not be the price but rather the dedication of the acquiring firm to the company's stated values. But the Chappells were unable to find such a buyer and came to believe that they could not sell their business without compromising their own values, which they were unwilling to do.[18] Ten years later in 2006, however, they sold 80 percent of Tom's of Maine to the Colgate-Palmolive Company.

The Chappells later explained that two major factors compelled them to sell controlling interest in their company to Colgate-Palmolive. One, they realized that remaining an independent company, given the consolidation of the retail industry (e.g., in pharmacies and supermarkets), was becoming increasingly risky and hence a strategic partner was needed to bring the business to scale. Second, they discovered that Colgate-Palmolive had people with very deeply held values of caring and teamwork. The Chappells also learned that the majority of Colgate-Palmolive employees had great longevity with the company—which they felt was a good gauge for how the organization treated its people. Further, they learned that Colgate-Palmolive had showed respect for the other companies they had acquired over the years and allowed them to remain somewhat autonomous under their corporate umbrella.[19]

Table 10.2 Acquisitions of Values-Centered Companies

Company	Buyer	Factoid
Aveda	Estee Lauder	Sold for $300 million in 1997
Ben & Jerry's	Unilever	Sold in 2000
The Body Shop	L'Oreal	Sold for £652 million (€945 million) in 2006
Honest Tea	Coca-Cola	Sold 40% for $43 million
Tom's of Maine	Colgate-Palmolive	Sold 80% in 2006
Stonyfield Farm	Danone	Sold 40% in 2001 and 85% by 2003

Much like Tom and Kate, Bennett Cohen and Jerry Greenfield of Ben & Jerry's rejected an offer to be acquired by M&M Mars, because the food giant had a reputation for exploiting the community and the environment. The founders later accepted an offer by Unilever—a company that they felt was more socially responsible. Gary Hirshberg and Samuel Kayman believed the sale of Stonyfield Farm to Danone could actually have a positive impact on the environment. Hirshberg speculated that Stonyfield could "infect" the number two yogurt seller in the world with Stonyfield Farm's "organic bug" and in this way make an even greater positive impact on the environment.[20]

Stay Private if Possible

A large majority of the companies in our sample (almost 90 percent) were privately held at the time of the study or until their acquisition by larger (mostly) public companies. Even the bigger companies in our sample preferred being private. One would expect that most conventional companies would prefer the IPO option because going public tends to be financially rewarding for both the entrepreneurs and their investors. However, the general consensus among our entrepreneurs seemed to be that they could exercise the balance between financial and social goals more effectively as private entities.

Gary Erickson says that Clif Bar is today dabbling in environmental innovations that its public-company peers do not have the freedom to touch and for this reason he has no intention of taking Clif Bar public. The company's intention is to stay private so it can continue to do good works. "I've seen what happens to companies that become public companies. . . . They lose the values that were set up," says Erickson. "Clif Bar is like a kid. You want to see it go off and do something meaningful."[21]

Jeffrey Hollender of Seventh Generation learned the hard way that being private was best suited for his business. The company completed an IPO in 1993 only to become private again a year later. While being public, its stock price dropped significantly because the investment community did not appreciate the company's prospects even though it was growing. Seventh Generation with its "green" mission and products, it seems, was ahead of its time. In 1994, Seventh Generation needed additional capital, but Hollender's faithful group of early investors did not want to put money into a public company. They wanted their investment to go toward the firm's growth rather than as dividends to shareholders. As a consequence, in an unusual move just a year after it went public, Seventh Generation went through a complicated process of buying back the shares of investors and becoming a private company once again.

In hindsight, Hollender feels that reverting to private company status was a wise decision. "I've only got 20 shareholders to communicate with," Hollender says.

They are more sophisticated. They understand the business. They are long-term strategic investors. They aren't really worried about what happens on a quarter-to-quarter basis. They are more worried about how the company is progressing toward its three-year and five-year goals. I tell people that I've had board meetings where I've missed my sales and profit numbers for the quarter, and the board was thrilled because that's only one of 20 things they're looking at.[22]

Given his experience, Hollender believes that being private is the sensible route for a multiple bottom-line company.

The Body Shop's Anita Roddick was disillusioned by her experience with the public markets. She took her company public in 1984 with the conviction that, as a public company, The Body Shop would have "tremendous potential and power to do good in the world."[23] But years later she complained that her dream of "ethical capitalism" had faded. She asserted, on several different occasions, that managing a balance between profits and social causes was highly difficult for a public company.[24]

Be a Different Kind of Public Company

Although several of our values-centered firms have had negative experience as public entities, the fact is that the public markets can be a critical source of capital for a company's growth and long-term survival. In general, companies are able to access financial resources much more easily and cheaply as public entities. And, in today's competitive business world, ready access to the financial markets can be a source of competitive advantage. Most responsible companies considering going public, however, have two major concerns: First, that the objectives of the company (i.e., triple bottom-line) and those associated with its public status (financial) may be incompatible, and second, that the public market may react unfavorably to companies with idealistic objectives, even if the company is performing well financially.

As described earlier, five of our values-centered companies, Interface Carpets, Whole Foods, The Body Shop, Starbucks, and EV Rental, have taken the IPO route to become and remain as publicly traded entities. In all those cases, however, their public company status has not prevented our values-centered firms from continuing to pursue a socially responsible agenda. They have been able to sustain this seeming contradiction in part by making their values and sustainable business practices an integral part of their business model. These firms proactively publicize what they stand for and how they operate, and convincingly argue that their financial success depends on the ability to pursue their social environmental mission. Both consumers and investors are aware of their triple bottom-line mission and, in many cases, have bought into their atypical business philosophy. These companies demonstrate that it is possible to take advantage of public markets for growth capital while still maintaining their integrity.

Interface Carpets is a very good example of a public company that continues to pursue sustainability in all aspects of its business practice. Ray Anderson, founder and long-term chairman of this large carpet manufacturer, has made his vision well-known to the public: To become a leader in industrial ecology by first becoming a sustainable corporation and eventually a "restorative" enterprise. Anderson defines sustainability as "the means of managing human and natural capital with the same vigor we apply to the management of financial capital."[25] To realize this vision, he and his management team have clearly laid out and communicated a plan aimed at achieving sustainability.

Anderson was not always this blunt about his environmental and social mission. In fact, in the early days, he was silent about his motives because he was concerned about public market backlash. There was no press release to proclaim the company's quest for sustainability. Anderson didn't even announce his intentions to shareholders at the company's annual meetings. This could have been a wise decision since few people in the 1980s and early 1990s believed that going green could equate to an increase in shareholder returns. In fact, speaking about sustainability probably would have turned off many investors. "Over the years, we've been very careful with how we've dealt with shareholders on the issue [of sustainability]," Anderson admits. "Frankly, we didn't have a whole lot to report in those early years."[26] But he finally came out of the closet, so to speak, in a major way in 1997, confessing his quest for sustainability in front of an unlikely group of fellow CEOs and businessmen at a North Carolina State University business conference.

Still, Anderson took small steps without subjecting his company to major investment or risk. At first, he changed the little things, e.g., putting recycling barrels for soft drink cans on plant floors and recycling bins for paper in the offices, or searching for greener manufacturing materials that weren't made from petroleum products. Then, as his newfound conservationism became bolder, he took on larger and more innovative projects. For instance, Interface installed at its LaGrange facility a $15 million machine that made the company's Cool Blue carpet tiles out of discarded and defective carpet tiles. The same plant also began using energy generated by the city of LaGrange's landfill—tapping and burning the methane produced from the decay of organic matter. This latter initiative earned the company an "Energy Partner of the Year" award in 2006 from the EPA.

The efficiency of Interface's new technology and processes, however, did not show up financially for a long time. The company reduced waste by 60 to 80 percent at each of its factories in the first three-and-a-half years. That reduction saved $67 million according to an environmental accounting system the company invented to keep track of its progress. But starting in the late 1990s, Interface's profits dropped by about 20 percent each year, causing industry analysts familiar with Anderson's sustainability mission to be skeptical. The talk in manufacturing circles was that environmental initiatives cut big chunks out of a company's profits. "It was tough," Anderson recalls. "There was never, never, not one thought of turning back. But it was very frustrating to know that the things you were doing to become sustainable were not showing up as being profitable."[27]

Anderson courageously stuck with his plan, a difficult stance for a public company CEO. Even in the midst of the economic downturn, he continued to pursue sustainability. The company invested millions of dollars in more efficient and environmentally beneficial equipment and processes such as machines capable of reclaiming yarn that otherwise would be trashed.

As the commercial carpet industry made a modest comeback in the new century, Interface emerged from the slump with a competitive advantage. Interface's sustainability mission became one of the company's strongest selling points. When Dell, Microsoft, and Starbucks bought Interface's carpet for their respective corporate headquarters, they did so in part because of the company's environmental commitment. "This thing that seemed like it was altruistic in the beginning has turned out to be really, really good for business," Anderson argues. "It's just a better way to bigger profit."[28]

Anderson's courage and resilience paid off. Like many values-centered entrepreneurs, Anderson could not have achieved his balanced business success if he hadn't been willing to stick with his plan for the long haul.

Chapter Takeaways

Interestingly, the values-centered approach combined with concern for social impact seems to cause entrepreneurs to develop and operate with a longer time horizon. Our entrepreneurs' self-imposed higher standards make it difficult for them to grow hastily, sell, or go public with their companies. Nonetheless, companies like Interface and Starbucks demonstrate that a public company can continue to operate responsibly, all they need is an effective business model, good communications, and courage.

- Think long term, think legacy. Plan to stay with the company for a long time.
- Have patience. Grow a company at a steady and healthy pace to build a sustainable operation.
- Think twice before selling the company while your mission is not completed. If you do sell, be thoughtful about to whom you want to sell your company. Make sure the acquirer will carry on the mission of the company.
- Stay private if possible. As a public company, communicate your vision so that customers and investors buy into it.

11

Make Giving a Priority

I had such a string of good fortune in my life . . . Those who are most lucky should hold their hands out to those who aren't.
—Paul Newman, actor and founder of Newman's Own[1]

Money is only important in how it acts as a tool for social change.
—Laura Scher, founder and president of Working Assets[2]

We have known quite a few entrepreneurs over the years. Many of them in their earlier years have shared with us how badly they want to give back once their business was successful. It's a familiar story—how their business is not about the money; how they want to help others; or how they or their business will donate much of their earnings to charities.

Our experience, however, is that most entrepreneurs don't honor these cavalier promises when their companies become mature and profitable. Time turns memories dim and alters feelings. Some successful entrepreneurs may give marginal amounts. Others wait until late in life and choose gifts that become monuments to their immortality. Of course, there is nothing necessarily right or wrong with giving any amount at all at any time in one's life. It's a personal decision. We are not being judgmental. Our observation is simply that people not deeply committed to giving have difficulty with it.

In contrast to the typical entrepreneur, our values-centered entrepreneurs tend to give substantially, in a variety of different and significant ways, and often relatively early in their companies' development. This chapter describes our entrepreneurs' philosophical approach and commitment toward giving. It also presents a spectrum of their methods and forms of giving as well as the benefits that they may derive from giving.

View Giving as an Important Function of Business

Values-centered entrepreneurs, like other entrepreneurs, work hard to make money. But for many of them, giving away a part of their companies' earnings is an important function of their business. Yvon Chouinard of Patagonia made it crystal clear in his book that providing money for environmental causes was one of the principal reasons he got into business in the first place.[3] Similarly, giving was the primary motive for Timothy Haahs in starting his highly successful architectural firm. At New Belgium Brewery, philanthropy is considered the second most important core value of the company, right after environmental protection. Gary Erickson and Kit Crawford of Clif Bar believe that giving back is a critical component to being "a business with a heart."[4] Blake Mycoskie, the founder and CEO of Tom's Shoes, calls himself designer and "Chief Shoe Giver."

Because giving is of primary importance, most of our entrepreneurs did not wait until their companies became mature. They started giving modest amounts early in their companies' life-cycle and gave incrementally more over time as their businesses became more established. For instance, at Working Assets, there was no procrastination when it came to giving. In its first year, 1985, the company donated to charities $32,000—a significant portion of its income. About 20 years later, between the years 2004 and 2006, the company gave away more than $3 million each year. Since its founding, Working Assets has generated over $60 million for various progressive nonprofits.[5] Further, Tom's Shoes, a very young entrepreneurial firm with no profits to speak of, has incorporated giving into its core business model: The company gives away a pair of shoes for each pair it sells. "I always thought I'd spend the first half of my life making money and the second half giving it away," says Blake Mycoskie. "I never thought I could do both at the same time." This ambitious model has made it difficult for the company to turn a profit thus far. "Selling online has allowed us to grow pretty rapidly, but we're not going to make as much as another shoe company, and the margins are definitely lower," he admits. "But what we do helps us get publicity. Lots of companies give a percentage of their revenue to charity, but we can't find anyone who matches one for one."[6] Mycoskie adds, "I believe Tom's is going to give away millions of shoes one day."[7]

Institutionalize Your Giving Programs

To formalize their commitments to giving, many of our values-centered entrepreneurs established formal, institutionalized programs. Such institutionalized giving is frequently treated as an essential function of the business, right along with accounting and marketing. Some of them, even, have the status of the founder's "pet project" and consequently receive more personal attention than even the conventional business functions.

Some of our companies set up corporate foundations (not-for-profit entities) to formally administer their giving as well as to provide vehicles through which their customers and employees can be encouraged to participate. The typical structure, displayed in Figure 11.1, is as follows: Company ABC sets up a foundation, Foundation ABC, and makes an initial gift and/or ongoing financial commitment. The foundation, usually headed up by the entrepreneur, gives directly and indirectly to targeted causes and charities. Generally, the companies persuade their managers

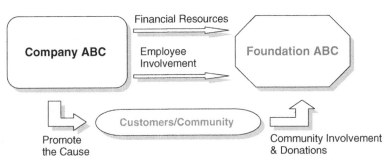

Figure 11.1 Typical Relationship between Company and Foundation

and employees to get involved as donors and/or volunteers. The companies may also promote awareness of their causes through their business practices, i.e., through marketing materials and activities aimed at soliciting donations from customers and the broader community.

While the basic structure described above is common and is utilized widely by many corporations, the commitment and level of effort is more profound among our values-centered organizations. Anita Roddick in discussing The Body Shop Foundation asserted:

> It isn't one of those awful tax shelters like some in America. It just functions to take the money and give it away. We are active in all of the most unpopular causes, whether it's human rights or the poor independent farmers who are endangered species. We are really doing grass roots community organizing and building.[8]

A number of our companies have established quotas for their annual giving. Migros led the way when it instituted a so-called "cultural levy" or percentage as part of the statutes governing the organization. Under this covenant, the federation's regional cooperatives are pledged to contribute a minimum of one half of 1 percent of their gross retail sales for cultural, social, and political policy purposes. In similar fashion, the central organization (the FMC) is pledged to contribute 1 percent of its turnover (akin to gross revenue). Since the inception of the cultural levy, contributions have increased almost every year; in 2006 they totaled over the equivalent of $98 million.

To institutionalize its giving, Patagonia set up an Environmental Grants Program in 1985. The program is funded by what the company called its "Earth Tax," a yearly levy of 1 percent of sales or 10 percent of pre-tax profits, whichever is greater.[9] In this way, the company commits itself to continuous funding of the program even in years when it does not have profits. The program is known to every employee inside the company and many customers, which further strengthens the company's commitment. By 2008, Patagonia and its foundation had given away more than $25 million to over 1,000 organizations.[10]

Other companies in our sample have demonstrated similar levels of commitment: Ben & Jerry's endowed its foundation with a one-time gift of $45 million and 50,000 shares of common stock in 1985. The firm's annual contribution to the foundation has been set at 7.5 percent of pre-tax profits. Stonyfield Farm created a "Profits for the Planet" program under which the company donates 10 percent of pre-tax profits annually to organizations that serve to protect and restore the environment. Tom's of Maine through its "Tom's of Maine Grant Programs" has committed to giving 10 percent of its profits to worthy environmental and social organizations. Working Assets places 1 percent of its revenue in a donation pool for annual distribution. Clif Bar devotes the equivalent of 1 percent of revenue to community causes, including, for example, giving money to breast-cancer prevention and encouraging employees to volunteer their services on company time to Habitat for Humanity.

Champion givers, Tim Haahs and his 48 employees have committed to donating at least 20 percent of profits (wow!), both directly, and through the Timothy Haahs Foundation, to charities and churches serving the needy in the Philadelphia area. Moreover, in 2002, Haahs moved his office into a building that he designed which includes a 12,000 square-foot community center with an auditorium and meeting space that he makes available to non-profit agencies free of charge. A sample collection of institutionalized giving programs are listed in Table 11.1.

Two of the firms on our list, Tom's Shoes and New Belgium Brewery, have tied their giving to units of products sold. Tom's Shoes, as mentioned, has coupled its giving program to the sale of its products—shoes. Thus, for every pair of shoes the company

Table 11.1 Sample Institutionalized Giving Programs

Company	Giving Amount (Yearly)	Recipients
Ben & Jerry's	7.5% of yearly pre-tax profits	Progressive social causes, including neighborhood development and environment.
Clif Bar	1% of revenues	Community causes including breast cancer, culture, and the environment.
Newman's Own	100% profits	Cystic Fibrosis Foundation, Harlem Restoration Project, and many obscure little organizations.
Patagonia	1% on sales or 10% of pre-tax profit, whichever is greater	Grassroots environmental organizations and individuals.
Salesforce.com	1% equity, 1% product, and 1% time	Nonprofits working on various education and poverty related issues.
Stonyfield Farm	10% of pre-tax profits	Projects that serve to protect or restore the environment.
Tim Haahs Associates	20% of pre-tax profits directly and through its foundation	Charities and churches serving the needy in the Philadelphia area.
Tom's of Maine	10% of its pre-tax profits	Environmental and social organizations.
White Dog Café	20% of pre-tax profits	Locally owned sustainable farms and businesses.
Working Assets	1% of revenues	Organizations in the areas of civil rights, peace, environment, and social and economic justice.

sells, it gives a pair free to an indigent Argentine child. New Belgium Brewery donates $1 to philanthropic causes for each barrel of beer sold the prior year. The donations are allocated to the various states in proportion to their percentage of overall company sales. Funding decisions are made by the company's Philanthropy Committee which is composed of several levels of employees and includes owners, area leaders, and production workers. New Belgium is always on the lookout for charitable organizations that demonstrate creativity, diversity, and an innovative approach to fulfilling their mission and achieving their objectives.[11] Since its inception, the company has donated more than $2 million to such organizations in the communities where it does business.

It is noteworthy that our values-centered companies' giving far exceeds, in percentage terms, that of conventional corporations. According to Giving USA Foundation, corporations on the average give 1.2 percent of their profits.[12] This number is substantially lower than the 7.5 percent to 20 percent that many of our values-centered companies give. Also, recall that at Patagonia, Tom's Shoes, Working Assets, New Belgium Brewing Company, and Clif Bar, giving programs require that donations be made whether or not they make a profit. And, of course, no organization is more committed to giving than Newman's Own, the salad dressing and sauce company founded by actor Paul Newman and A.E. Hotchner. This company, structured as a non-profit organization, gives away all its excess incomes other than that needed for capital investments and contingencies.

Targeted Giving to Maximize Impact

It may surprise the reader that giving is not a simple process. For starters, identifying charities or needs that ideally match a company's cause is not as easy as one might assume. Thus, many of our values-centered entrepreneurs and their firms devote significant time and effort to finding organizations that satisfy their giving criteria.

Newman's Own has a special challenge because it is intent on giving to organizations that are outside of the mainstream of philanthropy. The founders have sought out "obscure little organizations that can't generate the publicity necessary to attract the attention of donors."[13] A good example was the donation of a new school bus for the Hope Rural School in Indiantown, Florida, a school for the children of migrant farm workers. Without a replacement for its condemned school bus, the school would have closed, and the children would have been deprived of an education. The nuns at the school had written letters to numerous well-funded charities but received no positive responses. Paul and Hotch, however, upon discovering their need sent them a check for $27,000 for a new bus. Thirteen years later after this bus had worn down, they happily sent them a check for a replacement.

Clif Bar, whose values converge around health and the environment, gives to causes that are in line with these interests. For example, the company has established the "rripL³ Fund" which is a grant program that supports smaller grassroots organizations in the areas of community services, culture, and the environment. It also gives away many of its energy bars to people who are homeless and hungry in the San Francisco area. In 2003 alone, the company gave away over 1 million bars!

Tom's of Maine's Grant Program is highly structured: It is divided into four general areas: education, the arts, the environment, and indigenous peoples. Approximately 40–50 grants per year are awarded either in the form of a one-time award or a multi-year pledge. Most are in the $500–$5,000 range with larger amounts reserved for the multi-year pledges. Beneficiaries have included Harvard Divinity School's Center for the Study of Values in Public Affairs, the Maine Audubon Society, and elementary education programs in Maine that teach about the environment. Other donations have gone to the Rainforest Alliance, Maine Women's Fund, Maine Business for Social Responsibility, the National Parks and Conservation Fund, and a project in Portland, Oregon to protect its regional watersheds.

A high-profile project funded by Tom's of Maine was "Reason for Hope," a PBS documentary about the scientist/conservationist, Dr. Jane Goodall. The company viewed this sponsorship as a natural fit because it shared common values, i.e., the environment and education, with Dr. Goodall. Prior to sponsoring the television special, the company for two years had been contributing to the Jane Goodall Institute and the related "Roots and Shoots," an international environmental and humanitarian teaching program. In support of this program, the company included coupon inserts with its products that encouraged customers to mail back the coupons; in return, Tom's promised to donate one dollar to the program for each coupon returned. Additionally, the company offered to pay the $25 initiation fee for any school or community wishing to establish a Roots and Shoots program.

Another program that Tom's of Maine has run for years assists those displaced by disasters. In 2004, for instance, Tom's of Maine joined a number of other Maine companies in sending aid to the Gulf Coast after the region had experienced a series of devastating hurricanes. Specifically, Tom's of Maine prepared packages of toothpaste and deodorant for displaced residents. The company has also made product donations to other needy causes, one example being to the Red Cross for families in war-ravaged Kosovo.

Salesforce.com has donated its salesforce and customer relationship management software to nonprofits so that they can "focus more time on their social mission and increase their efficiency."[14] Today, Salesforce.com's productivity-enhancing software system is being used by over 2,700 non-profit organizations around the world for managing a wide range of activities including constituent relationships, fund raising campaigns, volunteer opportunities, and program delivery. Donating its software is perfectly consistent with the Salesforce.com Foundation's mission to help organizations (particularly those that can least afford it) further their social mission, deepen their impact, and better the lives of those in need.

A few of our values-centered companies, in lieu of or in addition to making gifts, operate their own in-house programs where they give aid directly to their causes. Judy Wicks of the White Dog Café, for instance, has run various programs including an annual dinner at the Graterford State Prison, the White Dog PUPPY mentoring program for kids, and Urban Retrievers, a community service organization for young people.[15] She also has a program designed to spotlight the economic and ethnic diversity of Philadelphia. To promote this program, she encouraged her own affluent and suburban dining clientele to patronize inner-city neighborhood restaurants.

Similarly, The Body Shop has not only made donations through its foundation but has run a variety of initiatives on its own. For example, it has partnered with IKEA in an effort to make a real difference for the environment by establishing the Business Leaders' Initiative on Climate Change (BLICC). BLICC teaches other companies how to measure, report, and reduce their greenhouse gas emissions.

As part of its philanthropic program, Dancing Deer Bakery founded the Ginger-bread House Project. Its staff members and volunteers visit homeless shelters through-out the Greater Boston area to make gingerbread houses with mothers and their children. The company also has a partnership with One Family Inc., a non-profit organization dedicated to finding lasting solutions for family homelessness. To con-tribute to this cause, called Sweet Home, Dancing Deer sells baked goods on its website (http://www.dancingdeer.com/sweethome). Thirty-five percent of the sales goes to One Family which in turn uses this money to provide education, job-training, child-care, and housing for the homeless. Dancing Deer also uses eBay as an avenue for generating donations. The company has created a line of gingerbread houses decorated by the Boston Bruins, Boston Celtics, New England Patriots, and Senator John Kerry, among others, to sell on eBay. In 2006, the 93 gingerbread houses sold on eBay raised over $100,000 for the company's Sweet Home project.[16]

Perhaps the granddaddy of all in-house programs is Migros's Club School pro-gram which is funded through the company's cultural levy. Here, Migros's regional cooperatives run a network of adult education schools that collectively constitute the largest adult education organization in Switzerland. Currently, approximately 600 different subsidized courses are offered in such diverse areas as languages, general edu-cation, artistic skills and handicrafts, social skills, and professional training. The cen-tral federation also runs some internal programs for the handicapped, senior citizens, and remote mountain communities, as well as targeted underdeveloped counties.

All in all, the impact of our companies' giving programs has been significant. Newman's Own has given away nearly $200 million over the years to a variety of needy charities. Since 1985, Working Assets has donated $60 million to progressive causes. Magic Johnson Foundation has raised more than $20 million for charity and helped send more than 3,000 students to college. It's been rumored that Magic Johnson has given away more to charities than he had made as a professional basketball player.

Encourage Employees to Give

A number of the values-centered companies, in lieu of or in addition to making gifts, encourage employees to contribute their time and talent on company time. Patagonia, for instance, has a long-standing policy under which workers are offered five days of paid leave each year for volunteer activities at their children's schools.[17] Furthermore, under the Patagonia Internship Program employees may take a leave for one or two months at full salary and benefits to work for a non-profit organization, usually on some aspect of environmental activism. The program has been exceptionally popular with the company's employees; some 150 of them participated just during its first five years of operation.[18]

As brought up in an earlier chapter, Salesforce.com employees are encouraged to donate one percent of their working time to the community. Examples of the firm's employees' volunteer activities are feeding the homeless, tutoring kids, participating in community beautification and restoration projects, providing expertise to non-profits, and assisting with disaster relief. By 2008, nearly 85 percent of the firm's employees had participated in the program donating more than 77,000 hours to help feed the hungry, combat homelessness, teach children to read, and improve the environment among other activities. The company had also donated in excess of $12 million to non-profit organizations, and supplied Salesforce licenses to more than 3,500 nonprofits in 56 countries around the world.

Tom's of Maine's policy on employee volunteerism represents an important avenue through which the company tries to live its mission. Employees are encouraged to devote five percent of their paid work time (two hours per week or two and a half weeks per year) doing volunteer work for non-profit organizations of their choosing. Unlike the targeted programs that its foundation runs, the volunteer chores have been as varied as the interests of Tom's diverse workforce. In one unique example, an employee brought her dog once a week to a nursing home to provide comfort and companionship for the residents.

Clif Bar also promotes employee volunteerism on and off company time to such causes and projects as Habitat for Humanity, Angels Island Restoration, Diabetes Camp, and Company-Wide Community Service Day. In 2008 alone, the company employees donated 5,062 hours of their time, a substantial increase from 2,371 hours in 2005.

Timothy Haahs & Associates' principals and employees are offered flexible work schedules to participate in philanthropic activities ranging from food drives and charity walks, to serving on boards of directors of non-profit organizations. Novica, the online retailer, allows its employees to work on and participate in events for Novica Foundation, the nonprofit that makes loans to the Third World artisans. Even Small Dog Electronics, perhaps the smallest company on our list, has encouraged its employees to donate hundreds of hours of work to local schools, libraries, and Special Olympics.

Encourage Customers and Partners to Give

In addition to setting the standard for corporate giving in their respective industries, several of our companies have inspired or persuaded their customers and business partners to become involved as well. Working Assets has been particularly innovative in involving its customers. The procedure goes something like this. First, each year customers are invited to nominate non-profit organizations as potential funding recipients. After an independent foundation evaluates the efficacy of supporting the hundreds of nominees, the firm's employees in conjunction with the Board of Directors select 50 organizations for the annual donations ballot. At the end of the year, customers vote on how to distribute the donations among them. Consequently, Working Assets' customers can feel confident that their voices are being heard and that they are involved in the decision process. Working Assets also makes it extremely convenient for customers to donate: customers are encouraged to "round up" their monthly long-distance bills, with the difference going to the company's giving program. Additionally the company may make special appeals for additional round-ups and donations to address immediate needs such as emergency relief efforts.

Robert Milk of Novica.com has recently started the Novica Foundation to provide affordable loans to struggling artists in the Third World who need working capital. Milk's strategy is basically to encourage and mobilize his customers, art lovers from the West, to lend money to the artists of their choice. Milk was able to quickly identify hundreds of artists and artist groups interested in participating in this program. He has also been able to leverage the firm's list of thousands of "Novica friends"—the loyal customers and big fans of Novica artists. The prospective lenders and borrowers are brought together through the existing Novica website.

Tom's Shoes also encourages customers to get involved in more ways than just buying a pair of shoes. The company website prominently displays the statement "Passionate People and Companies Wanted." Further down on the same page it proclaims that "Ideas wither or die without action. Get involved" and offers ways for customers to participate in the company's cause. For instance, founder Blake Mycoskie has attracted some 240 customers who told him they would volunteer to work on shoe drops at their own expense. In response, Mycoskie organized a $2,000 trip consisting of two days of sightseeing and four days of volunteer work.

Calvert Funds' business model empowers its customers to make a social statement. By 2007, Calvert had more than 400,000 investors, with $15 billion in assets, who were committed to making a difference while also making money for themselves. Customers have invested in one or more Calvert funds because of the company's socially responsible investment practices. To identify companies to invest in, Calvert's equity funds employs a "Double Diligence" research process which requires both a rigorous review of financial performance and a thorough assessment of corporate integrity. Moreover, the Calvert Foundation has teamed up with the Ford, MacArthur, and Mott foundations to establish a fund for individuals and institutions, seeking to channel investment into disadvantaged communities with the long-run goal of helping end poverty. Through this fund, people can safely invest in low-income communities while benefiting from a professionally managed portfolio that exercises rigorous due diligence and the ongoing monitoring of investments.

Giving for Competitive Advantage?

We sincerely doubt that any of our values-centered entrepreneurs give because they expect profit in return. The numbers just don't work that way. But we do believe that there are benefits that arise from giving.

First of all, firms that promote themselves as being socially responsible would look hypocritical if they did not give above the national average to worthy causes. It is simply part of the overall profile necessary for credibility.

Secondly, giving affords the company exposure to people and segments of society that might not otherwise give the company or its products a second thought. Although it is hard to measure its effect, it is generally acknowledged that a certain amount of giving is beneficial to business. That is the reason, for instance, that store managers of regional and national chains have small funds that they are expected to use for charitable giving within their community. It is considered community relations, and most store managers would concede that, in addition to bolstering the firm's public credibility, it probably brings in a few new customers and also helps cement the loyalty of some current customers. But there is no way of proving whether it pays off financially or not.

Consider here one of our values-centered companies—say Tom's of Maine. The company contributes to a variety of nonprofits. It is not unreasonable to believe that some people associated with these charities would, the next time they need toothpaste, pick up a tube of Tom's of Maine. But again, this is not the reason that the company supports these charities. If it were, Tom's would undoubtedly choose larger, more visible charities for maximum exposure. Or, take the Novica Foundation which enables customers to provide loans to struggling artists. This program could lead to future benefits for Novica's business, i.e., Novica as a company can potentially profit in the long run from more and better artists, and more loyal and involved customers. To the best of our knowledge, however, no one at Novica believes that this program will result in substantial profits. If the management team were focused on profits alone, it would certainly pursue other projects with stronger financial upsides.

Thirdly, a company's commitment to giving can help in attracting and retaining employees because they like being associated with an employer who has a socially responsible reputation. Some observers even believe that this association makes them more productive on the job. Timothy Haahs, for example, is sincere when he says that the secret to his architectural firm's success is its giving. We suspect that he is over-simplifying but he may also be on to something. Quite possibly the company's giving program has furnished him and his employees with the opportunity to think about the meaning of their work in a broader context and to realize that by providing superior results for their clients they are in a position to be a force for the greater good. After all, only the most hardened would see making money for the company's shareholder as the moral equivalent of supporting a noble cause.

Before moving on, we should mention here that some of our more jaded students have suggested that our values-centered firms, as well as other companies, donate to charitable causes because it saves on their taxes. It is true that donations reduce a firm's tax liability but that amount is always less than the amount of the donations. In other words, a charitable donation reduces the company's total taxable profit but the reduction in tax paid is always less than the size of the donation. How much the company's giving reduces its tax bill during any year depends on its marginal tax rate. Typically, companies realize about a 40 percent saving. Thus, although the tax deductible feature does make the giving more financially palatable and perhaps encourages a higher level of giving, it can never be the sole reason for making donations.

To sum up this chapter, even though there are a number of good business reasons for giving we do not naïvely believe that our firms engage in charitable giving because they expect a return on their "investment." The principal purpose of their giving is to contribute to society in still another way—i.e., in addition to superior products, happier employees, healthier environment, and so on. But at deeper level there is perhaps another factor in play. Giving seems to be a great source of personal satisfaction for our values-centered entrepreneurs. Tim Haahs even sees it as a source of spiritual fulfillment. In his words:

> . . . those who are simply striving after making as much money as possible. They will also never truly obtain what is most important . . . However, compare this with those who are seeking a greater purpose for their lives. They are the ones who will ultimately be the most satisfied in life . . .[19]

Chapter Takeaways

We cannot say that you will be more profitable if you follow these principles. But it's clear that many of our values-centered entrepreneurs follow them and it helps them have a fulfilling career:

- Make giving a priority and start early.
- Make giving an important function and institutionalize it within your company.
- Give substantially but also target your gifts for maximum impact.
- Encourage employees and customers to get involved.
- Giving makes you happy (and helps other feel happy as well).

12

Be a Role Model for Others

What I am trying to do [is] leave a legacy for . . . minority people . . . I've always considered
myself more than just a basketball player.

—Magic Johnson[1]

We are here to test and prove that the success of a for-profit company whose driving force
is to serve others can be equal to or greater than those companies whose driving force is to
maximize profits.

—Timothy Haahs, Timothy Haahs & Associates.[2]

Most entrepreneurs we have known over the years seem to enjoy sharing their war
stories. Perhaps it is because they felt lonely in their struggling days or because they
believe they have a lot to share with others. Most of them also seem to feel a special
bond to aspiring entrepreneurs and are usually more than willing to lend a hand.

Like most entrepreneurs, our values-centered entrepreneurs are enthusiastic about
sharing their business experiences with other practicing and aspiring entrepreneurs.
For many of them, however, sharing their experiences is not just something that is
enjoyable to do, but an important part of who they are and what they stand for. They
want their companies to be role models for others. They want other entrepreneurs
and mangers to follow and learn from what they do.

For example, Samuel Kaymen and Gary Hirshberg, founders of Stonyfield Farm,
wanted their company to be a corporate model for other small and large firms
to emulate. Tom Sineath and Eric Henry of T.S. Designs suggest that they are
not in the T-shirt business, but in the business of showing people the business
model of the future.[3] They want to teach other firms how to be greener, more sustainable, and more profitable. Ray Anderson of Interface Carpets is perhaps the
most grandiose in his vision. He asserts that the "fever for sustainable or responsible business practices," of which he is clearly a leader, would spread and change
capitalism itself.[4]

Given that being a role model is an important goal, our values-centered entrepreneurs work hard to be exemplary in their management practices. Then, they
willingly share their lessons and "secrets to success" with other entrepreneurs, small
and larger businesses, and even the general public. Many of our entrepreneurs form
consulting firms, take on mentees, and create or join consortiums to pass on the

knowledge. Some even write books, go on talk shows, and let the media cover their philosophies and business practices. Table 12.1 lists some of these commonly used methods by which our entrepreneurs attempt to serve as role models.

Share Your Secrets with Other Entrepreneurs

Most of our values-centered entrepreneurs, especially those that began their companies before the 1990s, had no choice but to invent their unconventional way of doing business on their own. There were no textbooks or guidelines on how to start or develop a socially responsible for-profit venture, certainly not 20 years ago. Neither were there existing business models available to imitate. Anita Roddick of The Body Shop recalled: "Because I was a historian, I was looking around for anybody, anybody, in any way back in history . . . that had a different perspective or language to business . . . but I found nothing."[5] Roddick and most of the entrepreneurs on our list, until recently, were unable to find business strategies to emulate or role models to follow.

Perhaps it's because they experienced the frustration of not having mentors and role models that so many of our values-centered entrepreneurs today welcome the opportunity to share their business experience and philosophy. No one feels the obligation to share and serve as a role model to others more than Tim Haahs of Timothy Haahs & Associates. While Haahs often talks about helping people, he is not just talking about people in need of health care, education, social, and other services—people whom he and his company are proactive about supporting. Haahs recognizes that his fellow entrepreneurs need help as well—in the form of purpose and direction. He feels, moreover, that his company has a special destiny in the world, to prove that "the success of a for-profit company whose driving force is to serve others can be equal to or greater than those companies whose driving force is to maximize profits."[6] He said the following to us in an interview:

> I do believe it is important to share our business model with other entrepreneurs. The way we do business, especially in regards to our mission and core values, is extremely unique. The effect that it has on the overall environment of our company, and the difference it has made in people's lives is extremely important. If other organizations can benefit from mirroring our model we encourage them to do so . . .
>
> Our mission and core values are an extremely important part of our company and the way we do business. We do promote our values widely so that we can try to serve as a model to others . . .[7]

Table 12.1 Common Methods of Being a Role Model

- Be truly exemplary.
- Share your "secrets to success" with other entrepreneurs, especially in your purpose and direction.
- Take on a mentee or two.
- Do interviews with the media.
- Write about yourself, e.g., an article or maybe even a book.

Haahs's desire to help other entrepreneurs build companies with a higher purpose has grown as requests to speak publicly about his business model have multiplied, and audiences have responded enthusiastically to his message. "People are just amazed when I tell them our financial status," he says. "They come up to me and say, 'I didn't know you could have a money-making, for-profit company with this type of mission statement. It's unheard of.' "[8]

Increasingly, business people around Philadelphia and around the U.S. want to know how they can do it like Timothy Haahs & Associates. Some ask if it is OK for them to see Haahs's mission statement. Haahs gladly tells them that his mission statement is not copyrighted and available for viewing on his website. "In fact," he once said, "my mission is partly to see other entrepreneurs adopt this kind of spirit in their firms."[9]

Yvon Chouinard of Patagonia was one of the early role models for aspiring socially orientated entrepreneurs. Chouinard has long believed that his greatest contribution to the world would not be the direct impacts of his business operation or its philanthropy, but rather its role as an example of how other businesses could be managed for the good of society. After all, the mission statement at Patagonia is "To use business to inspire and implement solutions to the environmental crisis." Chouinard, however, may not have fully comprehended the purpose of his business until he considered selling it. It was then that he came to the conclusion that, "the real good that Patagonia could do was to use the company as a tool for social change and a model to show others that a company can do well by taking the long view and doing the right thing."[10]

A sort of a godfather in the area of responsible entrepreneurship, the Patagonia founder has over the years taken the time to offer personal advice to other values-centered entrepreneurs. For instance, in 2000 when Gary Erickson and Kit Crawford of Clif Bar wondered whether or not to transition all their products to organic, they met with Yvon and Melinda Chouinard. Erickson recalls, "We went climbing in Yosemite and talked about whether to extend a brand of organic or convert all of our brands." After some discussion and listening to Chouinard's views, Erickson knew what he should do. "It was a pretty easy decision," Erickson added, "I want my company to be where theirs is when Clif Bar is 30 years old."[11] For Erickson, Patagonia under Chouinard's leadership was a superb role model for Clif Bar.

Like Chouinard and Haahs described above, Chris King of Chris King Precision Components feels a special obligation to be a role model to other companies—particularly to those in the manufacturing sector. When asked if he would like other companies to follow his business practices, he responded enthusiastically, "Absolutely, I would like other companies to learn what I do and emulate me."[12] Chris King Precision Components has been a leader in implementing environmentally sensitive and innovative manufacturing processes for the cycling industry, and other companies in the manufacturing sector have been taking note of its novel methods and unorthodox philosophy. The company has also been a living proof that one can manufacture products in the United States and still be profitable. Furthermore, King and his employees have been more than willing to share their story with others in the hope that it will make a difference. "We're proud of what

we've proven is possible," says Jason Houston, head of King's Group Vibe and Consciousness Program.

> We hope that by sharing what we've accomplished, we can inspire others to consider doing
> the same. The best thing that could happen would be that someone comes along, sees what
> we did, and completely outdoes us. We'd love to keep finding out that there is still so much
> more we can do, and then do it.[13]

Clearly, our values-centered companies do not try to hoard their innovative practices that they worked hard to develop. In fact, they share them with others without
reservation. They encourage their partners, unrelated firms, and even competitors to
copy their ideas and practices to the extent they are transferable.

Share Experiences with the Public

Gary Hirshberg, co-founder of Stonyfield Farms, seemed surprised to learn that
senior executives of Fortune 500 companies were interested in his management
practice. He once remarked, "I've been sitting in roundtables lately with CEOs of
some of the largest corporations in America. And these people spend most of their
time at these luncheons asking me questions about my little $30 million business."[14]
Clearly, mainstream businesspeople are curious about our values-centered companies. Moreover, as a result of the business scandals of the past decade there is little
doubt that interest in the topics of social responsibility and ethical behavior has
grown substantially in recent years.

Given the growing interest in this topic from corporate executives and the general
public, in addition to other entrepreneurs, many of our values-centered entrepreneurs have publicized their experiences through various websites, newspaper
articles, and other media outlets. They have willingly reached out to a larger audience,
beyond their employees and everyday customers. Some have allowed themselves to be
written up as business school case studies, e.g., Anita Roddick of The Body Shop,
Howard Schultz of Starbucks, Seth Goldman of Honest Tea, and Sarah Hoit of
Explore Inc. Others, including the founders of Ben & Jerry's, The Body Shop, Tom's of
Maine, Patagonia, Salesforce.com, Seventh Generation, and Starbucks have written
(in some cases, multiple) books about their business experiences and management
philosophy. Most recently, in 2008, Magic Johnson published a book titled *32 Ways
to Be a Champion in Business*. Marc Benioff, founder of Salesforce.com, has used
his writing aptitude to publish two popular books. His first book, in 2004, was
Compassionate Capitalism. The book offers a model as to how companies of all sizes
can leverage their employees, equity, products, and relationships to benefit the communities in which they operate and the company itself. Benioff followed in 2006 with
The Business of Changing the World which essentially is an expansion of the same
theory that the world can be materially benefited by the actions of corporations.

We should note here that our entrepreneurs' efforts in getting their stories out
undoubtedly had the positive side effect of strengthening public awareness of their
brands. Although this was not the main purpose in promoting their tales, it is, of

course, likely that these secondary benefits crossed the minds of our entrepreneurs. After all, they are triple bottom-line thinkers.

Broad Air Conditioning occupies a unique position—a green company in China that makes products innovative enough to compete with U.S. companies. Co-founder Zhang Yue's outgoing demeanor does more than influence employee values at Broad; he utilizes his unique skills to also influence the Chinese government, the U.S., and beyond. By attending environmental conferences, delivering lectures, and writing essays, Zhang Yue has become an internationally renowned social entrepreneur. Most recently, he served as a co-chairman of the Sustainable Buildings and Construction Initiative (SBCI), a part of the United Nations' Environment Program.[15] The SBCI's objectives are to develop methods for constructing and demolishing buildings in a sustainable manner.

Timothy Haahs of Timothy Haahs and Associates says that he hopes to take his "business evangelism" to another level. He wants to share his ideas with a wider audience, and devote more time to helping entrepreneurs build their businesses based on the premise that success is about more than just the bottom-line. Like some of our other entrepreneurs, Haahs plans to write a book and even start an organization of some kind. "It came to me," he recalls, "that I want to write a book about leadership based on community-oriented entrepreneurship and pull back from work to travel around the country to speak about it. Maybe even create an association of like-minded entrepreneurs."[16]

Aveda, the prominent skin care company whose mission includes environmental leadership, publishes an annual Coalition of Environmentally Responsible Economies (CERES) report outlining its environmental goals, achievements, shortcomings, and projects for further improvement. Obviously, no one twists the firm's arm to write about its environmental efforts and challenges. Aveda stated in its 2005 CERES report that it publishes its continuous improvement efforts to "inspire others."[17]

Pacific Community Ventures (PCV), a socially responsible private equity company, has received renewed recognition in the investment community, after it successfully raised its third private equity fund in 2008. The initial skepticism surrounding its viability has increasingly turned into cautious admiration as well as curiosity as to how the company manages to balance serving communities and turning a profit. To help answer this question, the firm annually produces a "Social Return Executive Summary," which is a detailed report illustrating the relationships between the financial success of its portfolio companies and the betterment of the California communities where they are situated as well as the state as a whole. Increasingly being seen as a legitimate model, PCV (along with a couple of other socially responsible funds) has a chance of being a role model in the private equity industry in the same way as Calvert has been a role model in the mutual fund sector.

Issuing a report or publishing a book are not the only ways to gain visibility. The mainstream media frequently plays a big role in creating recognition for our responsible companies. The recent popularity of rankings offers salient examples. Calvert, for instance, has much benefited from its perennial spot on the "100 Best Companies in America for Working Mothers." This award is particularly noteworthy because Calvert is in the financial services industry, known for being hypercompetitive and unfriendly to women. Calvert has scored in the near top of its class in the categories: pay scale, opportunities for advancement, support for childcare, and the availability of family-friendly benefits. As a shareholder activist, Calvert does not just talk about what its portfolio companies should do, but serves as a true role model for them. Similarly, Starbucks and Whole Foods are consistently ranked in *Fortune* as being among the best companies to work for. Impressively, Whole Foods has been recognized by *Fortune* as one of the "100 Best Companies to Work For" for eleven consecutive years (1998–2008) ever since the rankings began. Whole Foods in addition to being lionized for its employee-friendly policies is also well-known for its pro-environment programs and practices. Like others in our sample, it's a triple bottom-line exemplar.

Finally, we as authors should recognize the enthusiastic support we received from the entrepreneurs and companies that we approached for help with the book. Without exception, they were eager to share information with us—for which we are most grateful.

Inspire Other Firms to Be Responsible

Our values-centered companies' efforts to be role models may be working. There are several clear cases of companies that have been inspired by the example of our torchbearers. Take New Belgium Brewery for instance. While New Belgium is well known for its award-winning beer, at the core of its mission is the charge to serve as a role model in the business world. And, this seems to be happening. Specifically, at least two breweries have followed in New Belgium's footsteps by converting entirely to wind power. Both New York-based Brooklyn Brewery and Utah's Uinta Brewing Co. have made the switch to wind power and cited New Belgium's commitment as a source of inspiration.[18] Co-owner and chief branding officer Kim Jordan of New Belgium, whose mission statement is "to operate a profitable company which is socially, ethically and environmentally responsible, that produces high quality beer true to Belgian brewing styles," is not surprised about its success as an inspirational role model.[19] She explains: "We've had core values and beliefs as a company before we ever made any beer."[20] As New Belgium Brewery expands its distribution network nationwide, it hopes to also extend its moral influence in the industry.

It is rumored that Salesforce.com's 1/1/1 (i.e., giving 1 percent of time, product, and equity) giving model has influenced at least one notable convert, Google. Just as Salesforce.com vested its foundation with 1 percent of the firms equity, Google (in typical not-to-be-outdone Googlistic fashion) took the value of 10 percent of the 3 million shares from Google's initial public stock offering and used those funds to establish the tax-exempt Google Foundation.[21,22]

Perhaps as a sign of ultimate flattery, there are companies that have not only imitated some of the management practices of our values-centered firms, but also have copied their core business models. For example, since Calvert pioneered the concept of socially responsible investing (SRI) in 1976, numerous other firms have followed suit. A relatively large number of socially responsible mutual funds have been formed over the last 30 years, including Citizen's Funds, GAMCO Asset Management, Inc., Legg Mason Investment Counsel, Parnassus Investments, and Sierra Club Mutual Funds, among others. Companies in the private equity industry have also followed and created socially responsible funds, some of which include Boston Community Capital, Investors' Circle, and our Pacific Community Ventures. In total, Social Investment Forum's 2005 Report on Socially Responsible Investing Trends identified $2.29 trillion in total assets under management using one or more of the three core socially responsible investing strategies—screening, shareholder advocacy, and community investing.[23]

In terms of advocacy, Calvert furnishes a dramatic example of industry social leadership. In 1982, in protest against apartheid, Calvert Social Investment Fund (CSIF) was the first U.S. mutual fund to prohibit investment in companies doing business in South Africa. By banning investment, Calvert helped heighten public awareness of apartheid and focused attention on divestment as a form of political and economic pressure to end the repression and injustice. Other funds and companies followed Calvert's lead and a massive divestment movement began that eventually helped bring down apartheid.

After Nelson Mandela praised the role of economic sanctions in isolating the apartheid regime and called for its end in 1993, Calvert was the first U.S. SRI firm to lift its South African investment ban. At the same time, Calvert called on companies that continued to operate in or had returned to South Africa to make positive contributions—with special attention to the country's need for jobs, skills training, support for black-owned business, housing, and equal rights in the workplace. In more recent years, Calvert has begun a similar campaign to support a free and peaceful Sudan. Calvert has partnered with the United Nations in an advisory role that has focused on utilizing the company's expertise to create a Sudanese divestiture initiative. Clearly, standing up for human rights is inherent in the firm's philosophy. Through its shareholder activism, investment criteria, internal corporate policies, and philanthropic programs, Calvert has inspired other firms to act.

Patagonia's CEO, Yvon Chouinard, not only has pioneered the practice of systematic company giving to charities, he has inspired hundreds of businesses to follow. Dedicated to the notion of sustained giving, Chouinard in 2002 co-founded (with Craig Mathews, owner of the Blue Ribbon Flies company) an alliance called 1% For the Planet which solicits other companies to pledge 1 percent of their yearly sales to non-profit environmental organizations. Remarkably, the alliance's membership has grown rapidly since 2002 to over 1,100 businesses in 37 countries. As of 2008, the members had contributed over $42 million to environmental groups.[24]

Perhaps the most inspirational and influential role model of all is Muhammad Yunus, founder of Grameen Bank. This selfless academic started lending his personal money to poor women in his locality out of his desire to help "just one person for one day."[25] Because of the difficulty of working with established banks in his native Bangladesh, Yunus eventually formed Grameen Bank with the mission of lending to the poor. It turned out that over 95 percent of the loans went to indigent women to start diminutive enterprises such as making and selling baskets. Yunus's unconventional business model, now known as microfinancing, became a huge success. To understand the magnitude of Grameen's success, consider some of the numbers below (as of March 2009).[26]

- 7.75 million total borrowers, 97 percent of whom have been women.
- 2,545 branches covering 83,967 villages.
- U.S.$7.78 billion dispersed to borrowers, out of which U.S.$6.91 billion has already been repaid.
- Disbursed U.S.$951.48 million during the previous 12 months alone (from March 2008 to February 2009).
- 97.93 percent loan recovery rate.

Inspired by Yunus's success, people all around the world have followed in his footsteps pursuing similar approaches in their own communities and countries. Today, there are microfinance institutions in more than 100 countries around the world.[27] No other social venture we know of has been replicated to this extent and no other values-centered entrepreneur is so widely admired.

During the first twenty years, neither Muhammad Yunus nor Grameen Bank received much recognition (although some, including former U.S. President Bill Clinton were early fans). Yunus, however, has received significant and deserved accolades in recent years. For his work with the Grameen Bank, he was named an Ashoka Global Academy Member in 2001.[28] In 2006, Yunus and Grameen Bank were jointly awarded what Yunus called "the most coveted award"—the Nobel Peace Prize, "for their efforts to create economic and social development from below."[29] He also has won a number of other awards, including the Ramon Magsaysay Award, the World Food Prize, the Sydney Prize, and the Ecuadorian Peace Prize. He was invited and gave commencement addresses at MIT in June 2008 and Oxford University in December 2008, and has been awarded 26 honorary doctorate degrees.[30] He welcomes all such honors because he sees them as a platform to spread his message of eradicating poverty.

In recent years, he has published two noteworthy books, *Banker to the Poor* and *A World Without Poverty: Social Business and the Future of Capitalism* in order to share his passion and model for reducing poverty. Yunus has also become more vocal on the world stage, as one of the founding members of Global Elders and as a director of the United Nations Foundation. Despite Yunus's success, people who encounter him are often touched by his humility as well as his out-of-box ideas. People are surprised to discover that he never sought wealth for himself, witnessed by the fact that he turned Grameen Bank into a cooperative and made himself an employee with a modest annual salary. Entrepreneurs around the world interested in replicating the Yunus business strategy can't help but also be inspired by the person.

Indeed, the success of the Grameen paradigm, i.e., providing financial services to poor or low-income clients, has sparked similar efforts in numerous countries throughout the developing world and even in some industrialized nations, including the United States (there is now a Grameen branch in New York) and Great Britain. Microfinancing has become a popular international movement, widely acknowledged as a potential tool in reducing or eradicating poverty. Today, microlending is offered by a broad genre of organizations including informal financial service providers, membership organizations (e.g., credit unions), NGOs, and even major formal financial institutions such as Citibank. According to the *MicroBanking Bulletin*, by 2006, there were 704 microfinance institutions (MIFs) that were serving 52 million borrowers ($23.3 billion in outstanding loans) and 56 million savers ($15.4 billion in deposits). Of these clients, 70 percent were in Asia, 20 percent in Latin America, and the balance spread through the rest of the world.[31] By 2004, researchers estimated that more than 3,000 institutions were serving approximately 665 million customers who were poorer than those who were served by the commercial banks.[32] Clearly, Yunus has had an immense impact in the world of finance as well as on the world of poverty.

Chapter Takeaways

Our values-centered entrepreneurs attempt to serve as role models to other companies in their respective industries and beyond. Specifically, they would suggest:

- Mentor other entrepreneurs.
- Share your experiences and practices with other companies and the general public.
- Encourage other companies to emulate your goals, policies, and even your business model.
- Inspire other firms to change their business practices in meaningful ways.

13
Concluding Thoughts

When you have this type of company, you have to be selfless.
—Julie Lewis, founder of Deja Shoe, Inc.[1]

We launched this study to explore what is unique, different, interesting, and special about a growing class of entrepreneurs and their companies that we designated as values-centered. Most of the world calls them social entrepreneurs but we chose a different appellation because we wanted to distinguish clearly between social entrepreneurs who found for-profit enterprises from those who build not-for-profit enterprises. We identified 46 such entrepreneurial firms that we felt met our rather loose criteria and also were engaging or interesting. We studied them in depth, some in more depth than others, and distilled ten commonalities that we called principles or guidelines. Not all of our firms exhibited all of these principles but the majority of the firms displayed the majority of them. Our thought was that these guidelines could provide a helpful framework for budding values-centered entrepreneurs.

In reviewing our study we realized that there was one overarching commonality inherent in the very nature of our firms and actions of their founders and managers that we need to emphasize. This is the notion that there must be a shrewd balance between environment/social mission and sound business strategy. We didn't include it explicitly in our guidelines because it's really a summary point or, better, a general paradigm. It could be added as an admonishment following each of our guidelines: "but, be sure to take into account maintaining a balance between mission and running a profitable business." It is, in essence, the definition of a values-centered firm. The company must generate sufficient cash flow and profit if it is to fulfill its mission.

The business landscape is littered with unrealistic entrepreneurs who have gone out of business. There is no specific data on this point but it is well known that over 50 percent of new ventures fail within five years. Hence, we think it safe to assume that values-centered ventures also fail at least at this rate and possibly a higher rate (because of the extra demands and the tendency to focus on mission to the detriment of profit). As with any venture, values-centered ones fail for two principal reasons: (1) a flawed business concept, and (2) poor execution. No noble mission will prevent a business with a series of missteps from failing. Consider two examples that we are familiar with.

Deja Shoe

Deja Shoe, Inc. was founded in the early 1990s by Julie Lewis and two former Avia (a large athletic shoe company) executives, Bruce MacGregor and Scott Taylor. Julie, an avid environmentalist, was intent on establishing a sustainable shoe company. She enlisted MacGregor and Taylor to help her with the business side of the venture. The original strategy was to produce casual shoes from recycled or sustainably harvested materials, a first in the footwear industry. The new materials were to be procured where they could be found, manufactured into footwear components principally in developed countries, and then shipped to Asia for low-cost assembly. Once the shoes were put together, they would be shipped to the United States, the principal market.

Part of the original plan was to market the sustainable footwear through "green" outlets; however, with the help of unexpected high-profile media exposure, large retailers such as LL Bean, REI, Nordstrom, and Bloomingdales wanted to carry Deja's initial product line. Seduced by the attention, the company decided to quickly shift gears and go for a big introduction in the mainstream market. To finance the venture, Deja was able to secure equity funding in the amount of $2.5 million from three venture capital firms.

Unfortunately, sales of Deja's initial line in March 1993 were very disappointing especially in the big stores. These retailers quickly shifted their promotions to other products. Deja's management believed that the key reason for the poor showing was that the firm had to switch from using recycled material (which proved to be defective) to a canvas material made from eco-fiber late in the design phase.[2] The eco-fiber clearly was not as environmentally exciting or imaginative as making shoes out of recycled baby diapers—the founders' initial ideas for material. Further, because of its high-cost operation, the company was forced to price its canvas shoes twenty to thirty dollars above competitors' canvas shoes.

Deja's management reacted to the setback by raising a second round of equity (and then a third and fourth round) to design and bring out a new line featuring principally sustainably harvested vegetal leather from the Amazon rainforest. Sales of the new line in fall of 1995 were higher than the 1993 line and management was encouraged. But cash flow was still insufficient to sustain the fledgling company through the year. Hence, Deja once again went back to its investors for additional funding. This time, one of the venture capital firms refused and the company was forced to look elsewhere for the money required to continue operations. In mid-1995, unable to secure the needed funding, Deja Shoe, Inc. voluntarily liquidated assets to satisfy its creditors.[3]

Monday morning quarterbacking suggests that Deja made a series of missteps in its business judgment. Among others, it tried to do too much too fast. Because of the decision to target the mainstream market combined with pressure from the venture capitalists to meet projected targets, the company was forced to bring out products before they were perfected. Combine these pressures with the steep learning curve Deja faced because of its sustainability focus and dedication to using strictly eco-friendly materials, and the odds were just overwhelming against survival.

In the final analysis, Julie Lewis's enthusiasm for making a profound and immediate sustainable impact blinded her and the other executives to the necessity of balancing the quest for sustainability with sound business judgment required to run a successful firm. It should also be noted that Deja might have done better if its management had been more cautious with fundraising and more patient with its growth objectives as suggested in this book.

Just Desserts

Our second example is Just Desserts, a once iconic San Francisco-based bakery products firm. Just Desserts was founded in 1974 by the husband and wife team of Elliot Hoffman and Gail Horvath. The couple started by supplying Bay Area restaurants with desserts and invested the profits in establishing retail stores. The first store was opened in late 1974. The basic business model was to fashion a chain of bakeries/coffee shops that specialized in desserts and would become neighborhood hangouts. The company's several bakery products were 100 percent natural; there were no artificial ingredients. The concept took off and over the next quarter century, the company grew to $12 million and encompassed ten bakeries and a production facility employing 140 people at its peak.[4]

In 1986, Elliot won the Small Business Administration's "top award as California's small business person of the year for his $6 million-a-year operation." Subsequent to receiving the award, he gained considerable recognition in the Bay area and started devoting some of his time to speaking engagements. During one of these talks, he met Catherine Sneed, a counselor at San Francisco County Jail. Sneed had developed a program using gardening as a rehabilitation technique for prison inmates (the metaphor was that inmates would nurture life instead of destroying it). Elliot became intrigued with the concept and set upon extending it. He bought a plot of land close to Just Desserts' production facility where recently released inmates, homeless and other troubled souls would grow fruits and vegetables to be sold to his bakery as ingredients for its products. He also provided the "students" (his term for the participants) with counseling on practical matters such as how to open a bank account and the importance of regularly coming to their jobs.[5]

Elliot became enthralled with the project and progressively spent more and more time in the garden and consequently less time at the company. The garden project led to other projects such as a City of San Francisco tree planting program that was subcontracted to his garden workers.

Passionate about the need to create social change and convinced that he could make a difference, he parlayed his garden project into a local school program. At one point, after months of planning, he and a group of some 800 volunteers, including high-level corporate executives, "descended upon an elementary school located in a disadvantaged neighborhood near the bakery, armed with $280,000 worth of donated supplies. They built gardens, retaining walls, and automatic watering systems; upgraded the laboratory and gym facilities."[6] As a result of Elliot's social activism, Just Desserts earned an amazing amount of free press which undoubtedly boosted company sales.

It was during the 1990s when Elliot was becoming increasingly socially active that Starbucks and other coffee shops were rapidly expanding in every major city in North America including San Francisco. Elliot and Gail perceived this trend as a major threat to their business because these competitors could readily sell complementary products such as cakes and cookies. The couple hastily altered Just Desserts' strategy in response. They shifted emphasis from retail to wholesale, securing local accounts with chains such as Whole Foods, Costco, and yes, even Starbucks. By 2000, the company had reached a tipping point. Elliot and Gail wanted Just Desserts to become a national distributor but realized that this would require a much larger production facility. Because real estate prices in San Francisco were obscenely high, the owners decided to move to East Oakland where jobs were badly needed and the City Council had offered the company a $1.5 million loan. To build its larger, more modern facility, the company had to take on an additional $12 million in loans. This move was a huge leap for Elliot and Gail because they had always relied on internally generated capital for growth.

Just Desserts moved to its new facility in August of 2001. Unhappily, this was not the best of times for expansion and taking on debt. With the burst of the dot-com bubble, the economy was contracting and the September 11 terrorist attack exacerbated the downturn. The company's wholesaler clients responded understandably by reducing their inventories of baked goods.

Just Desserts, to raise cash, sold its retail stores and persuaded the Oakland City Council to forgive one half of its $1.5 million loan. The company also approached Dawn Foods with a proposal to sell its wholesale business. The discussions had dragged on for almost nine months when the large international bakery supplier decided to back away from the potential deal. This was the final blow. Just Desserts filed for bankruptcy in July 2003.[7]

Was the collapse of Just Desserts simply a case of a small business with aspirations of becoming a large wholesaler of bakery products being a victim of bad timing and bad luck? Perhaps! Seldom can even great strategies overcome bad timing and bad luck. But one can speculate that had the company decided to expand four or five years earlier, it would have been in a much stronger position to weather the recession. Alternatively, the business might have been better served by a strategy built around strengthening the company's established brand image as a bakery/coffee house, e.g., by redesigning its retail facilities and strengthening its menus. If Elliot had better balanced his enthusiasm for social causes with his commitment to the business, would Just Desserts' fate have been different? No one can say for sure. But certainly, the odds for survival would have been higher.

We salute those who have tried and failed. There is nothing shameful or humiliating about an entrepreneur who envisions serving a cause and comes up a little short. Failure is an essential, albeit distasteful, element of the market system.

Additionally, we salute those values-centered entrepreneurs who have demonstrated that our economic system can be used successfully for purposes other than simply enriching those who have power. Given the recent financial meltdown and the headlines of excessive greed and arrogance on Wall Street and elsewhere in the business system, many people feel disillusioned and even betrayed. We need people like

Timothy Haahs, Yvon Chouinard, and Tom Chappell to show the world that our capitalist system is broad enough to accommodate goals other than just economic ones. Our market system clearly has flaws. As Muhammad Yunus has reminded us, capitalism has not worked out very well for the vast majority of the world's population. Furthermore, it is well known that the market system does not account for the environmental externalities that in the aggregate are resulting in perilously declining ecosystems throughout the world.

Values-centered entrepreneurs try to make the world better in some small, limited, but significant way. They shine through the avarice that, correctly or incorrectly, colors the prevailing image of our free enterprise system. As business school professors we are encountering more business students than ever who are highly interested in corporate social responsibility and social entrepreneurship. We hope this trend will grow and that values-centered entrepreneurship will be an important part of it. We trust that our findings will offer helpful guidelines for the reader who aspires to participate in this movement. And, we look forward to some of the readers building the type of business organizations that we will want to write about in the future.

Part 3
Case Studies

Case Study 1

Gottlieb Duttweiler and Migros*

> It's where I buy my food and everything I need to survive. I like how they set up their shops, I like their products, I like that they have cheap stuff for poor people and luxurious things for the rich. They need not to sell alcohol and tobacco and they support cultural and social institutions with a certain amount of their profit. Bravo Mr. Duttweiler.
> —Tanja Burgdorfer, a Migros customer[1]

Gottlieb Duttweiler was one of the world's first values-centered entrepreneurs. He launched a small grocery business, which he named Migros, in Zurich in 1925. It was founded with the idea that he wanted to "give back" to the people of Switzerland. Today Migros is Switzerland's largest supermarket chain as well as its largest employer (approximately 81,000 employees). Moreover, it is also viewed by many as an important Swiss "social institution."[2]

Duttweiler's original business model was to sell six basic foodstuffs out of five converted Ford trucks, making regular stops on the streets of Zurich. Because of this low-cost distribution system and his willingness to accept low gross margins, he was able to price these staples 20 percent to 40 percent below the prevailing retail price. Many Zurich housewives readily accepted this novel concept and Migros grew rapidly. Within a month of start-up, Duttweiler purchased and converted another four trucks to "stores-on-wheels" as they came to be known. He opened his first permanent store in Zurich in 1927. During the next three years, his stores-on-wheels established themselves in Bern, Basel, and St. Gallen, and several more permanent stores were opened in Zurich. Furthermore, the original six-item product line had expanded manifold.

At first, competitors paid little attention to Migros but the company's accelerated growth soon was perceived as a genuine threat by the grocery establishment, and the response was aggressive. Customers and employees were insulted, threatened, and even physically attacked. Newspapers were pressured not to accept Migros ads and manufacturers of nationally advertised brands were forced to boycott Migros. In response, Duttweiler started his own manufacturing plants producing his own private brands. Competitors retaliated with drastic price reductions on items carried by Migros but Duttweiler countered by broadening his product line and further expanding geographically.

By 1933, Migros had made major inroads in the Swiss grocery industry. It had grown to 100 permanent stores and 45 stores-on-wheels. In a desperate effort to halt

* Much of the information in this case is taken from E. Gray, "Gottlieb Duttweiler and the Perpetuation of Social Values at Migros," *Journal of Business Leadership* 6, 2 (Fall/Winter 1993): 51–62.

Migros's alarming growth, its competitors organized themselves politically and pushed through the Swiss Parliament an "emergency ordinance" prohibiting expansion by chain and department stores, including the broadening of their product lines. This blatantly anti-Migros measure effectively arrested the firm's precipitous growth and led Duttweiler to make two critical decisions. One was to diversify into travel and tourism. It was the depression era in Europe and many Swiss hotels were hurting badly. Duttweiler, seizing the opportunity, signed up a series of hotels in a plan to offer cheap vacations. For example, his "Hotelplan" offered an eight-day, all-expense holiday for as little as $45. These vacation tours caught on and today the Migros travel company is the second largest in Switzerland.

Duttweiler's second critical decision was to personally enter politics. In 1935, he and six cohorts were elected to the National Council and became the core of a new political party known as the "Ring of Independents."

In 1941, during the early days of World War II, Duttweiler made his most defining decision. He converted Migros into a cooperative or, as he put it, he "gave the company to its customers." The structure of the new cooperative was patterned after the Swiss national government. There was a central organization called the Federation of Migros Cooperatives (FMC) which managed centralized functions such as manufacturing, central purchasing, business diversification, and policy coordination. There were also several regional cooperatives (presently there are 10) which ran the company's retail operations. Formal authority in the new organization flowed from the members (customers) to the regional cooperatives to the FMC.

In relinquishing his ownership of Migros and then turning his estate outside of Zurich into an amusement park, Duttweiler sacrificed about $3.75 million of his personal fortune, keeping for himself only $250,000. He, after the reorganization, stayed on as Chairman of the FMC Board of Directors at a salary of $9,000 a year. In 1951, he stopped taking this salary.[3]

At the end of the war, in 1945, using his political influence, Duttweiler was successful in getting the ordinance prohibiting retail expansion lifted, and Migros forthwith resumed its dynamic growth. In the early 1950s, the company introduced supermarkets to Switzerland, and in 1970 it opened the first of what would be many Super Migros Markets. These stores were larger than the traditional supermarkets and carried clothing and other non-traditional products, and frequently anchored shopping centers that included a number of independent stores. The company also diversified into a variety of other businesses and developed additional manufacturing capacity.

Today, with revenues in excess of $16.4 billion, Migros is one of the largest business organizations in the world, ranking 451 on the 2007 Fortune Global 500. The company not only controls over 25 percent of the food market in Switzerland but also is highly diversified into such businesses as travel, restaurants, banking, furniture stores, gasoline stations, and international language schools. Additionally, it is an important contributor to Swiss culture and society. Although Gottlieb Duttweiler died in 1962 his business philosophy and the corporate culture that he embedded at Migros has endured.

Duttweiler's Philosophy

Gottlieb Duttweiler was truly an entrepreneur/philosopher. He was a man of action but also a man of contemplation who thought deeply about the place of business in society. He used the term "social capital" to capture his concept of the ideal economic order which was a free market coupled with a high degree of social responsibility for capital. He established his company in the 1920s when the world was torn between the competing ideologies of capitalism and socialism. He clearly understood the advantages of a self-regulating market economy over a state-run economy where individual freedom is necessarily limited. But he also recognized the dangers of an economic system based on the unfettered power of capital exercised by private individuals. He envisioned social capital, where management has an equal obligation to both the economic and the social needs of society, as a middle and desirable track between capitalism and socialism.

Duttweiler's socio-economic philosophy and personal values were operationalized at Migros through strict adherence to two strategic goals: (1) providing economic value for its customers and (2) responding to the cultural and social needs of Switzerland. The first goal, providing customer value, has been the focus of Migros's business strategy since its inception. The firm gained a "toe hold" in the retail food market by offering consumers budget-priced grocery staples. Indeed, Duttweiler concocted the hybrid name, Migros, to communicate the notion of being halfway between wholesale and retail. It would be a mistake, however, to perceive Migros as merely a discount operation. At its very core, the company seeks to provide value for its customers. It strives to have the same quality as national brands but at a significantly lower price. To illustrate, Migros currently sells a line of fashion watches, called M-Watches, which are patterned after the high-profile Swatch line. The M-Watches, which have become quite popular, sell at approximately 20 percent below Swatches and by all accounts are of equal quality. Quality is clearly an important value in Switzerland and Migros's success can be traced to the simple fact that it is seen as offering quality for less. The company's reputation, moreover, transcends national boundaries. Many German, French, and Italians are known to cross into Switzerland to shop at Migros markets.

Although Duttweiler saw raising the value quotient as an important way to give back to the Swiss people, he also believed in investing directly in the cultural and social infrastructure of the nation (the second strategic goal). Early on, as part of the statutes governing the organization, a "cultural percentage" was established. Under this covenant, the regional cooperatives were pledged to contribute at least one half of 1 percent of their gross retail sales for cultural, social, and political policy purposes. Similarly, the FMC was pledged to contribute 1 percent of its turnover for these purposes. Since the enactment of the cultural percentage, contributions have increased almost every year and in 2006 were over $98 million. A principal use of these funds is for the Migros Club Schools which are subsidized schools run by the several regional cooperatives and collectively represent the largest adult education program in Switzerland. Today, some 600 different courses are offered in languages, general education, artistic skills and handcraft, social skills, and professional training. The company also sponsors a large number of cultural events such as concerts, ballets, and art exhibits. Additional funds are also contributed for the development of Swiss artists and art. A recent example is the introduction of a private record label, Musiques Suisses, which features little-known works of Swiss music.

In the social sphere, Migros runs internal programs for senior citizens, the handi-capped, remote mountain communities, and even under-developed countries. It also makes contributions to a variety of charities. But interestingly, in accordance with Duttweiler's preferences, historically only about 8 percent of the cultural percentage has been spent for social purposes whereas almost 80 percent went to the cultural area (with the remainder going toward political causes and overhead). Duttweiler gave priority to cultural programs because they were not being supported by the Swiss government whereas the government provided many social services. He also felt that cultural activities would touch a much wider spectrum of Swiss society than would targeted social programs.

In addition to the prominence of its cultural and social activities, Migros, perpetu-ating Duttweiler's philosophy of social capital, has became an environmental leader in Europe. It was one of the first European companies to eliminate CFCs in aerosols, switch to vehicles with catalytic converters, reduce the use of PVCs in packaging, and significantly increase the efficiency of its water and electricity usage. More recently, with the concern for sustainable development, the company has converted much of its furniture line to Forest Stewardship Council (FSC) certified wood. It is also offer-ing more "fair traded" grocery items in its supermarkets and is now marketing the world's first "fair traded" biofuel (grown in an environmentally sustainable manner with a fair price to the farmer).[4] Migros's environmental programs and activities are not funded through the cultural percentage but, rather, through the company's regular business accounts.

Case Study 2
Stonyfield Farm*

Milking organics to reset agriculture, change diets, and save the world: A yogurt-maker's mission to grow a business culture of doing well by doing good.

> The question we asked ourselves when we started the company was: Is it possible to create a business that could help be part of the solutions to our planet's ecological challenges while also making money? The answer today is a resounding yes.[1]
>
> —Gary Hirshberg, CE-Yo of Stonyfield Farm

> The best thing a man can do for his culture when he is rich is to endeavor to carry out those schemes which he entertained when he was poor.[2]
>
> —Henry David Thoreau

Stonyfield Farm, presently a subsidiary of French food products conglomerate, Groupe Danone, is the world's largest producer and marketer of organic yogurt. With sales reaching $320 million and a consistent annual growth rate of over 20 percent since 1983, Stonyfield has been a remarkable success story in one of the fastest growing segments of the food industry.[3] In order to achieve such success, the company has had to undergo considerable change since its inception. Stonyfield has attempted to stay true to its roots of environmental and social responsibility, but growing from a non-profit single-family farm to a multi-million-dollar subsidiary of a multinational company has required certain sacrifices. Indeed, the company's dilemma is telling of the organic food industry as a whole: As it grows from a cottage industry to big business, it has the opportunity to spread its chemical-free gospel to an enormous audience—but whether it can operate on a global scale without compromising core values or causing unintended damage remains to be seen.

History

When Samuel Kaymen founded Stonyfield Farm in 1983 he did not set out to create a multi-million-dollar yogurt company. Initially, he set about creating small batches of

* This case was prepared by Trevor Zink under the direction of Professor Edmund Gray, Loyola Marymount University.

yogurt from his grandmother's Ukrainian recipe in order to fund his true passion—a non-profit organization called The Rural Education Center (TREC), committed to educating farmers and the general public on the merits and techniques of organic farming. Milking a small number of Jersey cows by hand to create an all-natural yogurt that he and his family sold to local markets, Kaymen showed by example what he taught through TREC.

A year before starting the company, Kaymen invited Gary Hirshberg, a staunch environmentalist who had long been involved in organic agriculture through his own nonprofit, to serve on the TREC board of trustees. Hirshberg had aspirations to spread environmental awareness through a profitable business, and agreed to work with Kaymen on the Stonyfield project. Both men were committed to socially responsive management practices, believing that business could help solve the problems plaguing society. Kaymen, an engineer by training, assumed product and production responsibilities, while Hirshberg headed the business operations. After accepting the position of president and chief executive director (now officially referred to as the CE-Yo), Hirshberg wrote a business plan that secured $35,000 in loans and allowed the company to sell 150 cases of yogurt for $56,000 the first year.[4]

The company's original business plan was to produce yogurt from milk purchased from local dairies as well as from on-site production. The company would pay the dairy farmers a small premium to help support the added expense of producing milk without employing hormones, chemical fertilizers, or pesticides. The plan also included the future purchase of additional cows from small farmers for expanded on-site production.

The early years were difficult. As Hirshberg's wife, Meg, recalls, "Most of our victories were merely disasters averted . . . We lost money on each cup sold."[5] The two men handled all facets of the business, including milking cows, delivering yogurt, stocking shelves, repairing equipment, and developing new products. After the first year, because the on-site milking operation was consuming too much of their time, the partners decided to sell their cows back to local farmers. Through the hardship, Kaymen and Hirshberg remained totally committed to making the company a success. Even when Kaymen fell sick and was briefly hospitalized (likely the result of being overworked), he continued to work from his hospital bed.[6]

The company scraped by through the start-up years and by 1986 was selling six flavors of yogurt for $658,000 annually. To handle its growing sales volume, the partners began looking for additional capital to expand and improve the manufacturing facility. An initial attempt to partner with a packaging company fell through when the packaging company unexpectedly fell into bankruptcy. Scrambling to save assets from repossession, Kaymen and Hirshberg spent over $400,000 of personal funds to restart production. Despite their efforts, the company still incurred a weekly loss of $30,000 for 10 weeks.[7] By early 1988, the need for new capital became critical; between this and other financial difficulties, the company had incurred a $1.4 million loss.[8] At first, the partners looked desperately for investors but had little success; as Kaymen mused, "Anyone in a necktie was fair game."[9] Subsequently, they decided to seek out a manufacturing partner. They found a potential partner in a Vermont dairy farm, but walked away from the deal when they discovered that the manufacturer was demanding nearly 100 percent of the company. By turning to their friends and family, as well as securing a loan from the U.S. Small Business Administration, the partners were eventually able to raise $2.1 million for the construction of their new plant.[10]

In 1989, Stonyfield moved 30 miles to its new manufacturing facility in Londonderry, New Hampshire. This 21,000 square-foot facility, named the Londonderry Yogurt Works Plant, was specifically designed for the company's needs and allowed it to achieve annual sales of approximately $4 million by producing 25 products in a dozen flavors.[11] However, the firm had yet to return a profit.[12]

With the move to the new plant, Stonyfield's financial situation began to improve. In response to competition over grocery store shelf space but with no funds for major commercial advertising campaigns, the company resorted to guerilla marketing tactics. The founders provided free product samples at grocery stores, and even admit to "sneaking yogurt cups into unsuspecting shoppers' carts as a marketing strategy."[13] In a clever ploy on his 30th birthday, Hirshberg requested that his friends go to the largest Whole Foods supermarket in Cambridge, Massachusetts and request Stonyfield yogurt. A week later, the store called and placed a substantial order with the company. Other promotional gambits included teaming up with vendors such as Rebecca's Café in Boston. This upscale eatery offered a free scoop of Stonyfield frozen yogurt on any dessert purchased. The café realized a 15 percent increase in dessert orders and Stonyfield gained additional market exposure.[14]

The company's continued efforts with innovative marketing strategies met with surprising results. Ten years after its inception, the company had grown to 85 employees and its sales had reached $18 million. By 1994, the company realized $22 million in sales.[15] Early that year, Stonyfield representatives arrived at the NBC "Today" show, gave away yogurt cups, and received a free on-air plug. Hirshberg even began using business cards with a 25¢ coupon on the back.[16]

In 1998, the company gave away 6.3 million cups of yogurt, continuing its crusade of turning people into yogurt eaters,[17] contributing to annual sales over $40 million.[18] Also in 1998, a major expansion of the Londonderry plant was completed. The revamped facility tripled the company's yogurt-making capacity so that by 2000, Stonyfield was producing over 80 different dairy products including all-natural refrigerated yogurt, organic yogurt, kid's low fat yogurt, organic nonfat frozen yogurt, soft-serve nonfat frozen yogurt, low fat ice cream, and its newest product, Yo Baby!—a whole milk yogurt product designed for infants and toddlers.[19]

In 2001, concurrent with Samuel Kaymen's retirement, Stonyfield entered into an acquisition agreement with Groupe Danone; over the next two years, the French company purchased almost 85 percent of Stonyfield's shares. Stonyfield sought such an arrangement not only to provide a return for original shareholders, but also because it wanted a larger partner to help it grow and enter mainstream markets as a means of achieving greater visibility for its sustainable business model. Danone was chosen because of its reputation for environmental responsibility. As part of the acquisition, Danone agreed to leave Stonyfield's management intact (including preserving Hirshberg as CE-Yo) and allowed them to pursue triple bottom-line objectives. Groupe Danone benefited from the acquisition because it afforded the company an immediate presence in the fast-growing organic and natural dairy food business.[20] However, in a very real way, the acquisition also catapulted Stonyfield Farm from being a values-based, family-run business into a subsidiary of a corporate behemoth, answerable to both shareholders and upper management.

Owners' Philosophy

Although Kaymen originally founded Stonyfield Farm, Gary Hirshberg is often referred to as the co-founder because he joined the firm in its infancy, assisted in developing the business, and played a major role in shaping its mission and strategy. The two men shared a strong conviction about the importance of corporate social responsibility. Both believed that companies owe more to society than simply remaining in business and earning a profit; corporate responsibility, they thought, means more than year-end donation tax write-offs. Rather, they felt that companies should be responsive to society's concerns through their operations, and also should become actively involved in important social and environmental causes. Their hope was to develop Stonyfield Farm into a corporate model for others to emulate.

Samuel Kaymen gained his world perspective growing up on welfare in Brooklyn, and his technical knowledge by studying electrical engineering.[21] Prior to devoting his efforts to the promotion of organic farming, he used his engineering knowledge while contracting for the defense and aerospace industries. However, his real passion took root when he moved to New Hampshire to start a subsistence garden with his wife. As he learned about agriculture, he grew increasingly concerned about American agriculture's heavy use of chemical fertilizers, pesticides, and inefficient machinery, as well as the demise of the small family farm. Gathering together like-minded organic growers in the area, Kaymen founded what is now known as the Northeast Organic Farming Association (NOFA), the oldest and one of the largest organic farming organizations in the United States.[22]

He continued his mission of spreading awareness and best practices of organic farming by founding The Rural Education Center (TREC) on his farm in Cornish, New Hampshire. Kaymen, self-described as a poor businessman, originally saw Stonyfield merely as a means to fund this school, and only later expanded his goals for the company. However, as demonstrated by his departure from the company upon the acquisition by Danone Groupe, Kaymen was never comfortable with the growth that caused the company to stray from its roots.[23]

Gary Hirshberg, by contrast, was a businessman as well as a social activist long before taking the reins of Stonyfield Farm, making significant contributions to organic farming and other areas including renewable energy and hydrology (he wrote a how-to book on water-pumping windmills),[24] gun safety, and income tax.[25, 26] Having grown up in New Hampshire the son of a shoe manufacturer, he was motivated to advocate for the environment after witnessing the toxic dyes flowing downstream from his father's factory.[27] Hirshberg was one of the first graduates of Hampshire College in Amherst, Massachusetts, and before joining Stonyfield Farm, he established the New Alchemy Institute, a non-profit environmental think-tank located in Woods Hole, Massachusetts. His research at the institute included organic agriculture, solar and wind energy systems, and renewable energy systems for food production.[28]

Hirshberg's overarching beliefs were best expressed in the mission statement he would later write for Stonyfield Farm, which envisions changing both the way people eat and the way corporate America conducts business (see Appendix A).

The 1983 federal budget cuts to alternative-energy programs both disappointed and worried Hirshberg. He concluded that a non-profit organization was no longer an effective conduit for his message of environmental responsibility and he decided that the corporate world offered a more persuasive channel for influencing people. He once said, "Any problem on earth will be solved if business makes it a priority. Any problem that has not been solved [remains so] because business has not made it a priority."[29] A 1983 visit to Disney World's Epcot Center both reinforced his belief in the ability of corporations to shape public opinion and convinced him that the prevailing opinion about food production was misguided. There, he watched chemical companies promote fertilizers, pesticides, and food processing as the wave of the future.[30] When given the opportunity to lead Stonyfield, he saw this as a potential platform for educating consumers on the advantages of organic farming—and corporations on the merits of sustainable business models.

Mission and Strategy

Although Stonyfield Farm's official mission emphasizes social and environmental responsibility, it does not neglect the conventional business goals of satisfying customers and providing a return to investors (see Appendix A). From the outset, Kaymen and Hirshberg earnestly believed that social responsibility and profitability can mesh together. Their business model was based on the belief that Stonyfield Farm could command a premium price for high-quality, differentiated products sold principally through specialty stores. Thus, the company's many conspicuous environmental and social activities have not only been genuine and well-intentioned, but also designed to attract customers and maintain their loyalty. The company's perilous infancy also provided Kaymen and Hirshberg valuable guidance, forcing them to recognize the need for maintaining margins as well as good intentions. Throughout, they believed that their firm could achieve a competitive position by selling a superior product and pioneering techniques in sustainable, lean operations.

Stonyfield Farm strives to produce the best-tasting, most healthful yogurt possible. Hirshberg has become famous for a quip about quality compromise: "Quality, quality, quality: never waver from it, even when you don't see how you can afford to keep it up. When you compromise, you become a commodity and then you die."[31] Following strict productions standards, all Stonyfield products are not only premium, but also certified Kosher. The company's recipe for quality involves several unique factors. First, it boasts the only product line with six live and active yogurt cultures including *L. reuteri*, which has been scientifically proven to improve the immune system and prevent gastrointestinal disease. Second, it uses only natural ingredients. For example, instead of refined white sugar, Stonyfield uses naturally milled sugar; its nonfat fruit juice-sweetened line uses agave nectar, a natural sweetener.[32]

Third, and perhaps most importantly, the yogurt has never contained milk from cows treated with the Bovine Growth Hormone (rBGH). The company vehemently opposes the use of this hormone for both economic and humane reasons.[33] Although the hormone increases the amount of milk that cows can produce, the increase in production tends to hurt small family farms by driving down the price of milk, tightening their margins. Stonyfield's management also believes that the use of rBGH is inhumane. Research indicates that cows given the hormone have reduced pregnancy rates and increased udder infections.[34] Critics of the hormone are also concerned that its effects on humans have not been adequately tested.[35, 36]

Since milk is the principal ingredient in Stonyfield Farm's products it represents a large portion of direct costs. Although the company could easily purchase cheaper milk from large dairies, its policy is to purchase strictly from family farms in New England. The company supports these farms for two fundamental reasons: First, the small farms contracted by Stonyfield utilize Jersey cows exclusively. These cows are renowned for their high-quality milk, which is believed to have a sweeter and creamier taste. Second, family farms use fewer pesticides, chemical fertilizers, and fossil fuels and therefore have a reduced negative impact on the environment. The company's vision reflects these policies: "To make pure and healthy products that taste good, while supporting family farms and protecting the environment."[37]

Environmental and Social Advocacy

Since its inception as a source of funding for TREC, Stonyfield has maintained an active role in various advocacy and educational programs. More than simply engaging in monetary philanthropy (which it does), the company has created programs to actively engage policy makers, other companies, and the general public in social and environmental causes.

One such program is entitled "Profits for the Planet." Each year, the company gives 10 percent of pre-tax profits in the form of grants to projects that preserve and protect the environment. In the 26 years of the company's existence, over $10 million has been gifted to hundreds of causes ranging from biodiversity protection to urban poverty reduction.[38] Competition for these grants is highly competitive, drawing creative ideas from a wide variety of applicants and groups.

Remembering its roots in education, Stonyfield also endeavors to teach consumers about a wide range of topics, from global warming to the use of hormones on animals. A series of videos on the company's website double as education on sustainable, natural farming and promotional materials for the company's products. Another program, called "Have-a-Cow," was started in 1990 as a cow "sponsorship" opportunity. Later, the program was changed to have an educational focus. The goal of the program is to inform people about dairy cows, dairy farm life and practices, and the value of preserving America's family farms. It also aims to build awareness and support for sustainable farming practices. The program has served as an effective platform for the company to connect with its customers, featuring mini biographies of farmers and cows, interactive information on various cow breeds, mini quizzes, and monthly updates written by the cows themselves.[39, 40]

The company also engages in significant social and environmental activism. A salient example is the company's opposition to rBGH, which it explicitly advertises on its yogurt cup lids. The company uses the lids, along with additional in-depth information on its website, to rally customers to take action, such as writing to the FDA to encourage the agency to withdraw its approval of the hormone. In the past, Stonyfield's management has also contacted local schools to request that their milk programs use only hormone-free milk.

Stonyfield, over the years, has engaged in a series of lid campaigns. The company uses the lids on its products as "little billboards" featuring environmental and political messages.[41] In 1996, the company urged its customers to protest proposed cuts in federal environmental spending through its "Flip Your Lid for the Earth" campaign. The company printed sample protest letters on the lids of 5 million yogurt cups and customers were asked to sign and send letters to their representatives.[42] The National Parks and Conservation Association joined Stonyfield in this campaign.[43] Other lid campaigns focused on such issues as global warming (1997/1998), combating children's hunger in the U.S. (1999), properly inflating tires to save gasoline (2001), the importance of voting (2004), healthier foods in the nation's schools (2006), opposition to the use of vBST, a synthetic bovine growth hormone (2007), and sustainable transportation methods, including a giveaway for a Trek bicycle (2009).[44] Not all of the company's lid campaigns generated positive publicity, however. Its campaign protesting handgun violence, for example, brought considerable controversy and even a few requests from supermarket managers to keep politics off grocery store shelves.[45]

Despite minor setbacks, Stonyfield's management believes that its environmental and social efforts pay off in the form of increased sales and widening distribution, as well as in recognition from the environmental community. The latter is evident from the company's many prestigious environmental awards. They include the Environmental Stewardship award from the Council on Economic Priorities, Corporate Conscience Award from the Council of Economic Priorities, the National Award for Sustainability from the President's Council on Sustainable Development, the Robert Rodale Environmental Achievement Award from the Rodale Institute, the Earth Day 2000 National Award for Sustainability, the 2001 Green Power Leadership Award from the EPA and the Department of Energy, and the National Conservation Achievement Award from the National Wildlife Federation for its commitment to sustainability.[46]

Pollution Prevention and Efficiency Programs

In line with the firm's overarching strategy, an array of policies and programs have been introduced for the dual purpose of minimizing the negative impact of company operations on the environment and promoting internal efficiency.

One such program was the company's campaign for solid waste minimization.

According to Gary Hirshberg, "anything that goes out the back door is lost profit."[47] Working with the University of Michigan's Center for Sustainable Systems, Stonyfield converted all of its container packing from high density polyethylene (HDPE) to the lighter weight plastic, polypropylene. Stonyfield also worked with manufacturing equipment designers to reduce product loss due to improperly filled containers. It is estimated that these changes obviated the manufacturing and disposal of over 100 tons of plastic per year. The company reduces organic waste by donating its edible food waste to local hog farmers (400,000 lbs in 1999).[48]

The company also systematically recycles aluminum, cardboard, and paper waste as well as much of its plastic waste. The company has initiated cutting edge technologies including on-site anaerobic wastewater treatment, solid waste elimination efforts, and a building designed to be certified at a LEED Silver level.[49,50] As of 2009, the company diverted over 18 million lbs of material from landfills through similar recycling programs.[51]

The company has long seen energy efficiency as a win-win opportunity because it not only reduces CO_2 emissions but also reduces operating costs. Along with the recent addition of the largest solar panel array in New Hampshire, which covers the factory roof, energy saving initiatives have included energy efficient lighting, motors, and refrigeration, and redesigning operating processes to include heat recovery. In 2008 alone, such initiatives saved the company over $250,000 and cut energy use by 8 percent while increasing production by 12 percent.[52]

In 1997, Stonyfield Farm became the first U.S. manufacturer to offset 100 percent of the carbon emissions from its facility. Since then, it has offset approximately 40,000 metric tons of CO_2 through a series of investments in offsite projects that mitigate greenhouse gas emissions. Examples of these projects include the replanting of deforested watershed and riparian habitat in Oregon, construction of a Vermont wastewater facility that utilizes excess methane (that was formerly flared) to run turbines that generate power for the New England area, and a wind power venture for the Sioux Indian tribe in South Dakota. Furthermore, the company has recognized that cow emissions are a major source of greenhouse gases, and is working on improved diets to reduce methane levels in bovine belches.[53]

Perhaps Stonyfield's most significant contribution to pollution prevention, however, is its policy of purchasing organic ingredients from local farmers. Company officials in 2000 estimated that as a consequence of its organic purchases, roughly 100,000 lbs of chemicals annually were not applied to American farmlands, thereby improving soil quality and reducing toxic runoff into fresh water sources. Also, this is an area where the company has recently reached a significant but elusive goal. Throughout most of the company's history, not all Stonyfield products were entirely organic, largely due to unstable supply and the high price of organic ingredients. In October of 2007, however, the company announced that its last remaining product line, fat free yogurt, had received the USDA organic seal and that its dairy products were now 100 percent organic. Gary Hirshberg called it a "monumental achievement." The feat was principally made possible by the large increase in the amount of U.S. farmland devoted to organic dairy farming.[54]

Corporate Culture and Policies

Teamwork and commitment to the company mission have been dominant dimensions of the Stonyfield culture. The company promotes this culture through employee training and professional development, and by fostering two-way communication at all levels of the organization. Employee input is encouraged and teams are frequently organized as vehicles to generate innovative recommendations. For example, teams with colorful appellations such as the "Cream Team" and "Where's the Milk" developed significant recommendations that resulted in more efficient operations. In 1998, Stonyfield employees participated in plant expansion decisions, including specific design suggestions. As part of the company's waste management program, employees periodically conduct "dumpster dives" to determine what is being thrown away. Also, each year, one employee receives the "President's Cash Award" for his or her waste reduction efforts, and financial incentives are extended to departments and teams that develop environmentally sound programs.[55]

Stonyfield offers an array of benefits to its employees, including free massages. Through an elected committee, workers have the opportunity to select their own health benefits plan. And perhaps most importantly, all employees participate in company profits through bonus and stock option programs. In fact, the first 15 percent of profits is allocated to this employee profit sharing plan and the next 10 percent is reserved for the company's "Profits for the Planet" program.[56]

Finally, Stonyfield Farm is one of a growing number of privately held firms that practices "open-book management," or the policy of sharing the firm's financial information with employees. The company initiated its open-book policy in the late 1980s after experiencing major financial losses. As a central component of this policy, semi-annual company-wide meetings are held to review financial performance.[57] Kaymen and Hirshberg firmly believed that being completely open with employees promoted loyalty—committed employees, in their view, were essential to the company's unique and successful strategy. "It's wrong to say that being socially responsible is what you do externally," Hirshberg explained. "You also must be healthy internally."[58]

The Future

Stonyfield Farm set out on a mission to change the world. Its founders envisioned a chemical-free food industry dominated by family farms, and they saw business as the most effective method to spread that message. In a very significant sense, they have achieved wild success in doing so. As the world's largest organic yogurt maker, Stonyfield purchases over 300 million lbs of organic ingredients each year, supporting more than 60,000 acres of organic farmland. Partnering with Groupe Danone they have been able to expand their vision overseas to England, Ireland, and France.[59]

This success, however, has not come without some trade-offs. For example, a 2006 *Business Week* article highlighted the fact that local family production will not be able to meet global demand for organic food. "It would be great to get all of our food within a 10-mile radius of our house," said Hirshberg. "But once you're in organic, you have to source globally." The article also alluded to the fact that Stonyfield may soon have to ship powdered milk from places as distant as New Zealand, though to date this has not become a reality.[60] The company does source packaging materials and ingredients like cocoa and fruit from China, Turkey, Ecuador, and elsewhere.[61]

Another of the company's huge successes has been to stimulate demand for organic products, thereby motivating other companies to manufacture, purchase, and sell them. However, this has had several unintended consequences. For one, the growing trend has begun to worry chemical manufacturers and biotechnology advocates, who have started anti-organic campaigns of their own.[62] Even more sinister, as large manufacturers and retailers such as Kellogg, General Mills, and Wal-Mart bring organics to the mass market a host of problems is introduced, including consumers' perception of organic "greenwashing," insufficient supply to meet demand, large-scale international sourcing of ingredients, an overall rise in the price of food, expanding farmland cutting into rainforests, increased water usage to grow pasture, and suppliers that bend the rules of what constitutes organic. Despite his role as father of the organic movement, Hirshberg is not spared these dilemmas—his continued leadership of the subsidiary is contingent on his ability to deliver double-digit growth.[63]

Hirshberg believes "the best way to predict the future is to invent it."[64] However, in a world where NGOs, consumer groups, regulators, families, and executives battle over whose values should prevail, whose needs will be met, and how best to feed the planet's burgeoning population, the stage is set for disruptive change. Stonyfield Farm continues to be a driving force in these developments. "The only way to influence the powerful forces in this industry," said Hirshberg, "is to become a powerful force." At that, he has clearly succeeded. What is less clear is the future direction of the agriculture industry and the ideal course for sustainable human development.

Appendix A

Stonyfield Farm Mission Statement

- To produce the very highest quality all natural and Certified Organic products that taste incredible.
- To educate consumers and producers about the value of protecting the environment and of supporting family farmers and sustainable farming methods.
- To serve as a model that environmentally and socially responsible businesses can also be profitable.
- To provide a healthful, productive and enjoyable work place for all employees, with opportunities to gain new skills and advance personal career goals.
- To recognize our obligations to stockholders and lenders by providing an excellent return on their investment.[65]

Case Study 3

King Cycle Group

> As potential consumers . . ., it becomes your responsibility to ask and be informed about the labor, management and environmental practices involved in the manufacture of your bike part or frame.
>
> —Chris King[1]

King Cycle Group, also known as Chris King Precision Components, designs and manufactures world-class cycling components. The company is renowned for its commitment to both product quality and sustainability. The trade journal, *Mountain Bike Review,* has praised its founder and CEO, Chris King, as a businessman who has proven that, "environmental and social consciousness and business success need not be mutually exclusive."[2]

The Early Days

Chris King developed what later would become his signature product, a sealed-bearing bicycle headset, during the summer of 1976 in his Santa Barbara garage. Early the next year, at the age of 20, he founded King Manufacturing, a contract machine shop that took work from industries as disparate as medical equipment, aerospace, microwave, and cryogenics. He also, however, continued to build headsets as a side line. Although demand for his headsets grew steadily over the next decade, most of the firm's machine time was still devoted to contract work.

Albeit developing headsets was simply a side business, it was King's passion. The headset is a critical bicycle component that connects the frame to the fork (the part that secures the front wheel and allows the rider to steer and balance the bike) and is constantly stressed by road conditions and the weight of the rider. Most serious road cyclers as well as mountain bikers were dissatisfied with the durability of conventional headsets because typically they did not last beyond a single racing season.

In 1987, Chris King sold King Manufacturing (less the headset business) to Medical Concepts, Inc. (MCI) where he also accepted the position of manufacturing manager. During the next four years while MCI grew to become a $30 million leader in the medical video imaging industry, King honed his manufacturing and management skills. At the same time, his sideline headset business began to take off and by 1991 there was an unacceptably large backlog of headset orders. King, subsequently, decided to leave his secure job at MCI and devote full-time attention to King Cycle Group. During the next couple of years, the company not only caught up on its backorders but also doubled sales. Concurrently, King was developing new products and in 1993 successfully introduced three new components—cogs, base plates, and wheelsets.[3]

Growth Pains

Shadowing the budding mountain bike movement of the early 1990s, demand for the company's products continued to expand. But with growth, new challenges emerged. One was the shortage of capital. King started the business with an investment of $10,000. Other than this initial capital, the company's growth was entirely financed from profits. In fact, it wasn't until 1999 that the company even took out a line of credit from a bank.

King's aversion to outside financing was the direct result of his experience with the initial $10,000 investment. Half of it was borrowed from his aunt and the other half came from another investor. In the early days, this investor became, in King's opinion, overly involved in the business even though he was not an experienced businessman. King decided then and there that he would finance the company internally to ensure that he had full control over its direction.[4]

Having limited capital, however, had implications for company policies as well as for its performance. For instance, to maximize margins, King decided early on to circumvent middlemen and distribute the company's products directly to retail accounts. He also had to insist on favorable payment terms from his customers to ensure that there would be sufficient cash on hand. Internal financing also dictated the slower growth pace of 20 percent per year (a rate that most firms would salivate over!) than the company otherwise could have achieved.

King Cycle Group also experienced critical human resource challenges because of its location in Santa Barbara. With growth, the company became increasingly constrained by worker shortages due in large part to the skyrocketing real estate prices in the Santa Barbara area.[5] Most of the company's workers were driving hours to and from work because they could not afford to live near the plant and it was next to impossible to attract new workers. Moreover, King's environmental sensibilities were offended by the air pollution created by the long commutes. For the company to continue to expand, King felt he had no choice but to relocate. "The tight labor market and expensive property in Santa Barbara has always made growth there difficult," he explained. "We had a lot of orders to keep up with and, on top of all that, we're always exploring new and innovative technologies."[6]

King chose Shasta County in Northern California as King Cycle Group's new home. In February of 2000, the company uprooted and relocated the entire operation 500 miles north to Redding, California. While 30 of King's 60 employees went along with the move, it was an incredibly stressful time for the company. In the months before moving, production fell 30 percent, employee morale dropped drastically, and new building construction fell far behind. However, the relocation process, although initially painful, offered the environment needed for the company's future growth.

Moving to Redding allowed King Cycle and its employees to enjoy a new, larger building, a better labor market, and a lower cost of living. During the four years following the move, sales accelerated and the company became national in scope. Expansion, however, led to a new set of challenges. The firm needed a different mixture of employees—especially needed were experienced professionals who could take the company to the next level. King recalls, "We couldn't seem to hire the educated professionals that we needed: engineers, programmers, planners, managers, and accountants. Those kinds of people were very hard to find in Redding . . . New city, new problem."[7] With company executives covering unfilled positions and putting in unmanageable hours, King knew that another move was imminent. Marketing Manager Chris DiStefano remembers,

> We checked out loads of places on paper, but looked seriously at Cambridge Massachusetts, Raleigh North Carolina, Boise Idaho, Philadelphia Pennsylvania, Austin Texas, Chicago Illinois, and Portland and Eugene, Oregon. It quickly became obvious that Portland was not only one of the very best fits for us, but it was also the closest. It was much easier for our employees to make the move from Redding to Portland.[8]

So, after spending months considering a variety of alternatives, the company finally settled on Portland. Company executives applied numerous criteria in selecting their new home. DiStefano recalls,

> Portland seemed to satisfy all of our company's needs. Plus, you can live in the country, or live downtown, go skiing or go see a play. There were outstanding bookstores and a huge music scene for such a small city. We thought that we would be able to find ourselves a good life here.[9]

In January of 2004, when the company and its employees were fully relocated, it became obvious to King and the other managers that they had made the right decision. "We moved to Portland for lots of reasons. Hiring great people was the most important one. We have hired some excellent people since we moved. There are new people in every area of the company and they brought intelligent ideas and decades of professional experience with them," said King.[10] By August, the company had all systems running and was manufacturing at a comparable rate to their Redding location. Chris DiStefano remarked, "This company moved two times in 5 years (1999 and 2003), and that took a lot out of our folks. Now, at over three years into our home here in Portland, I can say that we're moved in, settled in, and thinking only about the things that bike riders want us to think about."[11]

Focus on Quality—"There is Always a Market for the Best"

As far as Chris King can recall, his goal has always been to "make things that are good for society in a responsible way."[12] Since its inception, King Cycle Group has been making its products to the highest possible standards using the latest technology. King has often said, "There is always a market for the best. The top of the market is a small market but allows you to command your price."[13] King once bluntly wrote in a product catalog:

> It seems as though "good enough" has become the standard. There are many reasons substandard quality components are not good enough, here are a few of mine. Like most people, I have limited time to work on my bike and I don't like hassles, so the parts we design need to be easy to service. I certainly don't like to get stuck out in the middle of nowhere, so they also need to be reliable and durable.[14]

One of the salutary fallouts of his focus on quality has been the company's preference for working with American suppliers. King has come to believe that to make the highest-quality products he has to use the highest-quality materials—which he believes he can only find in the U.S.

Focus on quality has also been compatible with his desire to provide the best work environment for his employees. He maintains that happier employees make better products, and further, that it is easier to be a mean boss and much more challenging to be a kind boss who is inspiring. He explains, "If you want quality, you will have to make them want to produce quality."[15]

King's dedication to quality has also influenced him to value his independence from investors and business partners. Independence and control of the business are very essential to King because, as he sees it, this gives him the flexibility needed to make world-class products. He feels that partners or investors, to reduce costs, would likely push the company to outsource much of its operation and, with excessive outsourcing he fears he would lose control of quality.

Environmental Initiatives

Purchasing a Chris King headset or hub may be considered a vote for an exceptional level of quality unique among bicycle components, but it also helps support a company that has successfully combined good business with a strong, active, and effective environmental consciousness. Jason Houston, who is in charge of implementing King Cycle Group's Vibe and Consciousness Program explains,

> Environmental consciousness is a common, often empty, buzz word these days. But, right from the start, Chris has realized our reliance on the outdoors and we've always tried to act responsibly with that relationship in mind. Concern for the quality of life and a passion for being outdoors is why King Cycle Group exists. Awareness and mitigation of our environmental impact is fundamental to our operating philosophy.[16]

Chris King's concern for the environment ignited when he began cycling in high school in the 1970s, around the time the green movement started. He still refers to himself as a sort of a "hippie" who stumbled into business. King was a young adult when he witnessed the energy crisis of 1977. Conscious of both energy and environmental issues, he vowed never to needlessly harm the environment for sake of money. Today, his company focuses on minimizing its ecological footprint.

The major environmental challenge for King from day one has been manufacturing, which by its very nature is polluting. His headsets are made from aluminum and steel which are mined from the earth, purified and formed using less-than-green processes, and then hauled around on big trucks that spew air pollution. The headsets are carved by machines fueled by electricity provided by dams. They are lubricated by petroleum products pumped from deep in the ground. The colors that make the headsets attractive require the use of several strong chemicals and the boxes they are shipped in are made from trees. King and his employees realize that they cannot completely eliminate the polluting nature of their manufacturing business, but they continually strive to reduce it.

In addition to waste and pollution minimization in the manufacturing process, Chris King also believes that product quality plays a significant role in the company's sustainability performance. Chris DiStefano explained: "One of Chris' fundamental issues is that we do make things, so we use energy and use resources, which we try to minimize. And the products we make, like our headsets, never need to be replaced, so they can occupy a useful place and stay there."[17] The pursuit of quality and sustainability, thus, are seen as reinforcing of each other at King Cycle.

The company's sustainability efforts are visible everywhere. Its facilities, from the beginning, were designed with sustainability in mind. The factory's exhaust system not only filters and cleans the air, but precipitates oil back into the systems for reuse. Natural light is used wherever possible, and thick insulation reduces the company's energy consumption dramatically. The company tries to recycle absolutely everything it can. For instance, all of the company's metal scrap is sent through a puck-making machine to squeeze the oil out. By using a 400-lb hydraulic press to squeeze the pucks, manufacturing oil can be used over and over again.[18]

King Cycle also incorporates environmental and social concerns in all its purchasing decisions. "Whenever we use anything—from the raw barstock to the forks in the kitchen—we consider its source and the big picture of how it all fits into our overall philosophy," stated King.

> For example, we will only purchase domestically produced metal. It's more expensive, but you never know what you're supporting buying the foreign stuff. In Brazil they clear-cut the forests and burn the trees to make the charcoal used for smelting the iron. If you buy steel from Brazil, you might as well be voting directly for the destruction of the rainforests. We will not risk supporting that sort of mentality.[19]

King has found that his environmental initiatives pay for themselves in most cases through the efficient use of resources and development of higher-quality products. One key exception is the photovoltaic cells (solar power) on the roof which, purely from a financial perspective, were not a profitable investment. Another costly investment is the company's anodizing line. Designed largely in-house, it is an engineering masterpiece. "Anodizing is typically a pretty nasty process," asserted ex-VP Matt O'Rourke:

> What we've accomplished is a completely computer controlled and fully automated zero waste water system. It is extremely efficient and all of the water is reclaimed, distilled, and

reused in a closed system—there is not even a drain in the floor. And it wasn't cheap—we
paid five to six times what we might have spent on a typical used line of similar size, but
it's worth it.[20]

In other words, while return on investment and payback are important to the
company, there are times when King is willing to incur higher cost to minimize
environmental harm.

Being a Good Citizen

In addition to his sincere concern for the natural environment, Chris King also
believes that "world peace starts at home" and for many years, his company has
exhibited a sincere social consciousness in its community. Jonathan Maus, editor of
BikePortland.org and one-time employee, comments:

> I worked with King Cycle Group back in Santa Barbara, California, right out of college and I
> can say that I have never come across a company so committed to being a good citizen. In
> addition to being one of the most earth-friendly companies in the world, King Cycle Group
> spends and donates thousands and thousands of dollars every year to nonprofits, trail
> building projects, and more. This may not seem like a ton of money compared to the
> millions a company like Nike can throw around, but this is a small, privately held company
> that makes bike parts, which isn't exactly a rich man's business. I don't mean to pontificate
> or anything but this company is the real deal, and that's increasingly rare in the business
> world these days.[21]

An example of the company's community efforts is its Pretty and Strong product
line of pink colored hubs, headsets, and components—from which 75 percent of
the profits go directly to the Susan G. Komen Foundation.[22] (The Komen Foundation
is a global leader in its fight against breast cancer, fulfilling its mission through
support of breast cancer research grants, meritorious awards, educational and science
conferences and community-based outreach programs around the world.[23]) The
other 25 percent of the money goes directly to breast cancer research. Marketing
Manager Chris DiStefano recalls, "The program was developed from an employee's
own family experience with breast cancer. Our first year we had a limited edition
headset sold only for a brief time around October, which is national breast cancer
awareness month. Response was overwhelming."[24] Since then, King Cycle Group
has been producing its signature headsets in the Pretty and Strong pink edition
every season.

King Cycle Group has also formed a partnership with former champion mountain
biker Hans Rey's Wheels 4 Life charity. Following a successful cycling career, Rey
traversed the world exploring remote cultures and making documentary films.
Through his travels, he learned that in many parts of the world a bike can make a
significant difference in a person's life—it could mean work, education, healthcare,
and a future. Rey founded the charity, Wheels 4 Life, to provide bicycles for people in
developing nations. King Cycle financially supports Wheels 4 Life by dedicating a
portion of the proceeds of its special edition DreadSet component line to the charity.

The colors of this line, red, gold, and green, were selected by Rey because they are generally recognized as the colors of Africa, where the first bikes were sent.[25]

King Cycle has engaged with its home community in numerous other ways. Chris King was an early advocate and sponsor of Trail Daze in Santa Barbara—a day where cyclists clean up the roads and trails they frequent. King would typically make pancakes to help get the clean-up started. Upon arriving in Portland, the company forthwith became involved with the city's burgeoning cycling community, first by renting flat-screen TVs for local bars so that cyclists without cable could watch the Tour de France. In the ensuing years, the firm has regularly sponsored and supported dozens of cycling events for charity and clean-up purposes. It was, for example, an early advocate of a Mt. Hood clean-up. Chris King recently donated $5,000, with plans for additional matching donations, to a safety education fund in honor of Brett Jarolimek who died in a fatal collision while cycling. King saw this tragedy as a way to increase safety awareness issues among cyclists.[26]

King Cycle Group also promotes the concept of "enlightened consumerism," the notion that consumers are ultimately responsible for their purchases. It encourages its customers and the community to not only look at the dollar cost of what they buy, but the social and environmental costs as well. Chris King exhorts, "As potential consumers . . . it becomes your responsibility to ask and be informed about the labor, management and environmental practices involved in the manufacture of your bike part or frame."[27]

Culture and Mission Alignment

Clearly, King Cycle Group's organizational culture revolves around the twin pursuits of excellence and social consciousness. Company employees are proud of the quality of their work and are dedicated to the company's mission. King recalls that there were times when he wanted to say to employees working on a component, "Don't you think this is good enough?"[28] But he couldn't utter those words because he worried that they might get offended. The workers, according to King, have become so committed to quality that their standards at times even exceed his expectations.

King tries to provide the best work environment for his employees. "Chris gets very long-term commitments from the people working here because the company focuses on employee wellness from a total environmental perspective,"[29] said marketing manager, Chris DiStefano. King, based on his past experience, believes that manufacturing workers in most companies are de-motivated because of arbitrary performance reviews and favoritism in promotions and raises. Consequently, to better motivate his employees, King developed a very detailed (81 measures), objective, and transparent system for determining pay scales and raises. Each employee can see exactly why he is paid his present salary and what skills he needs to improve to increase it.

About 30 percent of company employees ride bicycles to work on a regular basis. This number goes up during "Ride to work month" where employees who ride to work 20 days during the month can receive up to two days paid time off. A company goal is that every employee be committed to and practice sustainability on a daily basis. David Prause, Production Manager, explains the organizational commitment:

> To develop sustainable practices throughout an organization, everyone must be involved, the push for sustainability should be fundamental in how everyone thinks about things, fundamental in how everyone responds to issues, and fundamental in how everyone makes decisions . . . pursuing sustainability can't be brand or a department, sustainability needs to be a core value, in which everyone in the organization believes.[30]

King Cycle Group's cafeteria policies demonstrate how a little effort can go a long way to building a stronger and more sustainable culture. Café credits are given to employees who cycle, carpool, or walk to work. Commutes over 15 miles or after dark get extra credits. This is a meaningful incentive to workers because the in-house cafeteria makes some of the best food in the area and is offered at about cost—and is made from local organic produce, of course. Since almost all personnel stay on-site for the midday meal, gasoline consumption is reduced. Eating together also gives employees a chance to communicate with each other and build tighter bonds. Further, because the cafeteria is close to the factory, it allows for shorter breaks and, therefore, potentially greater productivity.

Cycling Forward

In February of 2008 Chris King announced that the company would begin to produce bicycle frames under the Cielo name. This move is a logical extension for the firm considering that Chris King was a hobbyist frame-builder long before his company took off and he became a household name for bicycle enthusiasts. By the mid–1980s, success forced King to drop his other interests and focus on running his growing headset business. But he never stopped thinking about frame-building and it always bothered him that he didn't have time to pursue this interest. Now, three decades later, the time seems right for the company to expand its product line and for King to indulge himself.[31]

King has no plans of retiring anytime soon. But he would like to see his company "run itself"—something he has been working toward for the last 30 years. For this reason, he has plowed back much of the earnings each year. He explains, "I don't need a lot of money. I have always viewed that profit is something that benefits the company not me . . . a company is a livelihood to your small society so it is important to ensure its health."[32]

King sees the company's mission as his legacy. He explains, "I don't need my business to survive me but I would like to carry forward the philosophy that the company is founded upon."[33] Consequently, he is in no rush to sell his business for profit like other entrepreneurs. He muses, "What do you do with a company that has your name?"[34]

When asked if he would like other companies to emulate his business practices, he responded enthusiastically, "Absolutely. I would like other companies to learn what I do and emulate me."[35] Perhaps King best summarizes his view on the role and legacy of his company with the following statement:

> We hope that by sharing what we've accomplished, we can inspire others to consider doing the same. The best thing that could happen would be that someone comes along, sees what we did, and completely outdoes us. We'd love to keep finding out that there is still so much more we can do, and then do it.[36]

Case Study 4

T.S. Designs, Inc.

We have to succeed. If we don't, people will conclude the only model that works is the "Wal-Mart model."

—Eric Henry[1]

T.S. Designs is a small niche textile screen printing contractor based in Burlington, North Carolina. Founded in 1975, T.S. Designs at its peak had revenues of $4 million and employed over 100 people. As a consequence of global trends, however, the company in more recent years was forced to downsize and has redefined its niche in the textile industry, emphasizing quick response, quality, and environmentally friendly products and operations. Its stated mission is to build a sustainable company that simultaneously looks after people, planet, and profits (the so-called triple bottom-line).

Early History

T.S. Designs was founded by Tom Sineath as a contract-based screen printing business. During the company's first several years of operation its current president and Sineath's good friend, Eric Henry, was a student at the University of North Carolina, Chapel Hill, where he also ran a small, start-up company marketing screen printed T-shirts to fellow students. Business was good but in 1978 Henry decided to leave school early to become a shareholder and full-time employee of T.S. Designs. Over the next decade and a half under Sineath's and Henry's leadership T.S. Designs grew and became an established and successful small business. Its value proposition was to provide exceptionally high-quality and innovative screen printing services for major retail companies. In its heyday, the firm printed for well-known brands such as Polo, Nike, Reebok, and Tommy Hilfiger, and was a subcontractor to big textile producers including the Vanity Fair Corporation, Sara Lee Corporation, and William Carter Company.

While T.S. Designs was establishing itself in the screen printing business, an ominous trend was unfolding in the textile industry. Companies were increasingly sourcing apparel in developing countries where labor and environmental regulations were lax or nonexistent and manufacturing costs were significantly lower. With the advent of the North American Free Trade Agreement (NAFTA) in January 1994 this trend accelerated. Most major U.S. brands moved their manufacturing south of the border to Mexico and Central America, and later to China, with devastating consequences for American textile workers—some 825,000 industry jobs were lost between 1994 and 2002.

Concomitantly, much screen printing work also migrated offshore, resulting in a glut of screen printing capacity in the United States. For T.S. Designs this translated into a double quandary—severely declining prices and a significant drop in volume. Per-print revenue and volume declined by more than 50 percent compared to pre-NAFTA years. T.S. Designs had little choice but to downsize, laying off the majority of its workforce (going from 100 to 14). The firm's leaders were also forced to re-think the company's goals and strategy as well as its overall philosophy and approach to doing business.[2]

T.S. Designs Reinvents Itself

In response to the poor financials of the 1995–2002 period, T.S. Designs redefined its market niche and developed a unique new business model. The new business model emphasized high-quality, rapid-response, inventorying organic T-shirt blanks, domestic sourcing, and utilizing an innovative new printing technology called REHANCE. This novel strategy was designed to respond to a perceived market demand for a combination of quick response, high quality, and environmental sustainability.

The values and philosophy underlying the new business model are set forth in the company's Vision, Values, and Mission Statement (see Figure A.1) which emphasizes sustainability and a triple bottom-line mission. Although Sineath and Henry had been concerned about the earth's deteriorating environment since the late 1980s, they credit their friend, Sam Moore, Vice President of Burlington Chemical Company,

---

- Our vision is to transform the world we live in, both in small and large measures alike. Creating economic, ecological and social prosperity while ensuring that future generations have the same opportunity. We envision a world where no harmful chemicals are produced, worn or discarded.

- Our mission is to build a sustainable company that simultaneously looks after the People, the Planet and Profits.

- Our values guide everything we do:
  - Serve our customers with the highest quality service
  - Deliver value in all products
  - Provide a high quality of life for all employees
  - Protect and restore our environment
  - Maintain a reasonable profit

Figure A.1 T.S. Designs' Vision, Values, and Mission Statement

Source: www.tsdesigns.com

who had developed a sustainability plan for Burlington earlier, with the inspiration and encouragement to transform T.S. Designs into a competitive, triple bottom-line company.[3]

REHANCE. Conventional screen printing places a surface coating on an already dyed and finished garment. The ink typically used for the coating is plastisol which contains PVC and phthalates. PVC presents a serious health risk because it releases dangerous dioxins during both manufacturing and disposal. Dioxins are one of the most toxic chemicals known to science. Phthalates are an additive to plastisol that give the ink stretch and are suspected of being a danger to human health.[4]

The origin of REHANCE dates back to 1995 when T.S. Designs started a dialogue with Burlington Chemical Company which had developed a novel technology that could alter cellulose fibers at the molecular level (known as nano-technology). T.S. Designs' leaders grasped the potential for the technology to address the quality and sustainability challenges facing the textile industry with plastisol ink. The two companies after approximately a year of work and roughly a quarter million dollar investment between them refined the technology for screen printing. The process resulted in three patents and was registered under the name, REHANCE.

Using the REHANCE technology, T.S. Designs can print an undyed T-shirt or other apparel product and then garment-dye it to a specified color. This eliminates the need to invest in a color inventory and allows for a rapid response to a variety of color requests. REHANCE also eliminates the plastic surface coating of plastisol ink which, in turn, permits the printed surface to breathe and not abrade over time. Because it has been dyed and dried at a high temperature, the process results in a garment that will not shrink.[5]

The company uses the lowest-impact reactive dyes consistent with its quality standards. The T.S. Designs' dyes require less salt, lower water temperatures and result in no heavy metals; consequently they leave a smaller environmental footprint than the conventional industry dyes. The company has experimented with natural dyes but has yet to find any that meet its quality standards for durability and color fastness.

Organic Cotton. As part of its new business model, T.S. Designs maintains an inventory of organic cotton, prepared for dye, T-shirt blanks that can be printed and dyed to customer specifications. Organic cotton is an important dimension of the company's sustainability posture because demand for this material promotes organic cotton farming as an alternative to conventional cotton farming which is one of the biggest consumers of pesticides in the world. Pesticides contaminate soil and water resources, and many of them are known or suspected carcinogens. Furthermore, traditional cotton farming is a heavy user of synthetic fertilizers which also find their way into the water system, contaminating the environment and threatening human health.

The supply of organically grown cotton in the U.S. over the past two decades has been uncertain. It reached a peak in 1995 and then severely declined. Most retail apparel brands in the United States using organic cotton have gone offshore to purchase this fabric at a lower price and, concurrently, to take advantage of low-cost manufacturing in developing countries. Although it is T.S. Designs' policy to source everything as close to home as possible, the firm has at times been forced to purchase its organic cotton overseas.[6]

Environmental Initiatives

Looking to reduce its environmental footprint, T.S. Designs has introduced a series of impressive green initiatives over the years. These green measures date back to the late 1980s when the company eliminated styrofoam coffee cups in the office and asked its employees to bring in their own mugs instead.

From this modest beginning the company's environmental measures have expanded in manifold ways. In 1992, T.S. Designs established a formal environmental management system (EMS) which guided the review from an environmental impact perspective of all new products and process before they could be implemented. A comprehensive multi-substance recycling program has been put in place. Post-consumer recycled paper is utilized to the maximum extent possible and significant amounts of electricity, as well as dollars, have been saved through more efficient lighting and temperature control technologies and planning.

In recent years, the company's green initiatives have become more innovative. As one writer put it, "Sineath and Henry treat their headquarters in Burlington, North Carolina, as a laboratory, seemingly missing no opportunity to express their commitment to the environment."[7] In 2003, T.S. Designs installed the largest solar tracking array (3 KW) in Alamance County with the goal of meeting 10 percent of its energy needs from renewable sources. Five years later the company augmented its solar energy capacity with the installation of a 8.6 KW array. The company also has a small windmill on its property which is tied in to its energy system.

Water reclamation is another recent sustainability initiative of the firm. A "gray water" system has been installed where water is taken from the warehouse ice machine and air conditioner condensate and pumped into barrels to be used for the company's toilets. The company has also installed a waterless urinal. These measures reduce the demand on the municipal water system for drinking-quality water.

Reclaimed water is also used to hydrate vegetation on company property including employee-tended flower and vegetable gardens. Each participating employee has his/her own small plot and is responsible for that plot albeit everyone is encouraged to help out. All of the gardening at T.S. Designs adheres to organic gardening principles, eschewing environmentally harmful pesticides and chemical fertilizers. Sineath and Henry conceive the gardens as a paradigm for teaching sustainability as well as a positive economic model for generating produce. They also see their organic farming and overall water reclamation efforts as an example that, hopefully, other companies will follow.

On its property, T.S. Designs hosts a green-built, automatic biodiesel pump station, fueled by Piedmont Biofuels, that is open to the public. It is 100 percent powered by renewable energy produced at T.S. Designs. The company also houses a 100-gallon batch biofuel reactor on the back of its property that services the members of Burlington Biodiesel Co-op, as well as T.S. Designs' box truck. Here, vegetable waste, collected from local restaurants, is turned into the fuel sold to co-op members. There is also a compost pile on the property that is used to provide the heated water required in the production of biodiesel fuel (inside the compost pile there is a 250-gallon water tank which stays at a constant 160–170 degrees). The company, further, has a smaller compost pile that heats a small greenhouse.[8]

Not surprisingly, as a direct result of its environmental innovations, T.S. Designs has been honored with numerous awards. As early as 1994, the company received the Governor's Award for Excellence in Waste Reduction. More recently, in another example, in 2004, the firm was presented with the Green Business Leader Award from Co-op America which recognized its work to, "create a greener world by using fair and sustainable methods."[9]

Supply Chain

Supply chain management is a critical component of T.S. Designs' business model but it is also a difficult balancing act. The company's sourcing strategy attempts to balance four factors. First, because the company inventories organic cotton T-shirt blanks it must seek out suppliers who can assure a constant supply of organically grown fabric. This can be a daunting challenge given the limited acreage devoted to organic cotton worldwide—increasingly organic cotton is coming from overseas sources. Second, because of the requirements of the REHANCE process the company must procure a much higher purity of fabric than is necessitated by the plastisol process. Consequently, the company works very closely with its suppliers. The need for close coordination is exacerbated by a third factor: insistence on the adherence to sustainable methods and standards up and down the supply chain. Finally, company policy requires sourcing from as close to home as possible throughout the chain. Eric Henry has said,

> In our view, to go outside your market for a product or service that your market can provide is not sustainable. Ideally, we'd like to go from organic cotton grown in North Carolina to a finished shirt in North Carolina. Ultimately, we think that's a big part of what sustainability is.[10]

This is not always possible however. During one period of time, a portion of the company's organic cotton was coming from Turkey and its T-shirt blanks were being cut and sewn at a cooperative in Nicaragua.[11]

Currently, T.S. Designs has two principal suppliers of T-shirt blanks, American Apparel and Mortex. American Apparel is a Los Angeles-based company that has made a long-term commitment to stocking organic cotton yarn. Mortex is a North Carolina-based apparel manufacturer that offers high-quality individualized design and quick response to customer needs. The company has been praised for its excellent employee benefits and epitomizes Henry's thrust for local supply.

T.S. Designs has purchased all the rights and patents to the REHANCE technology from Burlington Chemical Company, its partner in developing it, but Burlington still supplies many of the essential components. NC Green Power is yet another of the firm's suppliers. This independent, non-profit organization provides North Carolina residents with the opportunity to offset all or part of their electricity needs with renewable blocks of energy. By working with NC Green Power, renewable energy (including the firm's solar and wind generation) now fills about 50 percent of T.S. Designs' energy needs.[12]

People

When discussing T.S. Designs' planet, people, profits mission, Eric Henry likes to use the three-legged stool analogy, pointing out the obvious that without any one of its three legs the stool will not function. Nevertheless, he realistically admits that "T.S. Designs focuses on the planet part of the equation which in turn builds people and profit in its wake."[13] But this focus does not translate into the company mistreating or ignoring its employees. In fact, Henry refers to the firm's employees as, "our biggest and most valuable resource."[14] He explains, "Employees are one of our key assets and we continuously find ways to develop and mentor them. We create a respectful workplace where people are treated fairly and diversity is encouraged, maintain an open forum for discussion, and provide ongoing training in safety, sustainability, and personal development."[15] An example of the company's investment in its human assets is its financial support for employees taking continuing education courses. Workers whose first language is not English are especially encouraged to take English language courses.[16] Most recently the firm has been experimenting with a four-day production week designed to give employees extra time with their families. Early signs suggest that this policy is also increasing production efficiency.[17]

T.S. Designs' employees are also encouraged to be a part of its sustainability culture. The majority of the firm's employees, for instance, are responsible for their own garden plots where they grow vegetables or flowers. Moreover, the firm has developed a gardening sub-culture of community responsibility where people help out each other in tending the plots. Tom Sineath notes, "Each employee that participates has their own space to take care of, but there is a lot of community gardening that takes place."[18] In 2009 T.S. Designs will launch a large-scale garden in addition to the individual garden spots. This garden will grow food that will go to the employee lunches and some employees have signed up to volunteer to help and in turn they can take veggies home with them.

As part of the sustainability mission, T.S. Designs accepts responsibility for people well beyond its property line and especially throughout its extended supply line. In particular, the firm believes in "fair trade." To illustrate, in seeking an organic supplier, the company initiated discussions with Maggie's Functional Organics, a Michigan-based company. Maggie's was working with a worker-owned women's sewing co-operative in a part of Nicaragua that had just been devastated by a hurricane. The women built the sewing facility themselves and organized it such that all profits were plowed back into the business for long-term growth. They received fair wages and benefits. Maggie's was using the co-op to cut and sew organic apparel that it was selling in the United States. T.S. Designs, believing that Maggie's could be a reliable supplier of organic T-shirt blanks, worked diligently with both the company and its Nicaraguan supplier to establish the quality and delivery standards required by the REHANCE process. Eric Henry said that T.S. Designs felt an obligation to the women of the co-op to help bring them into the global marketplace. But he acknowledged that he also had a strong business motive in that the number of cut and sew operations in the United States was very limited and that Nicaragua was much closer geographically than China.[19]

T.S. Designs' executives also see local supply as a very important dimension of the firm's sustainability thrust. Their thinking is obviously greatly influenced by their experience in the North Carolina textile industry which, as mentioned, was ravaged by the migration of jobs to developing nations. But they also contend that local supply is more sustainable because it mitigates carbon emissions and pollution by eliminating long-distance transportation.[20] Presently, as discussed above, the company's two prime suppliers are located in North Carolina and California, and all of its organic inventory is made in the United States.

Recently however, T.S. Designs has helped organize a multi-entity initiative branded "Cotton of the Carolinas." The program's first harvest will result in about 15,000 T-shirts that will be available in early 2009. Cotton of the Carolinas is starting out by growing conventional cotton because no organic cotton is currently grown in the Carolinas (the hope is to eventually grow organic cotton but the jury is still out on this because of the local climate). The marketing emphasis of the program will be on "local" and "transparency." According to Eric Henry,

> We plan to make everything from the farmer to the sewer part of the background story that will be available via the website we will build. We want to do what the local food movement has done and tell the story behind the shirt which is, greatly reduce the carbon footprint and keep the dollars local. The tagline will be, Grown—Made—Sold—Here.[21]

The shirts, at least in the first couple of years, will be available for purchase only in North and South Carolina. For the first year's harvest, the supply line for the shirts will be approximately 700 miles (by comparison, a conventional T-shirt travels around 17,000 miles before reaching the ultimate customer). The complete path of the shirts (from farm through printing and dying) can be viewed on the organization's website. According to T.S. Designs' newsletter, "This program is yet another tool in our sustainability toolbox."[22]

The Future

Although the REHANCE process allows for a quicker response to customer orders and provides a much higher-quality product than conventional screen printing, the immediate marketplace response to T.S. Designs' new business model was disappointing. "The bottom line," commented Eric Henry, "is that big companies didn't care about REHANCE."[23] The conventional wisdom was that consumers want cheap T-shirts, not quality and sustainability. The company's pragmatic response was to

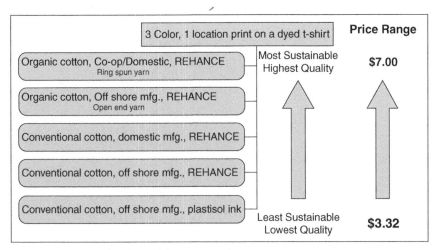

Figure A.2 T.S. Designs' Sustainable Print Options

Source: Eric Henry and Sam Moore, "Manufacturing and Selling a $4.00 T-Shirt in a $1.00 World," Greening of Industry Conference in San Francisco, California, October 13, 2003, p. 18. Costs have increased significantly since 2003 and REHANCE T-shirts now sell in the $10–$11 range.

offer customers a range of options running from the most sustainable/highest-quality/ highest-cost to the least sustainable/lowest-quality/lowest-cost option (see Figure A.2). In 2003, the top-of-the-line option—organic cotton, co-op or domestic production, and REHANCE—contributed only about 20 percent of the company's revenue. But it was the fastest growing component of the business. Since then, the firm has emphasized its triple bottom-line identity and focused on customers who value sustainability. T.S. Designs now merchandises primarily organic cotton T-shirts using REHANCE and the waterbased printing process. Whereas once the company's principal customers were major retail brands, now they include a more varied group of organizations such as, most recently, the Discovery Channel, Frog's Leap Winery, Greenpeace, and the Weaver Street Market Co-op.

T.S. Designs has been profitable for the last couple of years, but due to the recent economic downturn a small loss is forecast for 2008. The firm has also continued to expand its market niche and 2008 sales will be up for the year. An important question remains however: Will the company be able to cross over into the mainstream market with products that sell for two or three times the price of a conventionally produced T-shirt? Eric Henry is optimistic. He sees it as a matter of turning "consumers into citizens."[24] He extols the firm's philosophy, "We vote with our dollars so we have a responsibility how we spend those dollars in determining the community we want . . . it's the consumer who will decide what kind of business model will thrive in the future."[25]

Notes

1 Introduction

1. From *Maxims for Revolutionists*, 1903.
2. Justina Ly, "Riding a Green Wave," *Daily Breeze* (Torrance, CA), June 11, 2007, C1–C2.
3. Adam Lashinsky, "Kleiner Bets the Farm," *Fortune*, July 21, 2008, 97–104.
4. Debbie D. Brock, Susan Steiner, & Marina Kim "Social Entrepreneurship Education: Is it Achieving the Desired Aims?" *USASBE 2008 Proceedings* (2008), 0832.
5. World Commission on Environment and Development, *From One Earth to One World: An Overview* (Oxford: Oxford University Press, 1987).
6. T. N. Gladwin, J. J. Kennelly, & T. Krause, "Shifting paradigms for sustainable development," *Academy of Management Review* 20, 4 (1995): 874–907.
7. Marc Gunther, "Money and Morals at GE," *Fortune*, November 15, 2004. Retrieved May 22, 2008 from http://money.cnn.com/magazines/fortune/fortune_archive/2004/11/15/8191077/index.htm.
8. F. Byrne, "Dinner with the FT: Auction Man," *Financial Times*, March 25, 2006. Retrieved May 25, 2008 from http://search.ft.com/ftArticle?queryText=pierre+omidyar&y=0&aje=true&ct=0&id=060325000813&x=0&nclick_check=1.
9. "Gunter Paili Cleans Up," *Fast Company*, December 19, 2009. Retrieved May 20, 2008 from www.fastcompany.com/node/55003.

2 The Values-Centered Entrepreneur

1. M. Friedman, J. Mackey, & T. J. Rodgers, "Rethinking the Social Responsibility of Business: Putting Customers Ahead of Investors," *Reason Magazine*, October 2005. Retrieved February 8, 2007 from http://www.reason.com/news/show/32239.html.
2. Liz Claman, "Magic Means Business," *LA Times Magazine*, November 30, 2008.
3. M. Friedman, "The Social Responsibility of Business is to Increase its Profits," *New York Times Magazine* 33, 30 (1970): 122–127.
4. S. Prasso, "Saving the World with a Cup of Yogurt," *Fortune*, March 15, 2007. Retrieved May 22, 2008 from http://money.cnn.com/magazines/fortune/fortune_archive/2007/02/05/839919/index.htm.
5. B. Gates, "How to Fix Capitalism," *Time*, August 11, 2008, 40.
6. J. Elkington, "Towards the Sustainable Corporation: Win-win-win Business Strategies for Sustainable Development," *California Management Review* 36, 3 (1994): 90–100.
7. Adam Smith, *The Wealth of Nations* (New York: Modern Library, 1965), 651.
8. H. R. Bowen, *Social Responsibilities of the Businessman* (New York: Harper & Row, 1953), 6.
9. Joseph W. McGuire, *Business and Society* (New York: McGraw-Hill, 1963), 144.
10. Archie B. Carroll, "A Three-Dimensional Conceptual Model of Corporate Performance," *Academy of Management Review* 4, 4 (October 1979): 497–505.
11. Robert Hay & Edmund R. Gray, "Social Responsibilities of Managers," *Academy of Management Journal* 17, 1 (March 1974): 135–143.
12. John K. Galbraith, *The Affluent Society* (Boston: Houghton Mifflin, 1958).
13. Paul Newman died September 27, 2008.

14. David Y. Choi & Fred Kiesner, "Homeboy Industries: An Incubator of Hope and Business," *Entrepreneurship Theory and Practice*, September 2007: 769–790.
15. J. Gregory Dees, Jed Emerson, & Peter Economy, *Strategic Tools for Social Entrepreneurs* (New York: John Wiley & Sons, Inc., 2002), 195.
16. Note: we were slightly less stringent for our "Up & Comers" group as some did not have a history of multi-year profitability.
17. Anita Roddick passed away in October, 2007.
18. Kirk Hanson, *Social Evaluation of The Body Shop International 1995* (Littlehampton, U.K.: The Body Shop International, 1996).

3 Commit to a (Meaningful) Purpose

1. S. Diesenhouse, "Making a Difference: A Yogurt Maker's Culture of Caring," *New York Times*, sec. 3, col. 2, March 14, 1993, 13.
2. G. Kawasaki, recorded presentation at Stanford Technology Ventures Program. Obtained May 26, 2008 from http://edcorner.stanford.edu/authorMaterialInfo.html?mid=1171.
3. Lizette Wilson, "Executive Profile: Marc Benioff," *San Francisco Business Times*, July 25, 2003, 17, 51, 9.
4. Personal interview with author.
5. R. Rosenblatt, "The Root of All Good: Reaching the Top by Doing the Right Thing," *Time*, October 18, 1999, 88.
6. Retrieved February 12, 2008 from http://www.grameen-info.org/bank/index.html.
7. "The Interface Model: Ray's Story." Retrieved May 29, 2008 from company website http://www.interfaceinc.com/eur/company/sustainability/ray_anderson.asp?page=1.
8. Kauffman Foundation, "Giving to Entrepreneurship by Spreading the Gospel of Giving." Retrieved September 24, 2007 from www.eventuring.org.
9. Personal interview with Robert Milk, co-founder of Novica, March 31, 2008.
10. Company Interview, "Mel Jones: Sterling Planet," *The Wall Street Transcript*, February, 7, 2005. New York: Wall Street Transcript Corporation. Retrieved January 28, 2008 from http://www.twst.com/pdf/ABA615.pdf.
11. "Moving toward Sustainability: Working to Reduce Our Ecological Footprint," *Clif Bar Sustainability Newsletter*, 3 (Summer 2004). Retrieved May 6, 2009 from www.clifbar.com/uploads/default/Sustainability_Issue3.summer2004.pdf.
12. A. Roddick, *Business as Unusual: The Triumph of Anita Roddick* (Glasgow: Thorsons/HarperCollins, 2001).
13. Ben Cohen, co-founder of Ben & Jerry's Homemade Inc., in the article "Coming of Age," in Inc.'s tenth-anniversary issue, 1989.
14. Ibid.
15. Julia Boorstin, "No Preservatives No Unions Lots of Dough," *Fortune*, September 15, 2003.
16. P. Hawken, *Growing a Business* (Fireside: New York, 1988).
17. Company website, Retrieved November 24, 2009 from http://www.interfaceglobal.com/Sustainability/Our-Journey/Vision.aspx.
18. Retrieved May 30, 2008 from http://www.ecover.com/gb/en/About/Mission+UK.htm.
19. B. Cohen & J. Greenfield, *Ben & Jerry's Double Dip: How to Run a Values-Led Business and Make Money Too* (New York: Simon & Schuster, 1997).
20. Company website, Retrieved November 22, 2009 from http://www.timhaahs.com/index.php/site/mission.
21. Hawken, *Growing a Business*.
22. N. F. Koehn, "Howard Schultz and Starbucks Coffee Company," Harvard Business School Case Study, Vol. 801361 (2001), 40.

4 Raise Capital with Mission in Mind: Be Strategic, Resilient, and Cautious

1. Nelson Mandela, acceptance speech of the President of the African National Congress at the Nobel Peace Prize Award Ceremony, Oslo, Norway, December 10, 1993.
2. P. Newman & A. E. Hotchner, *Shameless Exploitation in Pursuit of the Common Good: The Madcap Business Adventure by the Truly Oddest Couple* (New York: Doubleday, 2003).
3. J. A. Timmons, *New Venture Creation: Entrepreneurship in the 1990s* (fifth ed.) (Irwin: Homewood, IL, 1999).
4. Personal interview with Timothy Haahs.
5. J. Mans, "Stonyfield Farm," *Dairy Foods* 99, 9 (September 1988): 76.

6. Retrieved on August 15, 2008 from company website http://www.innocentdrinks.co.uk/press/.

7. Amar Bhide, "Bootstrap Finance: The Art of Start-Ups," *Harvard Business Review* 70, 6 (November–December 1992): 109–117.

8. Ibid.

9. M. Bresnahan & G. Johnson, "For Magic, NBA was Halftime," *Los Angeles Times*, June 30, 2008, C-1.

10. Ibid.

11. Liz Claman, "Magic Means Business," *LA Times Magazine*, November 30, 2008.

12. Bresnahan & Johnson, "For Magic, NBA was Halftime."

13. N. F. Koehn, "Howard Schultz and Starbucks Coffee Company," Harvard Business School Case Study, Vol. 801361 (2001), 40.

14. A Special Day with Howard Schultz, Chairman and Chief Global Strategist, Starbucks Coffee Company, 2004 Entrepreneur of the Year, Lloyd Greif Center for Entrepreneurial Studies, University of Southern California.

15. Ibid.

16. Nancy Marcello, "Green Companies: The Body Shop International," Loyola Marymount University Case Study, 2003.

17. K. Valley & A. Gendron, "Iggy's Bread of the World," Harvard Business School Case Study, 9–801–282 (2001), 14.

5 Hire Talented Employees with Shared Values

1. Personal interview with Timothy Haahs, June 2008.

2. Personal interview with Robert Milk, co-founder of Novica, March 31, 2008.

3. R. Heneman, J. Tansky, & H. Camp, "Human Resource Management Practices in Small and Medium-Sized Enterprises: Unanswered Questions and Future Research Perspectives," *Entrepreneurship Theory & Practice* 25, 1 (2000): 11–26.

4. Y. Chouinard, *Let My People Go Surfing: The Education of a Reluctant Businessman* (New York: The Penguin Press, 2005).

5. K. Valley & A. Gendron, "Iggy's Bread of the World," Harvard Business School Case Study, 9–801–282 (2001), 14.

6. Personal interview with Timothy Haahs, June 2008.

7. E. Gray, "Gottlieb Duttweiler and the Perpetuation of Social Values at Migros," *Journal of Business Leadership* 6, 2 (Fall/Winter 1993): 51–62.

8. Tom Chappell, *The Soul of the Business: Managing for Profit and the Common Good* (New York: Bantam Books, 1993), 25.

9. E. Gray & K. Petrapoulos, "Green Companies: Tom's of Maine," Loyola Marymount University Case Study, 2002.

10. Personal interview with Robert Milk, co-founder of Novica, March 31, 2008.

11. Liz Claman, "Magic Means Business," *LA Times Magazine*, November 30, 2008.

12. David Choi, "Rhythm & Hues," Loyola Marymount University Case Study, 2005.

13. Ibid.

14. Interview with Laura Scher, July 11, 2008.

15. Company website. Retrieved on July 18, 2008, from www.designcouncil.org.uk/en/case-studies/all-case-studies/innocent-smoothies.

16. Ibid.

17. Chris King Precision Components website. Retrieved November 20, 2007 from www.chrisking.com.

18. Interview with Laura Scher, July 11, 2008.

19. Ibid.

20. A. E. Smith & Samantha Beerman, "How to Be Good," *Incentive* 180, 8 (August 2006).

21. Muhammad Yunus, *Banker to the Poor* (New York: Public Affairs, 2003), 103.

22. Ibid.

23. Choi, "Rhythm & Hues."

24. Ibid.

25. Donna L. Goodison, "Dancing Deer Prances to List of Top Inner-City Firms," *The Boston Business Journal* 21, 14 (May 11, 2001): 12.

26. "About Us," Dancing Deer Company website. www.dancingdeer.com. Retrieved December 4, 2007.

27. Stacy Perman, "Baking Principles into the Business," *BusinessWeek*, Small Biz Online. Retrieved December 7, 2008 from http://www.businessweek.com/smallbiz/content/dec2005/sb20051212_554808.htm.

6 Promote Your Company's Values

1. A. Roddick, *Business as Unusual: The Triumph of Anita Roddick* (Glasgow: Thorsons/HarperCollins, 2001).
2. Theodore M. Finney, *Hearing Music: A Guide to Music Appreciation* (New York: Harcourt Brace, 2007), 191.
3. S. Shane, *A General Theory of Entrepreneurship: The Individual-Opportunity Nexus*, New Horizons in Entrepreneurship Series (Cheltenham: Edward Elgar Publishing, 2003). Joseph A. Schumpeter, *Capitalism, Socialism, and Democracy* (New York: Harper, 1950).
4. Retrieved on May 18, 2009 from http://www.revfoods.com/browse/customer_testimonials.
5. J. H. Hollender & S. Fenichell, *What Matters Most: How a Small Group of Pioneers is Teaching Social Responsibility to Big Business and Why Big Business Is Listening* (New York: Basic Books, 2003).
6. Sami Grover, "The TH Interview: Eric Henry of TS Designs," Treehugger Online, March 12, 2007, retrieved March 20, 2007 from http://www.treehugger.com/files/2007/03/eric_henry_of_t.php.
7. Retrieved on July 24, 2008 from http://www.designcouncil.org.uk/en/case-studies/all-case-studies/innocent-smoothies.
8. Personal interview, March 20, 2008.
9. Ibid.
10. Ibid.
11. Retrieved May 20, 2008 from http://www.benjerry.com/company/history/xml/scrapbook_data.xml.
12. Personal interview, August 2008.
13. CEO Exchange, Episode 204: "The Built to Order Revolution," broadcast May 2001.
14. Personal interview, August 2008.

7 Build a Cohesive, Dedicated Organization

1. A Special Day with Howard Schultz, Chairman and Chief Global Strategist, Starbucks Coffee Company, 2004 Entrepreneur of the Year, Lloyd Greif Center for Entrepreneurial Studies, University of Southern California.
2. D. Batstone, *Saving the Corporate Soul—and (Who Knows?) Maybe Your Own* (San Francisco: Jossey-Bass, 2003).
3. A Special Day with Howard Schultz, Chairman and Chief Global Strategist, Starbucks Coffee Company.
4. Ibid.
5. N. F. Koehn, "Howard Schultz and Starbucks Coffee Company," Harvard Business School Case Study, Vol. 801361 (2001), 40.
6. F. Maraga, "Working Mother Gives Patagonia Honors," *Ventura County Star*, Business section, September 2, 1998, E06.
7. New Belgium Brewing Company. Retrieved on May 26, 2009, from http://www.knowmore.org/wiki/index.php?title=Image:New_Belgium_Brewing_Co.-logo.png.
8. Company website. Retrieved on May 26, 2009 from http://www.newbelgium.com/our-story.
9. "100 Best Companies to Work For," *Fortune*, February 4, 2008, 75–77.
10. D. Wann, "Brewing a Sustainable Industry," Terrain.Org: A Journal of the Built and Natural Environments. Accessed October 11, 2007 from http://www.terrain.org/articles/9/wann.htm.
11. Leah Carlson, "Quality of Life," *Employee Benefit News* 18, 5 (April 15, 2004): 53–55.
12. T. Chappell, *The Soul of a Business: Managing for Profit and the Common Good* (New York: Bantam Books, 1993).
13. See Stonyfield Farm case study in this volume.
14. E. Fuhrman, "Crafting Beers for Conscientious Consumers," *Beverage Industry* 98, 7 (July 2007): 30–35.
15. See Chris King case study in the book.
16. Personal interview, August 2008.
17. J. McCune, "The Corporation in the Community," *HR Focus* 74, 3 (March 1997): 12–14 and "Corporate Volunteerism at Tom's," www.tomsofmaine.com.
18. C. Adams, "Breakaway (Special Report): The Entrepreneurial Life—Upfront: Brushing Up on Values," *Wall Street Journal*, September 27, 1999, 6.
19. Retrieved January 15 from http://www.calvert.com/about_1537.html.
20. Salesforce.com press release. "The Center for Employment Opportunities Helps Programs Participants Return to the Workforce Through Salesforce.com's 1 Percent Product Donation Program." San Francisco. May 1, 2008.

8 Maximize Profits . . . With Some Exceptions

1. Widely quoted but original reference is not found.
2. D. Choi, "Novica," Loyola Marymount University Case Study, 2008.
3. D. Choi, "Rhythm & Hues," Loyola Marymount University Case Study, 2005.
4. J. H. Hollender & S. Fenichell, *What Matters Most: How a Small Group of Pioneers is Teaching Social Responsibility to Big Business and Why Big Business Is Listening* (New York: Basic Books, 2003).
5. S. Perman, "Scones and Social Responsibility," *BusinessWeek* Issue 3998 (August 21, 2006): 38.
6. Panel discussion, Global Social Venture Symposium, April 2007.
7. K. Meyer & K. Bollier, "Judy Wicks (B)," Harvard Business School Case Study, 996040 (1996).
8. K. Valley & A. Gendron, "Iggy's Bread of the World," Harvard Business School Case Study, 9–801–282 (2001), 14.
9. Perman, "Scones and Social Responsibility," 38.
10. Dancing Deer company website www.dancingdeer.com. Retrieved December 4, 2007.
11. Perman, "Scones and Social Responsibility," 38.
12. Louis Hau, "Newspaper Killer," *Forbes*, December 11, 2006. Retrieved on May 8, 2008 from http://www.forbes.com/2006/12/08/newspaper-classifield-online-tech_cx-lh_1211craigslist.html.
13. Ibid.
14. Ibid.
15. Retrieved on July 24, 2008 from company website (www.sterlingplanet.com).
16. Ibid.
17. Meyer & Bollier, "Judy Wicks (B)."
18. "The Green Enterprise: Frog's Leap." Retrieved November 17, 2008 from http://news.zdnet.com/2422–13748_22–210918.html.
19. Ibid.
20. The Leadership in Energy and Environmental Design (LEED) is a green building rating system developed by the U.S. Green Building Council (USGBC). LEED was created to define "green building" through a common standard of measurement. LEED provides a complete framework for assessing building performance and meeting sustainability goals. Based on well-founded scientific standards, LEED emphasizes state of the art strategies for sustainable site development, water savings, energy efficiency, materials selection and indoor environmental quality. LEED recognizes achievement and promotes expertise in green building through a comprehensive system offering project certification, professional accreditation, training and practical resources.
21. N. F. Koehn, "Howard Schultz and Starbucks Coffee Company," Harvard Business School Case Study, Vol. 801361 (2001), 40.

9 Minimize Your Environmental and Social Footprint

1. Kevin Wilcox, "CEO Challenges Delegates on Environmental Issues," County News Online, August 10, 1998. Retrieved November 14, 2008 from http://www.naco.org/cnews/1998/98–08–10/13.htm.
2. Y. Chouinard, "Patagonia: The Next Hundred Years," in *Sacred Trusts: Essays on Stewardship and Responsibility*, ed. M. Katakis (San Francisco: Mercury House, 1993), 112–121.
3. Company website. Retrieved October 12, 2008 from http://www.clifbar.com/soul/who_we_are.
4. China CSR Map. Broad Air Conditioning. Retrieved April 9, 2008 from http://www.chinacsrmap.org/E_Org_Show.asp?CCMOrg_ID=733.
5. Zhi Yi He, Meng Sun, & Paul W. Beamish, "Broad Air Conditioning and Environmental Protection," Richard Ivey School of Business, The University of Western Ontario, 2004.
6. R. Anderson, *Mid-Course Correction* (Atlanta, GA: Peregrinzella Press, 1998).
7. Ibid.
8. Ibid.
9. Company website. Accessed October 20, 2008 from http://www.ecover.com/gb/en.
10. ISO 14001 is a leading environmental management standard. It specifies a set of environmental management requirements for environmental management systems. The purpose of this standard is to help organizations to protect the environment, to prevent pollution, and to improve their environmental performance.
11. Anderson, *Mid-Course Correction.*
12. D. Choi, "Chris King," Loyola Marymount University Case Study, 2009.

13. "The Green Enterprise: Frog's Leap Winery." Retrieved November 18, 2008 from http://news.zdnet.com/2422–13748_22–210918.html.

14. *Green Steps Journal*, 2005, www.greensteps.org/stepone/tsdesigns.htm, 2–3.

15. E. Fuhrman, "Crafting Beers for Conscientious Consumers," *Beverage Industry* 98, 7 (July 2007): 30–35.

16. Ibid.

17. The Forest Stewardship Council (FSC) is an international network to promote responsible management of the world's forests.

18. Clif Bar 2004 Sustainability Report. Retrieved November 29, 2008 from http://www.clifbar.com/uploads/default/Sustainability_Issue3.summer 2004.

19. Gabriela Rodrigues, "Leading by Example: The Founder of Clif Bar Grows a Sustainable Company by Green Actions and an Unconventional Office." *American Forests* (Winter 2007). Retrieved on June 3, 2009 from http://findarticles.com/p/articles/mi_m1016/is_4_112/ai_n27149281/.

20. Ibid.

21. E. Pofeldt, "The Nurturer Eileen Fisher/Eileen Fisher Inc.," *FSB: Fortune Small Business*, 13, 8 (2003): 44.

22. SAI is a global standard-setting non-profit human rights organization dedicated to improving workplaces and communities best known for its SA8000 standard. The SA8000 is a voluntary standard designed by a multi-stakeholder advisory board, including representation from companies, trade unions, NGOs, suppliers, government agencies, certification bodies, social investment firms, and human rights activists. The standard is based on the following eight human rights components: Child labor, forced labor, health and safety, freedom of association, discrimination, discipline, working hours, and remuneration. Certified facilities like Eileen Fisher must integrate these standards into their management practice.

23. "Sizzle: Power Players," *Elle Magazine* 12 (December 2006), 72.

24. Liz Claman, "Magic Means Business," *LA Times Magazine*, November 30, 2008.

25. Alissa Walker, "Measuring Footprints," *Fast Company*, www.fastcompnay.com/magazine/124/measuringfootprints.html. Also, in *Fast Company* 124 (April 2008).

26. On LEED, see Chapter 8, note 20.

27. In general, contracts are available to the public through government websites, e.g., http://www.management.energy.gov/InterFlooringWO.pdf. Interface is also listed as an eligible contractor with Department of Energy as a Recycled Content Carpet vendor.

28. "The Green Enterprise: Gaia Napa Valley Hotel and Spa." Retrieved November 18, 2008 from http://news.zdnet.com/2422–13748_22–166046.html.

29. Company website accessed on February 20, 2009 from http://www.smalldog.com.

30. Ibid.

31. "The Green Enterprise: Gaia Napa Valley Hotel and Spa."

32. Ibid.

33. J. Makeower, "How Aveda is Changing the Complexion of Magazines," WorldChanging.com, October 30, 2005. Retrieved January 28, 2008 from http://www.worldchanging.com/ archives/003689.html.

34. B. Krumsiek, "Socially Responsible High Tech Companies: Emerging Issues." *Journal of Business Ethics* 43, 3 (March 2003): 179–187.

35. M. K. Phillips, "Social Investing for the Long Term," *Global Investor* 175 (2004): 9–10.

10 Stay With It for the Long Haul

1. D. Sayers, *Creed or Chaos? Why Christians Must Choose Either Dogma or Disaster* (Manchester, NH: Sophia Institute Press, 1995).

2. P. Hawken, *Growing a Business* (Fireside: New York, 1988).

3. Personal interview with Chris King, June 2008.

4. Ibid.

5. Ibid.

6. E. Gray, "Gottlieb Duttweiler and the Perpetuation of Social Values at Migros," *Journal of Business Leadership* 6, 2 (Fall/Winter 1993): 51–62.

7. Liz Claman, "Magic Means Business," *LA Times Magazine*, November 30, 2008.

8. A. Zibel, "Craigslist Founder Committed Outsider: Site's Creator Spurns Suitors to Preserve Independence," *The Oakland Tribune*, April 4, 2002.

9. Amar Bhide, "Bootstrap Finance: The Art of Start-ups," *Harvard Business Review* 70, 6 (November–December 1992): 109–117.

10. David Choi, "Working Assets," Loyola Marymount University Case Study, 2008.

11. Zibel, "Craigslist Founder Committed Outsider: Site's Creator Spurns Suitors to Preserve Independence."

12. Y. Chouinard, "Patagonia: The Next Hundred Years," in *Sacred Trusts: Essays on Stewardship and Responsibility*, ed. M. Katakis (San Francisco: Mercury House, 1993), 5–7.

13. Y. Chouinard, *Let My People Go Surfing: The Education of a Reluctant Businessman* (New York: The Penguin Press, 2005).

14. Gary Erickson with Lois Lorentzen, *Raising the Bar: Integrity and Passion in Life and Business: The Story of Clif Bar & Co.* (San Francisco: Jossey-Bass, 2006).

15. Ibid.

16. Eric Young, "Executive Profile: Gary Erickson," *San Francisco Business Times*, May 9, 2003.

17. Personal interview, June 2008.

18. Tom Chappell, *Managing Upside Down: The Seven Intentions of Values-Centered Leadership* (New York: William Morrow, 1999).

19. Ilana DeBare, "The World According to Tom's of Maine," *San Francisco Chronicle*, October 10, 2007.

20. Hollender & Fenichell, *What Matters Most*, 28.

21. Julie Schmidt, "Raising the Bar on How Business Gets Done: Clif Bar Is Good for You, Environment," *USA Today*, March 14, 2005, 11B. Retrieved on December 22, 2008 from http://www.usatoday.com/educate/college/careers/profile3-14-05.htm.

22. Joyce Marcel, "Profiles in Business: Jeffrey Hollender and Seventh Generation," *Vermont Business Magazine*, June 1, 2003.

23. Anonymous, "Anita the Agitator," *Time*, January 25, 1993.

24. Jane Simms, "The Queen of Green," *Director* (London), September 2000.

25. Michael Wall, "The Greenest Capitalist," *Creative Loafing*, March 8, 2006. Retrieved on March 5, 2008 from http://atlanta.creativeloafing.com/gyrobase/the_greenest_capitalist/ Content?oid=21703.

26. Ibid.

27. Company website. Retrieved on August 2008 from http://www.interfaceinc.com/eur/company/sustainability/frontpage.asp.

28. Ibid.

11 Make Giving a Priority

1. D. Lyn Hunter, "Paul Newman Challenges Corporations to Donate More: Forum on Philanthropy in Business' Lecturer Gives away Millions in Food Company Profits," *The Berkeleyan*, September 11, 2000.

2. Personal interview August 2008.

3. Y. Chouinard, *Let My People Go Surfing: The Education of a Reluctant Businessman* (New York: The Penguin Press, 2005).

4. Company website (www.clifbar.com).

5. Company website (www.workingassets.com). December 27, 2008.

6. Nadia Mustafa, "Shoe That Fits So Many Souls," *Time* 169 (February 5, 2007), C.2.

7. Ibid.

8. Dennis Hughes & Janice Hughes, "An Interview with Anita Roddick, Founder of The Body Shop and Author of Business as Unusual." Retrieved June 1, 2009 from http://www.shareguide.com/roddick.html.

9. United States tax rules allow corporations to deduct from their taxable income gifts up to 10 percent of the company's before-tax income. A company, of course, can donate more than 10 percent but would not receive a tax break for the marginal amount above 10 percent.

10. Stuart Nettle, "The Company I Hate to Love," February 19, 2009. Retrieved on June 1, 2009 from http://www.swellnet.com.au/surfpolitik.php?surfpolitik=Patagonia_190209.php.

11. Company website, www.newbelgium.com. Accessed October 11, 2007.

12. The Committee Encouraging Corporate Philanthropy, *Giving in Numbers* (New York: Author, 2007). Retrieved January 28, 2008 from http://corporatephilanthropy.org/research/pubs/GivinginNumbers2007.pdf.

13. P. Newman & A. E. Hotchner, *Shameless Exploitation in Pursuit of the Common Good: The Madcap Business Adventure by the Truly Oddest Couple* (New York: Doubleday, 2003).

14. Company website, http://www.salesforcefoundation.org/donation. Accessed May 1, 2008.

15. K. Meyer & K. Bollier, "Judy Wicks (B)," Harvard Business School Case Study, 996040 (1996), 12.

16. A. Wolfe, "Gourmet Suppliers Take Their Philanthropic Efforts to Ebay," *Gourmet News* (Yarmouth) 69, 1 (January 2004): 38.

17. N. Brooks, "When it Comes to Work Environment Some Employers are Mother Superior," *Los Angeles Times*, October 4, 1998, Sec. E, 5.

18. Patagonia, Inc., "Louder Than Words," Press Packet, 1998.

19. Personal interview with Timothy Haahs, June 2008.

12 Be a Role Model for Others

1. M. Bresnahan & G. Johnson, "For Magic, NBA was Halftime," *Los Angeles Times*, June 30, 2008, C-1.

2. Personal interview with Timothy Haas, August 2008.

3. Sami Grover, "The TH Interview: Eric Henry of TS Designs," Treehugger Online, March 12, 2007, retrieved March 20, 2007 from http://www.treehugger.com/files/2007/03/eric_henry_of_t.php.

4. R. C. Anderson, *Mid-Course Correction: Toward a Sustainable Enterprise: The Interface Model* (White River Junction, VT: Chelsea Green Publishing Company, 1999).

5. Anita Roddick's Keynote Speech, the Falcone Center for Entrepreneurship at Syracuse University, Friday, October 27, 2006.

6. Personal interview, August 2008.

7. Kauffman Foundation, "Giving to Entrepreneurship by Spreading the Gospel of Giving." Retrieved February 10, 2008 from http://eventuring.kauffman.org/Resources/Resource.aspx?id.

8. Ibid.

9. Ibid.

10. Y. Chouinard, *Let My People Go Surfing: The Education of a Reluctant Businessman* (New York: The Penguin Press, 2005), 5–7.

11. M. Burnham, "In Patagonia: Sustainable Industries," December, 5, 2005. Retrieved January 2, 2009 from http://www.sustainableindustries.com/sijnews/2044512.html.

12. Personal interview with Chris King, June 2008.

13. "Product Spotlight," *Mountain Bike Review*, June 2000. Retrieved on November 13, 2007 from. http://mtbr.com/spotlight/jun00/index.shtml.

14. B. Cohen & J. Greenfield, *Ben & Jerry's Double Dip: How to Run a Values-Led Business and Make Money Too* (New York: Simon & Schuster, 1997), 6.

15. United Nations' Environment Program Sustainable Buildings and Construction Initiative website, http://www.unepsbci.org Accessed April 6, 2008.

16. Kauffman Foundation, "Giving to Entrepreneurship by Spreading the Gospel of Giving."

17. Aveda Ceres Report, 2003–2005, accessed on February 17, 2010 from http://aveda.aveda.com/protect/we/ceresreport2003_2004.pdf.

18. Kristen S. Bastian, "New Belgium Brewing Brews Community Spirit," *Northern Colorado Business Report* 11, 5 (Fort Collins, November 25, 2005), B11.

19. G. Owsley, "Why Brand Veneers Must Reflect a Soul," *Advertising Age* (Midwest Region Edition) 78, 26 (June 25, 2007): 22–23.

20. Bastian, "New Belgium Brewing Brews Community Spirit."

21. www.google.org/foundation.html, accessed May 1, 2008.

22. Jon Swartz, "Benioff Book Has a Theme: Philanthropy," *USA Today*, July 23, 2007.

23. www.socialinvest.org/resources/research.

24. Retrieved on May 1, 2009 from www.onepercentfortheplanet.org.

25. Charlie Rose Show with Muhammad Yunus, August 26, 2007. Accessed May 1, 2009 from youtube.com.

26. Company website. Retrieved March 27, 2009 from http://www.grameen-info.org/index.php?option=com content&task=view&id=26&Itemid=164.

27. Charlie Rose Show with Muhammad Yunus, August 26, 2007.

28. "Muhammad Yunus, Ashoka's Global Academy Member, Wins Nobel Peace Prize" (October 12, 2006). Retrieved August 17, 2007 from http://www.ashoka.org/node/3798.

29. "The Nobel Peace Prize for 2006," NobelPrize.org. 2006–10–13. Retrieved on October 13, 2006 from http://nobelprize.org/nobel prizes/peace/laureates/2006/press.html.

30. Lists of his awards are found at Grameen Bank website, www.guzelsozler.web.tr/son-eklenen/6-yatakta-servisme.html, his personal website, and his profile at *Bangladesh News* website.

31. The MicroBanking Bulletin #15, *Microfinance Information eXchange*, 2007, 30–31.

32. Robert Peck Christen, Richard Rosenberg, & Veena Jayadeva, "Financial Institutions with a Double-Bottom Line: Implications for the Future of Microfinance," CGAP Occasional Paper, July 2004.

13 Concluding Thoughts

1. Deja Shoe, Inc., An Interactive Case Study, video, University of Michigan, Corporate Environmental Management Program (CEMP).
2. Eco-fibers are raw materials, used to manufacture textiles, that are grown without using pesticides, chemicals, or synthetic fertilizers, such as hemp or bamboo.
3. Paul Hardy, "Deja Shoe (A): Creating the Environmental Footwear Company," University of Michigan's Corporate Environmental Management Program (CEMP), 1996 and Paul Hardy, "Deja Shoe (B): Product Launch," CEMP, 1996.
4. Kevin T. Higgins, "Compassionate Capitalists: The Owners of Just Desserts Hope to Leverage a New $12 Million Bakery into a Major Share of the Super-Premium Cake Business," *Food Engineering* 74, 4 (April 2002): 49.
5. Alan Reder, *In Pursuit of Principle and Profit: Business Success through Social Responsibility* (Putman Publishing Group/Jeremy P. Tarcher, Inc., 1994), 36.
6. Ibid.
7. Pia Sarkar, "Bittersweet Journey: Founders Struggle to Key Just Desserts From Crumbling," *San Francisco Chronicle*, August 5, 2003, B–1.

Case Study 1: Gottlieb Duttweiler and Migros

1. http://www.lovermarks.com/nomination/4047.
2. Migros, Wikipedia, The Free Encyclopedia, en.wikipedia.org/wiki/migros.
3. "The Swiss Family Migros," *Time*, August 9, 1954.
4. "Gebana and Migros Team Up to Offer Fair Prices for Brazil," August 29, 2007, www.swissinfo.org.

Case Study 2: Stonyfield Farm

1. Gary Hirshberg, "Commencement Remarks" (University of New Hampshire, 2009).
2. Henry David Thoreau, *Walden, and On the Duty of Civil Disobedience*, ed. Cynthia Brantley Johnson (New York, Simon and Schuster, 2004).
3. Matthew J. Mowry, "Business NH 2009 Business of the Year Awards: Stonyfield Farm, Gary Hirshberg, Chairman, President and CE-Yo," *Business NH*, May 2009.
4. Funding Universe, "Stonyfield Farm, Inc.," http://www.fundinguniverse.com/company-histories/Stonyfield-Farm-Inc-Company-History.html.
5. Meg Cadoux Hirshberg, "Balancing Marriage and Business," *Inc.*, May 1, 2009.
6. Funding Universe, "Stonyfield Farm, Inc."
7. Ibid.
8. Courtney Claire Brigham, "Turning Heads of Giants," *Eagle-Tribune*, August 29, 1999.
9. Sheryl Julian, "Tang of Success," *The Boston Globe*, June 24, 1998.
10. Funding Universe, "Stonyfield Farm, Inc."
11. Mary Sit, "A Different Yogurt Finds a Niche," *The Boston Globe*, October 21, 1989.
12. Shelley Donald Coolidge, "Yogurt Maker Acts on Its Commitment," *Christian Science Monitor*, June 6, 1994.
13. Stonyfield Farm, Inc., corporate webpage, http://www.stonyfield.com.
14. Susan Greco, "Sampling with a Twist," *Inc.*, August 1992.
15. Coolidge, "Yogurt Maker Acts on Its Commitment."
16. Udayan Gupta, "Cause-Driven Companies' New Cause: Profits," *Wall Street Journal*, November 8, 1994.
17. Morgan, A. "The bigger they are . . .," *Success*, 46, 2 (February 1999): 62–65.
18. Emily Esterson, "One Holdout: A White Knight Who Won't Quit," *Inc.*, September 1988.
19. Stephanie Thompson, "Stonyfield Farm Serves First National Campaign," *Advertising Age*, January 3, 2000.
20. Stonyfield Farm, corporate webpage.
21. Roberta Reynes, "Something to Moo About," *Nation's Business*, August 1995.
22. NOFA Interstate Council, organization website, http://www.nofa.org/index.php.
23. Diane Brady, "The Organic Myth," *BusinessWeek*, October 16, 2006.
24. Sue Markgraf, "A Way with Windmills," *Dairy Foods*, August 1997.
25. Warren Hastings, "Free Gun Safety Locks Offered," *The Union Leader*, May 22, 1999.
26. "Pac Honoring Senators Who Voted for Income Tax Draws Criticism," *The Associated Press*, May 6, 1999.

27. Brady, "The Organic Myth."
28. Gary Hirshberg, "The Stonyfield Story," *The Journal for Quality and Participation* 21, 1 (1998).
29. L. Singhania, "Food Maker Manages to Mix Politics, Profits," *The Los Angeles Times*, March 21, 1997.
30. Hirshberg, "The Stonyfield Story."
31. ThinkExist.com, "Gary Hirshberg Quotes."
32. Stonyfield Farm, corporate webpage.
33. Reynes, "Something to Moo About."
34. Stonyfield Farm, corporate webpage.
35. Reynes, "Something to Moo About."
36. The United States Food and Drug Administration maintains the official position that the hormone is safe for human consumption.
37. Stonyfield Farm, corporate webpage.
38. Ibid.
39. Ibid.
40. Given the cow's unfortunate endowment of hooves instead of fingers, their handwriting is exceptionally poor. Thus, these updates are usually typed by trained human-bovine translators.
41. Glenn Hasek, "Waste Not, Want Not," *Industry Week*, August 9, 1999.
42. "Pragmatism an Ally in Fight against Environmental Funding Cuts," *Marketing News*, May 20, 1996.
43. Katherine Heinrich, "Flip Your Lid," *National Parks*, May/June 1996.
44. Stonyfield Farm, corporate webpage.
45. Julian, "Tang of Success."
46. Stonyfield Farm, corporate webpage.
47. Brigham, "Turning Heads of Giants."
48. Hasek, "Waste Not, Want Not."
49. Stonyfield Farm, corporate webpage.
50. At the time of press, the company had not yet submitted the building to the LEED certification process, so this claim is unverified.
51. Stonyfield Farm, corporate webpage.
52. Mowry, "Business NH 2009 Business of the Year Awards: Stonyfield Farm, Gary Hirshberg, Chairman, President and CE-Yo."
53. Stonyfield Farm, corporate webpage.
54. Ibid.
55. Hasek, "Waste Not, Want Not."
56. Reynes, "Something to Moo About."
57. Ibid.
58. Jacqueline Davidson, "Responsibility Reaps Rewards," *Small Business Review*, February 1993.
59. Mowry, "Business NH 2009 Business of the Year Awards: Stonyfield Farm, Gary Hirshberg, Chairman, President and CE-Yo."
60. Soon after the publication of the *BusinessWeek* article, Stonyfield released an official response on the company website, clarifying that it did not have any plans to source milk internationally. The response has since been removed.
61. Brady, "The Organic Myth."
62. Andy Rowell, "Organicised Crime—Anti-Organic Farming Analysis," *The Ecologist*, February 2001; see, for example, The Center for Consumer Freedom, "Busting the Myth of Organic Food"; John J. Miller, "The Organic Myth: A Food Movement Makes a Pest of Itself," *National Review*, February 9, 2004.
63. Brady, "The Organic Myth."
64. Gary Hirshberg, "Socially Responsible Investing: What Is Possible in These Times?," *Green Money*, Fall 2009.
65. Stonyfield Farm, corporate webpage.

Case Study 3: King Cycle Group

1. Chris King company website. Accessed January 24, 2008 from http://www.chrisking.com/involvement.
2. "Product Spotlight," *Mountain Bike Review*, June 2000. Accessed on Nov. 13, 2007 from http://mtbr.com/spotlight/jun00/index.shtml.
3. Chris King Company History. Retrieved January 25, 2008 from www.chrisking.com/company/comphistory.html.

4. Ibid.
5. Christine Larson, "On the Move: Relocating a Business Does Not Have to Mean a Lot of Heavy Lifting," *Wall Street Journal*, April 23, 2001, 8.
6. "Product Spotlight," *Mountain Bike Review*, June 2000. Retrieved November 13, 2007 from http://mtbr.com/spotlight/jun00/index.shtml.
7. Chris King: Relocation to Portland. Retrieved January 25, 2008 from www.chrisking.com/company/comp_history.html.
8. Ibid.
9. Ibid.
10. Ibid.
11. "Interview: Chris DeStefano," *Industry Outsider*. Retrieved January 25, 2008 from http://www.industryoutsider.com/?p=127.
12. Interview with Chris King, August 2008.
13. Ibid.
14. Chris King Staff. Mountain Bike Hall of Fame. Retrieved January 23, 2008 from http://www.mtnbikehalloffame.com/inductees.cfm?page=99&mID=178.
15. Interview with Chris King, August 2008.
16. "Product Spotlight," *Mountain Bike Review*, June 2000.
17. Ibid.
18. Anonymous, "Fab Five," *Bicycle Retailer and Industry News* (Laguna Beach), 16, 1 (January 1, 2007), 16–17.
19. "Product Spotlight," *Mountain Bike Review*, June 2000.
20. Ibid.
21. Jonathan Maus, "King Cycle Group Releases 'Pretty and Strong' Results," February 16, 2006, http://www.bikeportland.org/2006/02/15/king-cycle-group-releases-pretty-and-strong-results/. Retrieved January 24, 2008.
22. Ibid.
23. "Why Pink?" Chris King company website. Retrieved January 25, 2008 from http://www.chrisking.com/prettyandstrong/pink.html.
24. Ibid.
25. "Why Red, Gold, Black & Green?" Chris King company website. Retrieved January 25, 2008 from http://www.chrisking.com/involvement/wheels4life/colors.html.
26. Jonathan Maus, "Donations Large and Small Kick Start Bike Safety Fund." Retrieved November 29, 2007 from http://www.bikeportland.org.
27. "Asia Manufacturing," Chris King company website. Retrieved January 26, 2008 from http://www.chrisking.com/asiamfg/index.html.
28. Interview with Chris King, August 2008.
29. "Interview: Chris DeStefano," *Industry Outsider*. Retrieved January 25, 2008 from http://www.industryoutsider.com/?p=127.
30. Jonathan Maus, "Chris King Employees Speak about Sustainability at City Hall," http://www.bikeportland.org, May 4, 2007. Accessed January 22, 2008.
31. Jonathan Maus, "Chris King Rekindles an Old Flame," http://www.bikeportland.org, February 9, 2008. Accessed February 19, 2008.
32. Personal interview with Chris King, June 2008.
33. Ibid.
34. Ibid.
35. Ibid.
36. Ibid.

Case Study 4: T.S. Designs, Inc.

1. *Greensteps Journal*, 2005, www.greensteps.org/stepone/tsdesigns.htm.
2. Eric Henry & Sam Moore, "Manufacturing and Selling a $4.00 T-shirt in a $1.00 World," Greening of Industry Conference in San Francisco, California, October 13, 2003, 2–4.
3. Sami Grover, "The TH Interview: Eric Henry of TS Designs," Treehugger Online, March 12, 2007, retrieved March 20, 2007 from http://www.treehugger.com/files/2007/03/eric_henry_of_t.php.
4. www.ourstolenfuture.org/newscience/oncompounds/phthalates/phthalates.htm#health.

5. *Green Steps Journal*, 2005, www.greensteps.org/stepone/tsdesigns.htm, 2–3.
6. Henry & Moore, "Manufacturing and Selling a $4.00 T-shirt in a $1.00 World," 5–7.
7. *Green Steps Journal*, 2005, www.greensteps.org/stepone/tsdesigns.htm.
8. T.S. Designs' website, www.tsdesigns.com.
9. *Green Steps Journal*, 2005, 7.
10. Ibid. p. 5.
11. Henry & Moore, "Manufacturing and Selling a $4.00 T-shirt in a $1.00 World," 14–16.
12. Website, www.ts.whispertrail.com/about/partners.
13. Eric Henry, *Impressions Magazine*, November 2006, 21.
14. Bonnie Hutchinson, "T.S. Designs Land Use Plan," October 6, 2003, www.tsdesigns.com/landuse.htm.
15. Ibid.
16. Megan J. Shepard, "A Sustainable Business Model: TS Designs," *Back Home Magazine*, November/December 2005.
17. *T.S. Designs Newsletter*, September, 2008, 3.
18. *T.S. Designs Newsletter*, August, 2006, 2.
19. Henry & Moore, "Manufacturing and Selling a $4.00 T-shirt in a $1.00 World," 14–15.
20. Grover, "The TH Interview: Eric Henry of TS Designs."
21. Personal communication to the authors from Eric Henry.
22. Dated February 25, 2009.
23. *Green Steps Journal*, 2005, 2.
24. Henry & Moore, "Manufacturing and Selling a $4.00 T-shirt in a $1.00 World," 19.
25. Grover, "The TH Interview: Eric Henry of TS Designs," 5.

Index